ALSO BY RICK TRAMONTO

AMUSE-BOUCHE
WITH MARY GOODBODY

BUTTER SUGAR FLOUR EGGS: WHIMSICAL IRRESISTIBLE DESSERTS
WITH GALE GAND AND JULIA MOSKIN

AMERICAN BRASSERIE
WITH GALE GAND AND JULIA MOSKIN

Tru

RANDOM HOUSE | NEW YORK

RICK TRAMONTO

Photographs by Tim Turner

Tru

A Cookbook from the Legendary Chicago Restaurant

WITH **Gale Gand**

AND MARY GOODBODY

All rights reserved under International and Pan-American
Copyright Conventions. Published in the United States
by Random House, an imprint of The Random House
Publishing Group, a division of Random House, Inc.,
New York, and simultaneously in Canada by Random House
of Canada Limited, Toronto.

Random House and colophon are registered
trademarks of Random House, Inc.

Library of Congress Cataloging-in-Publication Data
Tramonto, Rick.
Tru : a cookbook from the legendary Chicago restaurant /
Rick Tramonto, with Gale Gand and Mary Goodbody ;
photographs by Tim Turner.
p.   cm.
ISBN 1-4000-6061-3 (alk. paper)
1. Cookery.   2. Tru (Restaurant).   I. Gand, Gale.
II. Goodbody, Mary.   III. Title.
TX714.T7325 2004
641.5'09773'11—dc22   2003069339

Printed in China on acid-free paper
Random House website address: www.atrandom.com

FIRST EDITION

9 8 7 6 5 4 3 2 1

Book design by Barbara M. Bachman

I would like to dedicate this book to my Lord and Savior, Jesus Christ, who always leads me down the right road and who brings me through every storm every time.

To my best friend and wife, Eileen Tramonto, who keeps me loved, humble, and close to God in this insane business.

To my sons, Gio, Sean, and Brian, who keep me laughing and on my toes at all times. I love you guys.

And to the greatest and most passionate staff on the planet. I love you. God bless you and thank you for what you do every day at Tru. You are amazing!

And, last but not least, thank you to my friend chef Pierre Gagnaire for the culinary seeds you planted in my creative life and for your inspiring cooking, which feeds my heart and soul. This book reflects some of the fruits!

Foreword

IT IS ALWAYS A THRILL FOR ME TO SEE YOUNG TALENT DEVELOP in this business, and over the years I've watched Rick Tramonto and Gale Gand grow personally and professionally. Although we are partners, Tru is really their restaurant. They eat and breathe it every day, and sleep and dream it every night. And it is largely because of their talent, drive, and commitment to excellence that Tru has been a success.

My ideas, inspiration, and direction for a restaurant project all start with the food. When Ricky came to work for us as a sous-chef at Avanzare in 1987, I saw he had great taste and a passion for food. The first time I tasted his pasta fagioli, I knew there was something special about him, and to this day I have never had beef short ribs that compare to his. But Rick not only had the talent, he had the desire. He has always been open to growing as a person and has that rare combination of talents: the ability to be wildly creative, a healthy regard for business, and a willingness to nurture and develop people.

Gale has the amazing ability to take old-fashioned desserts and make them new and fun. She approaches her work with a great sense of humor and playfulness. In 1987, when she did her first dessert tasting for me, Gale's lemon meringue pie was the best I had ever tasted and her French *cannelés* were so good that I took them home to eat the next morning for breakfast. Impressed with her talent, we hired Gale as the pastry chef at the Pump Room.

To expand their craft, she and Ricky moved to Europe for a few years, and eventually returned to Chicago. Back in town, Rick called to tell me he had a dream for a fine dining restaurant and thought the three of us should work together. We kept in touch, they created some wonderful ventures on their own, and when the time was right we set off to do Tru.

When you find people whose strengths balance your weaknesses, whose spark ignites your passion, and whose imagination takes yours to new heights, it is magic. I love Rick and Gale and the magic they have created at Tru. I am proud to call them my partners.

Richard Melman
Chicago, Illinois
2004

Acknowledgments

FROM RICK TRAMONTO:

Special thanks to Rich Melman, my mentor, my partner, my friend, my guru. I love you, and thanks for always believing in me.

Thanks to my friend and cowriter, Mary Goodbody, who helped me dish this into words in the early morning hours, to share with the world the beauty of Tru.

To my culinary partner, Gale Gand. It's been an extraordinary journey. Thanks and love.

Thanks to my longtime friend and brilliant photographer, Tim Turner, who keeps me focused and challenges me to make every dish the best it can be during those long but fun photo shoots. Plate it again, plate it again, plate it again, plate it again . . .

Thanks to my supportive and loving family, Eileen Tramonto, Gio Tramonto, Sean and Brian Pschirrer, Frank Tramonto, Paul and Dorothy Tramonto, and Ed and Mary Carroll, who have shown me how to live and breathe outside the culinary world.

Thanks to my spiritual family, pastors Gregory and Grace Dickow of Life Changers International Church for their love and blessings, and for feeding me the word of God. Also to Van and Doni Crouch, Pastor Keith and Dana Cistrunk, Brian and Kathy Potter, Dr. Creflo and Taffi Dollar, Bishop T.D. Jakes, Jesse and Cathy Duplantis, and Pastor James McDonald at Walk in the Word for their teachings and wisdom of the Word of God.

Thanks to my awesome agent, Jane Dystel, and my editor, Mary Bahr, and the great team at Random House for their trust and faith in this book and me, and who always make it seem easy and pleasurable. Special thanks to my sous-chefs, Mark Andelbradt and Jason Robinson, for helping me test and organize these recipes for three long years.

Thanks to my Tru partners, Rich Melman, Gale Gand, Scott Barton, Kevin Brown, Jay Steibre, and Charles Haskel, for their deep friendship and for giving me a stage to play on every day.

A special thanks to my management team for their amazing attention to detail and for cherishing the customer: Serge Krieger, Margaret McKinnon, Julie Drengberg, Al Lipkin, Jeffrey Wielgopolan, Paula Purcell, Jeffrey Ward, Jason Robinson, Lisa Mortimer, Stuart Davis, and Aaron Elliot. To my sommelier (the wine guy), Scott Tyree, for growing and tending our great cellar, and for his unique wine pairing with my food: Thanks for your "winey" vision. Thanks to my awesome eighty-member staff at Tru for their dedication and loyalty to excellence, and for making it happen every day.

I would also like to thank the city of Chicago, Mayor Richard Daley, and the food press for supporting me and allowing me to hone my craft in this great city.

Thanks to those who inspire me on a daily basis and who support my culinary efforts: Pierre Gagnaire, Emeril Lagasse, Julia Child, Oprah Winfrey, Jose Andres, Ferran and Albert Adrià, Jean-Georges Vongerichten, Alain Ducasse, Bobby Flay, Alfred Portale, Mario Batali, Patrick O'Connell, Nobu Matsuhisa, Martha Stewart, Guy Savoy, Juan Mari and Elana Arzak, David Bouley, Danny Wegman, Randy Zeiban, Gray Kunz, Norman Van Aken, Charlie Trotter, Thomas Keller, Martin Berasategui, Michael Lamonico, Daniel Boulud, Michael Chiarello, Wolfgang Puck, Francois Payard, Greg Bromen, Jean-Louis Palladin, Alan Wong, Tom Colicchio, Roger Vergé, Eric Ripert, Jean Joho, Fredy Girardet, Anton Mosimann, Raymond Blanc, Roland Liccioni, Gabino Sotelino, and the Roux brothers.

Thanks to my supportive friends who I rarely get to see because I'm working all the time. I love you guys. To Thea Gattone, thanks for your prayers for this book; thanks to Peter Lepore, Larry and Julie Binstein, Vinnie and Theresa Rupert, the late

Bob Payton and Wendy Payton, Debra Ferrer and Jim Visger, Tim and Mary Williamson, Marty (coach) and Dianna Lackner, Joan Cusack, Harold and Erica Ramis, Ina Pinkney (the breakfast queen), Jimmy Bonnesteel, Greg Bromen, Mark Piazza, Jim Kurtz, Patti Street-Steeb, Val Landsburg, Rochelle and Gary Fleck (thanks for all the great Chefwear), and all the folks at Lettuce Entertain You. You're the best.

A very special thanks to my vendors and the farmers whom I work with every day across the country. They work so hard to find and grow the best-of-the-best ingredients and products for me to use at Tru. The restaurant and this book would not be possible without you. Thank you and God bless you, big time.

FROM GALE GAND:

Thanks to my lovely husband, Jimmy Seidita, for putting up with my obsession for my work, my late nights writing, and for accepting that I still want to work with my ex-husband. To my son, Giorgio Montana Gand Tramonto, for bringing me all the rich and joyful experiences motherhood has to offer. To Rick Tramonto for a great ride. To Rich Melman for giving me a studio to do my art in. To my late mother, Myrna Grossman Gand, for my spunk, and to my dad, Bob Gand, for teaching me to ask for more out of life—when it's my life we're talking about!

FROM MARY GOODBODY:

Thanks to Rick Tramonto for entrusting me with this enormous project. It's been a challenge and a joy. Thanks to Gale Gand for sharing her talent and her friendship. Thanks to the cheerful and willing staff at Tru, who so generously shared their expertise with me. A very big thanks to Francine

Fielding for her conscientious and good-natured help editing recipes, and to Lisa Thornton for her help with everything. Thanks to our amazing agent, Jane Dystel, who knows how to get a project going and then keep it on track with an encouraging e-mail or friendly phone call, and to our patient and good-humored editor, Mary Bahr, always ready with a creative idea to make the book even better. And, of course, heartfelt thanks to Laura Goodbody, who supports her mother in so many ways—and always has.

Contents

FOREWORD *by Richard Melman* ix

ACKNOWLEDGMENTS xi

INTRODUCTION: *The Tru Story* xvii

CHAPTER ONE: *Hors d'Oeuvres* 3

CHAPTER TWO: *Amuse-Bouche* 15

CHAPTER THREE: *Cold Appetizers* 35

CHAPTER FOUR: *Hot Appetizers* 57

CHAPTER FIVE: *Foie Gras* 87

CHAPTER SIX: *Soups* 109

CHAPTER SEVEN: *Fish and Seafood* 129

CHAPTER EIGHT: *Meat and Poultry* 153

CHAPTER NINE: *Game* 183

Tru Desserts *by Gale Gand* 203

CHAPTER TEN: THE CHEESE COURSE 207

CHAPTER ELEVEN: DESSERT AMUSE-BOUCHE 219

CHAPTER TWELVE: DESSERTS 225

CHAPTER THIRTEEN: PETITS FOURS 249

CHAPTER FOURTEEN: *Basic Recipes* 259

SOURCES FOR HARD-TO-FIND
INGREDIENTS AND EQUIPMENT 283

INDEX 289

The Tru Story

THIS IS THE STORY OF A RESTAURANT IN CHICAGO CALLED TRU.
By the time Tru opened on a bright, sunny day in May 1999, Gale and I had been involved
in fifteen other restaurant openings. You'd think we could have done it with our eyes closed,
but opening a restaurant is incredibly stressful and agonizing.

While our experience meant we did not need a guidebook—we could write the guidebook!
—it also meant we were well aware of what could go wrong. Happily, the debut went
smoothly and we opened to critical praise and, better yet, booked tables.

In so many ways, this was the culmination of our dreams. Tru represented an opportunity
to open a fine-dining world-class restaurant. In doing so, we could touch thousands of diners
from both our beloved Chicago and around the globe.

We could put our mantra into action: fine dining with a sense of humor.

Getting to this point had been a long, exciting, and sometimes painful journey. Looking
back, much of what went before seems to have been a well-conceived progression of career
moves. Believe me, most of it was blind luck driven by an abiding love of food, a passion for
the table, and an obsession with all that goes into producing superb meals.

BEGINNINGS

When we opened Tru, Gale and I were seasoned chefs who had been in the business
for a number of years. I started when I was fifteen years old, working at a Wendy's in
Rochester, New York, where I was born. I owe a debt of gratitude to Dave Thomas,
Wendy's founder, who created a work environment where a kid like me, who didn't really
fit into school, could thrive, move up, and grab on to skills that would serve me for a lifetime.
Once I was bitten by the restaurant bug, I never managed to complete my formal education,
but my culinary education became a movable feast, eagerly consumed in one restaurant after
another, one city after another, even one country after another.

Before too long, Greg Broman hired me for the Stathallen Hotel in Rochester. Under

Greg's guidance, I began to understand what it takes to produce fine food and survive in a professional kitchen. While there, I met Gale, who had graduated from the Rochester Institute of Technology's School for American Craftsmen and, with Greg's coaxing, had decided to work in the restaurant. We both found our true homes in Greg's kitchen and are forever grateful to him.

Greg encouraged us to go to New York City. By the mid-1980s, I found myself cooking on the line at the Gotham Bar and Grill, while Gale worked at Jams. During our years in the Big Apple, we cooked in some of the best kitchens in town. We lived in a hot, stuffy fifth-floor walk-up in the West Village with a roommate and mice in the oven! It was all part of our New York experience. We were young and ready for anything.

I have been cooking for twenty-six of my forty-one years and can delineate stages of my self-taught professional education. The early days in Rochester, New York, were like culinary high school. When I moved to New York City and cooked in restaurants such as Tavern on the Green, Aurora, and La Reserve, I became a serious culinary college student. Later, I spent several years in Europe, where I completed a graduate course in fine cuisine. Finally, the years I have had the good fortune to work with Rich Melman of Lettuce Entertain You Enterprises have been intensive courses in the business of running a restaurant. My association with Rich truly has been a blessing.

I am not finished with this education; far from it. As long as there is one more technique to master, one more flavor combination to try, and one more customer to please, I will work at my craft. When you are a chef, you never stop learning.

As a self-educated chef, it has been important for me to read a lot, travel, and experience the cooking of others. I spent years doing just that whenever I

could, both in this country and abroad. In my quest to elevate my own craft to lofty heights, I am always inspired by the work of others.

CHICAGO BECOMES HOME

Gale and I hooked up with Rich Melman by chance. When Gale moved back to her hometown of Chicago from New York in 1987, I followed. She set up some interviews for me, one at Scoozi, a large restaurant serving progressive Italian cuisine. In the middle of the interview, I told the manager I wasn't interested in such large-volume cooking and got up to leave. The corporate chef stopped me, saying he thought I should meet "the boss." Neither Gale nor I had heard of Rich Melman or Lettuce Entertain You, but the next day Gale drove me to the corporate offices and ended up waiting in the car for two hours while I met with Rich.

Rich and I hit it off immediately. He was fascinated with my background and the humble beginnings at Wendy's that had led to line-cook jobs in some of New York's best kitchens. He was impressed that I had worked with restaurant legend Joe Baum when he opened Aurora. I explained that I did not want to cook in a big restaurant and Rich said he would find a place that would suit me, and to just trust him. I've been trusting him ever since. When Gale asked me what had happened, all I could say was that I had a job but didn't know where or for how much. She thought I was crazy! The job turned out to be at Avanzare (Italian for "to move forward"), a popular high-end Italian restaurant housed in the same space currently occupied by Tru. As it turns out, this space is a spiritual one for me.

I moved on to another restaurant, Bella Luna, in 1988 and Gale joined me as pastry chef. We had worked together at Gotham Bar and Grill and other restaurants in New York and so we knew this would be a successful alliance. It was; we got married at

Bella Luna. Gale made the cake, I catered the food, and *Food Arts* magazine ran the story about the celebration in their first issue.

Not too long after the wedding, we got a call from Bob Payton. I had no idea who this hale and hearty guy on the other end of the phone was, but he invited Gale and me to join him for breakfast at the Drake Hotel to discuss a job in England. We were curious. Bob ordered a huge stack of blueberry pancakes and a Diet Coke for breakfast and told us our names had shown up on lists of possible chefs he was considering to help him out. The job was "fixing" the broken restaurant at his five-star country-house hotel in England, and he seduced us with references to "sunny Leicestershire" in the United Kingdom. It was a remarkable performance. Bob, a former Madison Avenue advertising guy, pitched the job even as he interviewed us. The lure of Europe coupled with his larger than-life personality were too much for us to resist, and before we knew it we had signed up! In true Payton form, six weeks later work papers, green cards, and first-class airplane tickets arrived at our front door. We were off.

MUSEUM DAYS

Gale refers to the years we spent abroad working for Bob Payton and our shorter trips to Europe as our time in the museum. By this, she means we studied and observed much of what had gone before us. Gale studied art seriously before she began cooking, and, for her, museum visits are common but also treats to be savored. Certainly our time in Europe was one to be savored to the fullest.

Bob hired us to turn around the kitchen at Stapleford Park, where everything but the restaurant was first class. Within a year, we had earned Michelin's Red *M* and even the hardest-to-please food critics were impressed.

The hotel, about ninety miles from London, was absolutely beautiful. We lived in a grace-and-favor cottage on the estate with a thatched roof and tea roses by the front door. We also worked from morning to long after dark, which is not unusual when you are doing a total makeover of a menu, kitchen, and staff. It was consuming and exhausting work, but even so, we took every opportunity to slip away and see more of the world.

We sometimes said that the best thing about England was France. We were only a few hours from the finest restaurants in the world and Bob encouraged us to take advantage of this. He made calls to friends in the business to open doors and gave us the use of his many apartments in Europe. Bob's generosity was amazing. Whenever we had a few days off, we headed for France, Italy, Spain, Switzerland, Wales, or Scotland.

I refer to those years constantly throughout this book. The greatest chefs of Europe opened their hearts and kitchens to us, and consequently we learned an amazing amount. We ate at one fantastic three-Michelin star restaurant after another and compiled what we called the "Dream File," a compilation of our favorite ideas and most compelling experiences. We *staged* in as many of Europe's kitchens as we could, too. In the food business, to *stage* is to study for a prescribed time in another chef's kitchen without pay. The *stage* may be days or even months, depending on your relationship to the chef, his needs, and, to some extent, your budget and your ambition.

Being so close to France meant Gale and I could dine at Pierre Gagnaire's restaurant, significant because, more than any other chef, Pierre Gagnaire has defined the cooking at Tru.

Several years earlier, our friend Gabino Sotelino, the Basque chef-owner of Ambria, a Chicago restaurant, had urged us to eat in Gagnaire's restaurant in Saint-Etienne, France. Knowing how we felt about food and cooking, he thought we would relate to Gagnaire's style. We saved our money, flew to France, and booked lunch—and stayed for dinner. I got up the next morning and repeated lunch and dinner at the restaurant for two more days. I could not get enough of this young chef's food. I was blown away by his cooking, his presentation, and his very presence in the restaurant. He moved from kitchen to dining room with ease, talking with the patrons, serving dishes, and making sure the food was to their liking. Ingredient pairings were daring, with layers of flavors and textures. The entire menu was progressive with a firm foothold in the classics and a steady gaze toward the stars.

The restaurant was impressive, too. Small and elegant, it had earned three Michelin stars. The dining room was decorated with avant-garde artwork, including a bright yellow staircase in the corner that went nowhere, except in your imagination. I loved it.

By the time Gale and I landed at Stapleford Park in England, we had heard that Pierre Gagnaire had closed his first restaurant but had opened another, also in Saint-Etienne. When we got word from our friend chef Raymond Blanc that he had invited Pierre to his restaurant in Oxfordshire, we finagled a two-day-long *stage*. We connected with Pierre, cooked and talked with him, and a friendship was launched.

Today, Pierre owns Restaurant Pierre Gagnaire in Paris, where he has elevated his food to a new level and received the praise and respect he so richly deserves. Over the years, I have never passed up the chance to eat his food. I am incapable of eating only one meal at a time there and usually manage two or three in a row. I can never wait for the next course and am always on fire when I leave. I truly credit him with much of what Tru is today. He has become a generous friend who has embraced our careers and encouraged us every step of the way. A few years ago, he came to the United States to cook a dinner at New York's Gramercy Tavern with chef Pierre Hermé. I flew to New York. Anytime Pierre is around, I am there!

Our European travels enriched our souls and depleted our bank accounts. We had made several trips to Europe before our years working for Bob Payton, and every time we lugged home heavy suitcases filled with copper cookware, china, glassware, and linens. We stored it all in the basement of our suburban Chicago house, in the hope that one day we would open our own place.

One European jaunt stands out brilliantly: our pilgrimage to Paul Bocuse's restaurant in Lyon, France. This was years before we lived in England, and we were really still kids. I knew I wanted to have my picture taken with the great chef, so I rented a tuxedo in the States to take with me to France. We arrived on a Saturday night for our reservation and were crestfallen to learn the chef was not there. We waited and waited but he never showed up. The staff, sensing my extreme disappointment, suggested we return the next day before lunch. I struggled into my tux again and we paid for the expensive taxi ride to the restaurant. Bocuse was there! His English is limited and our French is far worse, but we managed to communicate and he agreed to a photograph. But, he warned, take two photos so that if your marriage ends you won't fight over the Bocuse picture! (This turned out to be a premonition. Years later, our marriage did end, but not our friendship and culinary partnership at Tru.) Bocuse then invited us to eat with him at a granite table in the corner of the kitchen. What an honor to watch the dance of such a fine-tuned kitchen! In so many ways, he set the bar for the level of hospitality at Tru.

Since that time, Bocuse has visited Tru. Chicago

culinary legend chef Jean Banchet brought him by one afternoon. We had short notice and literally polished our rows of copper pots in seven minutes! Bocuse walked through the kitchen and admired everything he saw—including a suckling pig we were just taking out of the oven—but still it was nerve-racking. Not unlike having your mother-in-law show up wearing white gloves.

On the kitchen wall next to the dining room door hangs a framed, signed poster of Paul Bocuse. This way, the master himself "sees" every dish that is carried from our kitchen to our guests.

TRU IS BORN

When Gale and I returned to Chicago from England, I went back to work for Rich Melman and Gale went to work for Charlie Trotter. It wasn't long before we became restless. I told Rich I wanted to open a cutting-edge fine-dining restaurant of my own and was met with encouragement—but with no firm offer for financial backing. So, we found Henry Adaniya, who had a space in nearby Evanston, a desire to open a restaurant, and a group of investors. We decided to give it a shot.

We opened Trio (named for the three of us: Rick, Gale, and Henry) in 1993 with the contents of our basement and very little money. We called it our starter restaurant. Although the restaurant never made much money for us, it turned us into "celebrity chefs." We got four-star reviews from the Chicago food press, and *Food & Wine* magazine gave us both Best New Chef awards. Food writers dubbed Gale "the Dessert Diva" and me "the Mad Scientist." We were honored, but it didn't take us long to realize that making a living in such a small space would be a constant struggle.

We then opened Brasserie T, a far more casual restaurant in Northfield, another Chicago suburb, and at the same time set about writing our first book,

American Brasserie. A year later we sold our share in Trio to Henry. The brasserie was 100 percent our own venture and for a few years we thrived. During the fourth year, we had a fire in the ventilation system, which forced us to close for two weeks. We had also opened a bakery, which further drained our resources, although it enabled us to write our second book, *Butter Sugar Flour Eggs.*

We continued to run the brasserie, struggling for another year and a half, but we knew it was only a matter of time before we closed. I remember Rich sitting down with us on the outdoor patio at Brasserie T one summer evening for what I can describe only as a "father talk." In his opinion, the restaurant was not going to make it, but on the other hand, he was ready to start talking about a fine-dining restaurant.

Tru at last!

THE TRU DREAM

Opening a restaurant is like a transatlantic steamship crossing. The rest of the world barely exists, yet you keep moving forward.

We went into partnership with Rich, which was crucial to us because we wanted ownership, desired culinary control, and needed a successful business partner. We had a budget of about $3.2 million, more than our wildest dreams could have predicted, and built our custom kitchen for about $1.2 million. I even had $100,000 committed to my other passion, designer china. Believe me, after years of running restaurants on a shoestring, this was pure joy. The amount of money was absolutely essential to opening a high-end restaurant in a major city. Still, money alone can't build a restaurant. It takes heart, passion, good, old-fashioned hard work, and, most of all, the Dream File.

It was Rich's idea to transform the Avanzare location into Tru. We gutted the space and started from scratch. This meant we were building Tru from the ground up. It's not unlike constructing a parallel universe. You are creating something very tangible from whole cloth and it can be heart-wrenching. Even as the wiring, Sheetrock, and plumbing were being installed, we were choosing fabric and napkins and deciding on the stain for the wood. Everything had to work together. Every detail had to be decided, reviewed, and revisited again and again.

At the same time, we were interviewing hundreds of potential employees. Staff can make or break any business, but if a restaurant staff cannot work as a well-choreographed team while presenting your vision to the public, the restaurant fails. Flat out.

We were still running Brasserie T, but, with its dwindling profits, the split of our marriage, and our expanding commitment to Tru, we decided the time had come to close the doors.

Since my days at Avanzare, I have had a long relationship and friendship with our managing partner, Scott Barton. He kept me balanced during the insanity of Tru's opening—"Mr. Cool, Calm, and Collected," we call him!—and was instrumental during this phase of planning and development. Nowadays, he helps us keep the finances on track, but back then he acted as general contractor while the restaurant was being built. When we traveled to Europe to research successful restaurants for this project, he accompanied us to get a handle on the source of our mission and vision.

Of course, we had opened restaurants before and so we knew what we were up against, knew how to figure the financial projections and make sure the business was a viable one. But this was more Rich's domain than ours, and *nothing* is more important. Rich is a master at balancing art and science when it comes to opening a restaurant. The art is the quality of the food and service and cherishing the customer; the science is running a financially healthy business. The restaurant's business model had to work on paper before we could break ground.

But what about the food? Carpets, napkins, money, waitstaff . . . all important, but when you get right down to it, it's all about the food. To my mind, nothing is more important. Before you open you must have a clear vision of the food. It defines the layout of the kitchen, the level of service, the ambiance of the dining room, the caliber of the staff—even the quality of the paper on which the menu is printed! We were lucky Rich felt the same way and believed chefs made good partners.

I wanted to serve a cuisine I refer to as progressive French. The roots of my cooking are anchored in the best European traditions and technique, but it's never stuffy or constrained. I look to the quality of raw ingredients, the season, the presentation, my whims, and my desire when I create a dish. I may rely on technique to execute it, but I never let it dictate the final outcome. For that, I look to what has inspired and thrilled me, and from there I trust my instincts.

When it came to planning Tru, Gale and I operated as one. Our vision was the same, we spoke the same language, we had traveled and eaten in the same places, and we were both totally committed to making Tru the best it could possibly be. We discussed everything, from whether to have salt and pepper on the tables (no) to the type of butter to serve (we tasted twelve before choosing our table butter). We tasted one foie gras after another, and rejected several types of caviar before deciding on some we liked. This scrutiny goes on to this day. We are our toughest critics, which is necessary for anyone who runs a restaurant. It's even more important when you compete on a national level with a restaurant of Tru's caliber; there is no room for error and you can never rest on your laurels. You must constantly move forward.

Rich came up with the name Tru, an acronym for *Tramonto* and *unlimited*—unlimited creativity, imagination, and possibility—and meaning be true to your food and your craft. Our logo is a Japanese-looking character and represents breaking out of the frame or thinking outside the box, something we try to do every day.

By the time we opened our doors, the restaurant was good. Now, five years later, it's very good. We are still working to make it extraordinary!

Designing the custom kitchen was one of the more satisfying aspects of getting Tru off the ground. Gale and I worked with kitchen designers from New York called Romano, Gatland, and the Boelter Company, a Chicago-based equipment outfit. There is very little I would do differently, except, like every cook, I wish we had more storage space, and I would like a real office. When I *staged* in French kitchens, such as those of Pierre Gagnaire and Michel Guerard, I found the French island design to be the most efficient, so we incorporated it into our design. This means the ranges face one another in a square. Instead of standing next to one another, shoulder to shoulder and facing a wall, our line cooks look directly at one another and so can communicate and observe what the others are cooking.

Tru's custom kitchen is designed with deep drawers that slide out beneath the workstations near the ranges, each fitted with small stainless steel bins for portioned and labeled ingredients for both cold and hot dishes. These can range from baby white asparagus to zebra-striped tomatoes and change daily depending on the menu. Each station is fitted with a custom knife drawer and we installed invisible garbage drops. A huge tilt braiser (a large kettle of sorts) of simmering stock sits in an accessible corner of the kitchen, and near it is a reservoir for cooking that stock down to a demi-glace. Finally, everywhere you look are soothing blue tile and copper pots, pans, skillets, and bowls. We have lots and lots of copper! Ours is a somewhat open kitchen and we welcome about fifty kitchen visitors a night. Anyone who dines with us is welcome to a tour of the kitchen.

We have two walk-in coolers and one walk-in freezer. It's not unusual to see whole lambs and pigs hanging in the larger cooler, as well as sides of beef, which we age ourselves. Large ice-filled plastic tubs hold whole fresh fish, which our prep cooks butcher daily for nightly service. This walk-in is fitted with an oak chest of drawers. Each shallow drawer is lined with moistened bamboo mats and organized to store and age Tru's extensive and amazing collection of cheeses, each one painstakingly and lovingly selected. We offer fifteen to eighteen cheeses a night, many of which are local; others are imported from the far corners of the country as well as from France, Italy, Spain, and wherever fine cheeses are made.

The smaller walk-in is for fruits and vegetables. In this temperature-controlled cool room is a colorful and tempting array of shapes and textures. We usually have ten to twelve varieties of mushrooms layered on sheet pans, a dozen different herbs, numerous amounts of baby vegetables, and countless melons, lettuces, root vegetables, and more.

Gale's pastry kitchen is off to the side of the primary kitchen, but, with its plate-glass window separating it from the office (which turns into the private kitchen-table and observation dining room at night) and its proximity to the overall action, it's very much part of the scene. Some of the pastry cooks arrive about ten A.M. and, working in shifts, stay until service ends around two A.M.

The pastry kitchen is outfitted with its own range, ovens, refrigeration, and workstations. For pastry and other work, there are granite countertops, and for preparing batters and doughs, an industrial-sized floor-model Hobart mixer (a large KitchenAid). In this sweet-smelling space, Gale and her staff of five prepare breads, cheese condiments, chocolates, candies, and desserts—including ice creams and sorbets. They also make the savory garnitures made with flour, such as the *tuile* cones for the savory sorbets. The number of brioche loaves baked in Gale's kitchen is phenomenal, because we power through them for foie gras and caviar presentations as well as for savory bread puddings and hors d'oeuvres.

Nightly, our kitchen is staffed by twenty cooks, which means there is one cook for every three guests. Three guys are on the fish station and three on the meat station. There are four cooks working on cold appetizers, one on hot appetizers and soups, one on *amuse-bouche,* and another whose only task is to build the caviar staircases (see page 37 for more on these). I have two dishwashers and two pot scrubbers who handle extremely fragile and very expensive china made by Rosenthal, Versace, and Limoge. We like to present food on unusual surfaces, such as glass, mirrors, and marble, and these, too, have to be washed. I always say our dishwashers are the most important people in the kitchen—after all, if they have a bad day and drop a stack of china, replacement costs are astronomical.

My sous-chefs and I act as expeditors and plate up the food, which means we check every plate that leaves the kitchen, garnish it, and make sure the busy cooks stay on track. All of us taste, taste, taste. This is absolutely vital, since on an average night fifteen hundred to two thousand plates leave the Tru kitchen. Nearly 80 percent of our customers order one of our collections—our interpretation of tasting, or degustation, menus. Unlike other tasting menus, at Tru if your table orders the Chef Tramonto Collection, everyone at the table gets something different. For a party of six, for example, this means six different cold appetizers, six different hot appetizers, six different soups, and so on. When a collection menu has eight or ten courses, serving it is challenging, to say the least, and demands precise coordination in the kitchen. While other tasting menus—the Market Collection, the Ocean Collection, and the Vegetable Collection, for instance—are more traditionally structured, they still represent a tremendous feat for the kitchen.

I designed the Tramonto Collections because when Gale and I traveled through Europe, our only consistent disappointment was that there was so little variety on the chefs' tasting menus. We wished we could have tasted twice as many dishes at one sitting. And so at Tru, our guests have this opportunity!

Tru's kitchen table is an intense experience, too. By day, I use the small room adjacent to the kitchen as my office. By night, it transforms into a private dining room. It seats up to six and is in use at least four nights a week—usually with a two-month lead time for reservations. Because of its location, the kitchen table can be reached through a private back door, which makes it popular with celebrities such as Michael Jordan, Oprah Winfrey, Billy Joel, Mick Jagger, and John Malkovich, to name a few.

THE DINING ROOM

My favorite color is blue, and so, with the help of Atlanta-based designer Bill Johnson along with Rich Melman, we planned the restaurant with only blue accents. Rich suggested a large, open white room in which our food could explode without many distractions, and that is what we have. The carpet, banquettes, and upholstered chairs are deep blue and black. Huge floor-to-ceiling windows are draped with gauzy white curtains, making our space private yet airy. From the bar, a stairway leads up to extra, semiprivate tables and a large private dining room.

We are extremely proud of our original contemporary art collection, which is one of the finest of any restaurant in the country. We work with Alan Koppel, a curator and gallery owner here in Chicago. We have works by Maya Lin, Yves Klein, Ed Ruscha, and Andy Warhol, among others. A large Peter Halley abstract painting dominates one wall, while two Vik Muniz photographs provide whimsy.

Before we opened, we occasionally met at Rich's house, where he has a spectacular Warhol of Jackie O in blue tones. Gale joked that the painting should hang in Tru because of its color and secretly we both coveted it. We didn't get it, but instead Koppel found us a turquoise Marilyn Monroe by Warhol, which really carries across the entire room.

TRU'S WINE PROGRAM

Since day one Scott Tyree has been our sommelier. I liked him the first time I met him for his sweet temperament and dry sense of humor—like a good wine. His commitment to the wine program has been unstoppable and he continues to make me proud as the program grows and becomes better all the time. We affectionately call him and his two assistants "the wine guys," which we consider a term of respect. Gale and I knew we needed to make a statement with our wine program, and to do so we needed choice and diversity. At any given time, our inventory is valued at close to $1 million. The cellar, which contains eighteen thousand bottles, turns over about three times a year.

In the early days, suppliers were reluctant to show us unusual or rare wines, but Scott's persistence and ever-growing knowledge have changed that, and we now have one of the most respected wine cellars in the Midwest and are working toward national ranking. Scott, who studied film at Northwestern University, was seduced by the wine-and-food industry when he worked in a bar and restaurant during college. After graduation, he worked at Shaw's Crab House in Chicago, where he proposed a wine program and increased sales dramatically. Today, he is a first-class sommelier. He passed the first two of three exams for the Court Masters Sommeliers on the first try, which is impressive.

Scott needs to keep up with five different collection menus a night, which may change weekly and always change seasonally. Our customers are sophisticated and demanding, and Scott says this makes his job more enjoyable because more often than not the exchange about the wine is enlightened and stimulating. Both Scott and I feel it's important to be open, gracious, friendly, even humble when discussing our large wine list, and never arrogant and always approachable.

Our staff is well versed, too, thanks to Scott's diligence. He holds tastings twice a week and assigns wine-producing regions to different members of the staff for research. They report back at the next tasting and everyone learns something new. At one point in his life Scott considered being a teacher, and our program allows him to pursue both this interest and his keen appreciation of wine. Scott wrote the wine notes that go along with the recipes in this book.

SERVICE

Our number-one goal is to give our customers the ultimate dining experience. In the culture of

Tru, we call it "cherishing the customer," which can be achieved only with a stellar team. We rely on Serge Krieger, the general manager, to make sure the waitstaff and other front-of-the-house personnel work together like a well-oiled machine. He is ably assisted by Paula Purcell, our senior captain.

During the first two years of operation, Scott Barton was very hands-on. He helped trained staff and set up our systems for inventory and purchasing. About six months after we opened, Scott hired Serge. The two worked together to make sure Tru's service was top drawer all the way. I was thrilled with Serge's background. He is steeped in the tradition of good service, having been raised in Europe, where he worked in some of the finest—and most exacting—hotels and restaurants, including three years with George Blanc. When he moved to the United States, he worked in New York for five years at the acclaimed Daniel restaurant. When he moved farther west, we became the fortunate ones.

To be profitable, we usually have two seatings every night. This means we need to "turn" the tables in between. It's all a matter of timing, and Serge and Paula make certain the waitstaff knows how to provide our customers with a leisurely dining experience that never feels rushed, but is choreographed so that the table is vacated when needed.

For the most part our staff is in this for the long haul. Our turnover is low and most of our employees have been with us for at least two or three years. I credit a lot of this to Serge, who embraces my philosophy of giving a job 100 percent—because otherwise, what's the point? This way, we have a culture in which being a waiter is an honorable profession. And at Tru, it's also lucrative. When Serge hires someone, he says it may be more effective to employ someone with a "golden heart"

than with a lot of experience. Even so, more than three-quarters of those who apply for jobs are turned down. We are selective and it pays off.

Paula needs about ninety days to train a new recruit. Each one must pass a series of tests, and taste as much food and wine as possible. They work hard in the dining room before they are considered trained, but once they meet the grade, no one is better at their job.

Serge has compiled a ten-page, densely typed, incredibly detailed manual of service for the staff. It begins with how guests should be greeted (" 'Good evening! Welcome to Tru. How may I help you?' ") and covers everything from water service ("If a guest requests ice water, bring a water glass filled with ice and pour still water into the glass") to placing glassware ("Glasses should always be set with the watermark pointing straight down to six o'clock"), serving ("Always serve women first and always move in a clockwise motion. Plates should be served from the left side with the left hand, unless this causes obvious discomfort, in which case the guest will be served from the right with the right hand"), and ends with resetting the tables ("begin to reset a table only after the guests have actually left the dining room. One never wants to give the impression that we are in a rush to get them out. [Yet] resetting tables is a matter of urgency. Soiled tables are unsightly for guests dining in the vicinity").

But this is not all there is to our service. It's organic, with the waitstaff responsible for anticipating our guests' every need. We have eight pairs of reading glasses for customers who forget theirs, ticketless valet service for cars, purse stools at the tables for the ladies, and escort service to the ladies' and men's rooms. We return forgotten credit cards with a bouquet of flowers, deliver luggage to hotels, rebook hotel rooms, and check on plane reservations if our customers request it. We supply disposable cameras if someone wants to take a commemorative photograph. We hold umbrellas for our guests as they walk to their cars, which, by the way, are running with the heater or air conditioner on when they leave the restaurant. We are all about taking care of people. I don't think you will find better service at any restaurant anywhere. We pride ourselves on silent, simultaneous, seamless service that is as unobtrusive as it is complete, professional, and welcoming. We call this the "the three *S*'s" of service!

We have thirty front-of-the-house staff, and on any given night twenty-five to twenty-eight are working. They arrive in the early afternoon, help set up, study the night's menus, polish glass and silverware, iron tablecloths, vacuum carpets, and do whatever is needed so that they are ready for business before the preservice meeting at 4:45. By 5:00, everyone is primed to go. It's showtime!

Opening and running Tru has been an extraordinary journey—but it has just started. Now the work begins. The restaurant business is not a sprint. As I told the staff on the day we opened and have repeated frequently along the way, this is a long-distance marathon and we intend to cross the finish line. Someday.

Tru

RICK'S STEAK AND EGGS

Serves 6

Steak tartar piled on small slices of brioche is a great little "wow" of an hors d'oeuvre. When I first traveled through France twenty years ago, I was intrigued by how many restaurants made steak tartar tableside. They brought the raw meat and the rest of the ingredients out into the restaurant and prepared the raw beef dish right then and there. When you make small amounts of tartar, as for an hors d'oeuvre or for tableside service, it's tough to incorporate much egg into the meat, and so I decided to play with the concept and top the tartar with a tiny fried quail egg for a jewel-like presentation. The egg mixes in your mouth with the meat and the flavors expand, so you get the flavorful effect of steak and eggs.

When you buy the tenderloin for this, talk to a reputable butcher and tell him you plan to serve it raw. Prime beef is the best choice, but if you can't get it, use the best choice beef you can find, such as Angus. Finally, while some recipes suggest chopping the meat in a food processor, I urge you to chop it by hand. The fat stays firmer and the final texture and flavor are more pleasing.

6 ounces beef tenderloin, cleaned and trimmed
¼ cup chopped capers
¼ cup chopped shallots
1 teaspoon Dijon mustard
1 teaspoon finely chopped flat-leaf parsley
Kosher salt and freshly ground black pepper
12 quail eggs
1 loaf Brioche (see page 280), cut into 12 slices
*   and toasted*
2 tablespoons white or black truffle oil
Cracked black pepper
2 tablespoons chopped fresh chives

1. Wrap the beef tenderloin in plastic wrap and freeze for about 30 minutes. This will make the beef easier to slice.

2. Slice the tenderloin into ¼-inch strips and then slice the strips into ¼-inch cubes. Put the cubed tenderloin into a small bowl and mix in the capers, shallots, Dijon mustard, and parsley. Season to taste with salt and pepper.

3. Heat 1 tablespoon of water in a large nonstick skillet over low heat. The water will prevent the eggs from sticking. Gently crack 6 of the quail eggs into the pan and fry for about 2 minutes or until the egg yolks are semi-translucent. Add a little more water if necessary to prevent sticking. Gently lift the eggs from the pan with a small, thin-bladed spatula and set aside on a plate. Repeat with the remaining 6 eggs.

4. To serve, spoon equal amounts of beef tartar on each of the brioche toasts. Arrange 2 on each of 6 plates and top each with a fried quail egg. Drizzle each with a little truffle oil and sprinkle with kosher salt, cracked black pepper, and chopped chives. Serve immediately.

HAMACHI-SALMON TARTAR SPOONS

Serves 6

I love sushi and sashimi. At Tru I take every opportunity to serve it as often as I can. The hors d'oeuvre course is perfect for serving this version of tartar-sashimi. The bright white hamachi and bright orange salmon provide stunning color contrasts. I was inspired to work with these colors by Peter Halley, the renowned American artist, whose painting hangs in our dining room and with whom I had the pleasure of collaborating on an artist-chef dinner series that blurred the lines between food and art. The two buttery fishes complement each other beautifully. Each is distinctively seasoned—the hamachi with ginger and lime leaves and the salmon with mint, lemon, oranges, and tequila—but they work well together. For the spoons, choose something fun with a pretty bowl or interesting handle, or both.

HAMACHI TARTAR:

¾ cup finely chopped hamachi

½ cup finely diced red onion

½ teaspoon finely chopped Kaffir lime leaves

¾ tablespoon fresh lime juice

2 tablespoons olive oil

½ teaspoon finely chopped scallion

¼ teaspoon finely chopped fresh ginger

Kosher salt and freshly ground black pepper

SALMON TARTAR:

¾ cup finely chopped Norwegian or wild salmon

1 teaspoon finely chopped fresh mint

2 tablespoons olive oil

Freshly ground white pepper

3 orange segments, finely chopped

3 lemon segments, finely chopped

1 teaspoon tequila (see Note)

Kosher salt

3 ounces hijiki seaweed, for garnish

Fresh chervil, for garnish

1 tablespoon Tramonto's Lime Dust, for garnish
  (see page 272)

1. To make the hamachi tartar, cut the tuna into even small dice. Toss with the onion in a glass or ceramic bowl along with the lime leaves.

2. Add the lime juice and olive oil and toss gently. Gently stir in the scallion and ginger, season to taste with salt and pepper, and refrigerate for no longer than 30 minutes.

3. To make the salmon tartar, in a small bowl, gently mix together the salmon, mint, olive oil, and pepper to taste. Cover with plastic wrap and refrigerate for no longer than 30 minutes.

4. Just before serving, mix the chopped orange and lemon and the tequila into the salmon mixture. Season to taste with salt.

5. Scoop about 1 tablespoon of the salmon mixture and, using 2 iced-tea spoons, form it into a quenelle (oval-shaped mound) on the tip of one of the spoons. Mound some hamachi tartar at the back of the bowl of the spoon. Garnish with some of the hijiki and decorative *plouches* (small bunches) of chervil, and sprinkle lime dust over the top. Repeat to make 5 more spoons.

NOTE: *Measure the tequila from some that has had the alcohol cooked off. Because you can't boil a teaspoon of tequila without it evaporating pretty quickly, I suggest you bring about 3 tablespoons of tequila to a boil, cook it for at least 1 minute to cook off the alcohol, and then measure a teaspoon from this. Discard the remaining tequila or, better yet, use it to flavor a soup or stew.*

ASSORTMENT OF DEVILED QUAIL EGGS
Serves 6

I grew up in a family that loved deviled eggs. My mom, Gloria Tramonto, made them all the time as a snack for us. I took this memory and transformed it into small, delicate quail eggs, more appropriate for fine dining than larger hens' eggs. I mix truffles with a third of the yolks, crimson beet juice with another third, and basil puree with the rest for rich, interesting flavors and colors and a festive appearance. These are not difficult but do require patience, which is why I recommend using a pastry bag with a plain or star tip to fill the tiny egg whites. Have fun with the presentation; put the eggs on glass mirrors or shiny silver trays.

6 quail eggs
½ cup mayonnaise
1 teaspoon paprika
Kosher salt and freshly ground black pepper
1 tablespoon finely chopped black truffles
1 tablespoon black or white truffle oil
2 tablespoons beet juice (from 1 medium beet)
1 tablespoon Basil Puree (recipe follows)

1. Put the quail eggs in a medium saucepan. Add enough cold water to cover the eggs. Bring to a boil and cook for 6 minutes. Drain and immediately submerge in ice-cold water. Peel immediately.
2. Cut the eggs in half lengthwise. Using a small spoon, very carefully remove the yolks and transfer to a small bowl. Set the whites aside.
3. Mix the mayonnaise and paprika with the yolks, mashing gently with a fork. Season to taste with salt and pepper.
4. Divide the egg-yolk mixture among 3 small bowls. Mix the truffles and truffle oil into the yolks in one of the bowls. Add the beet juice to another bowl. Stir the basil puree into the third bowl.
5. Pipe or spoon some of the truffled egg mixture into 4 egg-white halves. Repeat with the other 2 mixtures so that you have 12 filled deviled eggs.

BASIL PUREE
Makes about 1 cup

8 ounces fresh basil
1 bunch flat-leaf parsley
¼ cup cold water

1. Remove the leaves from the stems of the basil and parsley. Discard the stems.
2. In a saucepan filled with boiling water, blanch the basil and parsley leaves for about 10 seconds or until they turn bright green. Drain and immediately submerge in ice-cold water. Drain again.
3. Put the basil and parsley leaves in a blender. Add the cold water. Puree until smooth. Strain the puree through a chinois or fine-mesh sieve into a small glass or ceramic bowl. Discard the ingredients in the chinois.
4. Use immediately or cover with plastic wrap and refrigerate for a few hours.

KUMQUATS STUFFED WITH
CURRIED PEEKYTOE CRAB SALAD

Serves 6

This dish reflects my abiding love for citrus with seafood. I use tender, sweet Peekytoe crab, but you could substitute any high-quality crab. Peekytoe, blue crabs from the cold ocean waters off the coast of central Maine, are esteemed for both their body and their leg meat, while some other crabs, such as Jonah, are prized only for leg meat. Either way, choose the best crab you can, or, if you prefer, use cooked lobster here. I serve the crab mixture on top of tiny kumquats, which are small oval-shaped citrus fruits easy to find during their winter-through-early-spring season. Try key limes instead of kumquats, or use both key limes and kumquats, alternating the colors for presentation, and serve them on a bright, colorful plate. Lacking either, the crabmeat is good on tiny toast points.

8 ounces Peekytoe or other high-quality cooked
crabmeat, picked over to remove any shells
2 tablespoons olive oil
2 tablespoons fresh lemon juice
⅛ teaspoon curry powder
½ teaspoon kosher salt
1 teaspoon white pepper
1 tablespoon chopped fresh chives
6 kumquats
About 12 chives, chopped for garnish

1. Put the crab in a small bowl. Add the olive oil, lemon juice, curry, salt, white pepper, and chopped chives. Mix well.
2. Slice each kumquat in half lengthwise. Using a melon baller or small knife, scoop out a small amount of the kumquat flesh, leaving a thick shell. Fill each kumquat half with about ½ teaspoon of crab salad. Arrange the halves on a platter or other serving dish and garnish each with chopped chives.

PINK PEPPERCORN—CRUSTED BLUEFIN TUNA WITH TOMATO MARMALADE AND BUTTERMILK CRACKERS

Serves 6

The floral notes of these aromatic pink peppercorns with barely seared tuna appeals to me. I like them better than black peppercorns. They are sweet and slightly fragrant and, like all spices, taste best when freshly ground. The first time I saw pink peppercorns was twenty years ago at Paul Bocuse's famed restaurant in Lyon, France, where the waiter ground them at the table to finish a turbot dish. It was a revelation to me and I started experimenting with all sorts of peppercorns. The jammy marmalade I make to accompany the tuna has more of an onion than a tomato presence. Finally, I love these buttermilk crackers. They are wonderful with the tuna—crisp and crunchy, terrific with nearly any topping or on their own. Break them into unusual shapes with your fingers for a rustic look.

TOMATO MARMALADE:

2 tablespoons olive oil
1½ cups thinly sliced red onion
1½ cups peeled, seeded, and chopped vine-ripened
    tomatoes
⅓ cup granulated sugar
1 tablespoon finely chopped fresh thyme
1 tablespoon finely chopped fresh tarragon
Kosher salt and freshly ground black pepper

PINK PEPPERCORN—CRUSTED BLUEFIN TUNA:

½ cup pink peppercorns, toasted and ground (see Note)
1 6-ounce log bluefin tuna
1 tablespoon Clarified Butter (see page 279)
12 Buttermilk Crackers (recipe follows)

1. To make the marmalade, heat the olive oil in a large, heavy sauté pan over medium-low heat. Add the onions, reduce the heat to low, and cook, stirring from time to time, for about 20 minutes or until the onions are softened and golden brown. Stir in the tomatoes and sugar.

2. Reduce the heat to low and cook for about 3 hours, until the mixture is thick and jelled. Add the thyme and tarragon. Season to taste with salt and pepper. Set aside to cool completely.

3. To make the tuna, spread half of the ground peppercorns on a shallow plate. Roll the tuna log in the peppercorns to coat lightly.

4. Heat the butter in a medium nonstick skillet over medium-high heat. Sear the tuna for 3 to 4 minutes, turning to sear all sides.

5. Spread the remaining peppercorns on the plate. Roll the seared tuna in the remaining pepper to coat lightly. Slice into 12 equal pieces.

6. To serve, place a spoonful of the marmalade on a buttermilk cracker, lay a piece of the tuna on top of the marmalade, and set 2 of these on a plate. Repeat with the remaining crackers and tuna to make 5 more servings.

NOTE: *Pink peppercorns, available in many supermarkets and specialty stores, are not true peppercorns but are the dried berries from the* Baies rose *plant. Buy dried pink peppercorns and toast them in a dry skillet over medium-high heat for 30 to 40 seconds until fragrant. Transfer to a plate or sheet of wax paper to cool. Grind in a spice grinder or small food processor.*

BUTTERMILK CRACKERS

*Makes enough for
6 to 10 servings*

1 ¼ cups all-purpose flour
1 ½ teaspoons sugar
Pinch of kosher salt
5 tablespoons unsalted butter, cut into ½-inch cubes
10 tablespoons buttermilk
1 large egg white, lightly beaten
Kosher salt and freshly ground pepper for sprinkling

1. Preheat the oven to 350 degrees and position an oven rack in the center of the oven. Line a jelly-roll pan or large baking sheet with parchment paper.

2. In the bowl of an electric mixer fitted with the paddle attachment, combine the flour, sugar, and salt and mix at low speed until combined. Add the butter and mix until the mixture resembles coarse meal. Add the buttermilk and continue to mix until the liquid is absorbed and the dough starts to come together. Do not overmix.

3. Turn the dough out onto a lightly floured work surface. Shape into a disk. Wrap in plastic wrap and refrigerate for at least 1 hour or until firm enough to roll out.

4. Lightly dust the work surface and rolling pin with flour. Roll out the dough into a very thin sheet, about ¼ inch thick, dusting the work surface and dough with additional flour as needed. Prick the sheet of dough all over with a fork. Transfer the dough to the prepared pan. Unless the work surface was dusted with flour, the dough might stick. Use a spatula or another tool to release it gently from the surface. Brush the dough with some of the egg white and sprinkle with salt and pepper. Bake in the middle of the oven for 6 to 10 minutes or until golden brown. Transfer to a wire rack to cool completely. Break into irregularly shaped pieces to serve.

CHAPTER TWO

Amuse-Bouche

AN *AMUSE-BOUCHE*, SERVED BEFORE the meal begins, is meant to bewitch the eye and tickle the palate. They appeal to my belief that no one should take food too seriously, even while they are serious about food. At the end of the day, food should bring joy, excitement, and pleasure to the heart and soul, and there's no better way than with these little jewels.

Amuse-bouche should be lighthearted and provocative. The concept of a little bite at the table before the meal begins may be new to you, but once you grasp it, let your imagination run wild as you sample exotic or unfamiliar ingredients and try new cooking techniques. I love these so much, I wrote a whole book on the subject called *Amuse-Bouche*.

Use this little first course, too, to make use of decorative plates, antique cups, and Grandma's silver iced-tea spoons. Half the fun of *amuse-bouche* is the presentation, and it's gratifying to come up with oddball ways to serve them dramatically and playfully.

At Tru, I use pristine white plates, Asian-style bowls and spoons, sparkling shot glasses, sleek black trays, long-handled spoons and forks, mirrors, and granite and marble tiles. I also serve *amuse-bouche* in old-fashioned demitasse cups, finger bowls, heavy glass ashtrays, votive-candle holders, Depression juice glasses, and odd-sized cut-glass glasses, and on green-rimmed glass shelves, old-time wooden checkerboards, and small silver trays. Have fun!

ABOUT THE WINE FOR THESE RECIPES: These decadent little bites beg for equally stunning beverages. An opulent Tête de Cuvée such as 1990 Pol Roger *Cuvée Sir Winston Churchill* or the elegant, floral chilled *Sato no Homare* sake from Sudo Honke starts the meal off on a perfect high note.

17   *Red Watermelon–Lavender Juice with Yellow Watermelon Salad*

19   *Rabbit Roulade with a Salad of Frisée, French Beans, and Radish*

21   *Clam Foam on the Half Shell with Crispy Pancetta*

22   *Chilled Purple Peruvian Potato Soup with Chives*

23   *Carrot Parfait with Carrot Paint*

24   *Thai Snapper with Hijiki Seaweed, Lemon Balm Salad, and Yuzu Soy Dressing*

26   *Kumamoto Oysters with Passion Fruit Gelée on Aromatic Rock Salt*

27   *Red and Yellow Teardrop Tomatoes Stuffed with Goat Cheese with 100-year-old Balsamic*

28   *Deconstructed Insalata Caprese with Olive Oil Sorbet*

29   *Marinated White Anchovies with Green Olives and Tomatoes*

31   *Black Garbanzo Bean and Celery Salad*

32   *Prosciutto di Parma with Tricolor Melon and Mascarpone*

RED WATERMELON–LAVENDER JUICE WITH YELLOW WATERMELON SALAD

Serves 4 to 6

When I was a child growing up in Rochester, New York, we celebrated an annual lilac festival where families came together for a day of picnics and games. Lavender grew in the same areas as the lilacs, and I associate its light fragrance with the sweet watermelon from my mother's picnic cooler, which is why I pair the two here. I also recall wanting more of the juice from those sweet, pink melons, and so when I learned about juicing, I immediately started juicing watermelons. The juice is as sweet as can be, and the fresh lavender provides just a touch of floral perfume. I love the contrast of the yellow watermelon and mint salad with the bright red juice, and although I think it's a good idea to buy seedless watermelon because they are easy to serve, if you use seeded melon, the shiny black seeds make a sleek-looking garnish sprinkled on the plate alongside the shooter of juice.

Quarter of a small red seedless watermelon
(about 1 pound)
1 tablespoon coarsely chopped fresh lavender
Kosher salt
Quarter of a small yellow seedless watermelon
(about 1 pound)
1 teaspoon chopped fresh mint
1 teaspoon extra-virgin olive oil
Freshly ground black pepper
1 teaspoon Tramonto's Lime Dust, for garnish
(see page 272)

1. Using a large sharp knife, slice the rind from the red watermelon. Stud the watermelon flesh with the chopped lavender and then cut the melon into pieces small enough to fit through a juicer's feed tube.

2. Juice the watermelon. You will have about ¾ cup of juice.

3. Strain the juice through a chinois or fine-mesh sieve into a pitcher. Season to taste with salt. Cover and refrigerate for at least 2 hours or until chilled.

4. Using a large sharp knife, slice the rind from the yellow watermelon. Cut the flesh into strips approximately 1 inch thick and 3 inches long.

5. Put the slices of yellow watermelon and the mint in a large, shallow bowl. Drizzle with olive oil and toss lightly to mix. Season to taste with salt and pepper.

6. To serve, pour watermelon juice into each of 4 or 6 chilled shot glasses. Place each glass on a plate. Arrange equal amounts of the yellow watermelon salad next to each glass. Drizzle any remaining juice from the salad, and the lime dust, over and around the salad.

RABBIT ROULADE WITH A SALAD OF FRISÉE, FRENCH BEANS, AND RADISH

Serves 6

The matching of frisée salad with rabbit or duck confit is classic and I thought it would make a lovely little *amuse-bouche*. For this, I chose rabbit because it's lighter than duck and so much more unexpected. The flavors are the wonderful rich ones you find in French bistros and brasseries. When the great chef Alain Chapel was alive and running his eponymous restaurant in Mionnay, France, I had the great honor of eating there and spending time with him talking about food. He was a master of confit and had a lot of it on the menu the day I ate there. Since then, I have always included confits in my cuisine. He is a true personal hero and source of inspiration. I still cherish his cookbook that he signed for me in 1989. He is sorely missed.

3 cups shredded Rabbit Leg Confit (see page 190)
1 cup duck fat (see Note)
¼ cup white verjuice (see Note)
¼ cup finely chopped fresh thyme
2 tablespoons chopped chives
Kosher salt and freshly ground black pepper
1 head frisée (curly endive), roughly torn into pieces
¼ cup halved haricots verts or very slender green beans,
*   steamed until tender and cooled*
1 red radish, thinly sliced
¾ cup plus 1 tablespoon Sherry Vinaigrette (recipe
*   follows)*

1. Combine the rabbit confit and fat in a saucepan over low heat and heat gently for about 5 minutes or until warm.

2. Transfer the rabbit mixture to the bowl of an electric mixer fitted with the paddle attachment. Add the verjuice, thyme, and chives and season to taste with salt and pepper. With the mixer on medium speed, mix until blended. Alternatively, mix the ingredients in a large bowl with a spoon. It's easier to mix in an electric mixer.

3. Place a 10-inch-long sheet of plastic wrap on a work surface, with the long side facing you. Spread out the rabbit mixture along the bottom, leaving a 2-inch border at each end. Roll the plastic over the rabbit to make a log. Hold both ends of the plastic wrap and roll it along the work surface to tighten the roll. The roll should be about 1 inch in diameter. Prick a few holes in the log with a small pin to release any trapped air. Refrigerate for at least 3 hours and up to 24 hours.

4. Combine the frisée, haricots verts, and radish in a bowl and toss with ¾ cup of the vinaigrette.

5. Remove the plastic wrap from the log. Slice into ¼-inch-thick pieces. Divide the salad among 6 plates, arranging it in a mound in the center of each plate. Top each mound of salad with 4 slices of the rabbit confit and drizzle each with ½ teaspoon of the remaining vinaigrette.

NOTE: *To render 1 cup of duck fat, melt 1 pound of duck fat in a heavy saucepan over low heat. Cool slightly and then strain through a fine-mesh strainer or chinois.*

Both white and red verjuice can be bought in specialty food stores.

SHERRY VINAIGRETTE

Makes 3½ cups

½ cup coarsely chopped shallots
1 tablespoon Dijon mustard
1 cup sherry wine vinegar
1½ tablespoons chopped fresh chives
1½ tablespoons chopped fresh chervil
3½ cups extra-virgin olive oil
Kosher salt and freshly ground black pepper

1. Put the shallots in a blender and pulse until finely chopped. Add the mustard and vinegar and blend until well mixed. Add the chives and chervil and pulse several times until blended.

2. With the blender running, slowly pour the olive oil through the feed tube and blend until thoroughly combined and emulsified. Season to taste with salt and pepper.

3. Strain through a chinois or fine-mesh sieve. Use immediately or cover and refrigerate for up to 3 days. Whisk well before using.

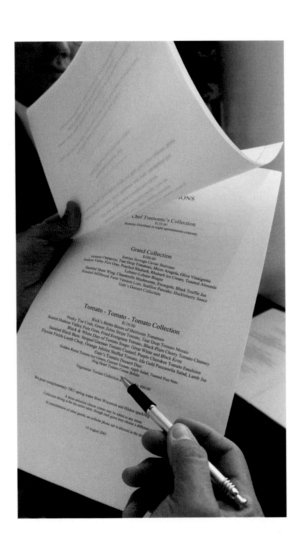

CLAM FOAM ON THE HALF SHELL
WITH CRISPY PANCETTA

Serves 6

One of the greatest clam chowders I ever had was when my friend chef Todd English came to cook with me at Brasserie T to promote his first book. Together we made the most incredible clam chowder ever! I think of this dish as clam chowder in a spoon. The foam relies on clam juice for its flavor and we serve it with the other ingredients essential to clam chowder: bacon (pancetta in this case) and potatoes. As the foam dissolves on your tongue, it almost tastes like you are in New England, eating clam chowder at a clam shack overlooking the water, and so it becomes a play on soup.

4 sheets gelatin
2 cups clam juice
Kosher salt and freshly ground black pepper
2 N_2O cream chargers
¼ pound pancetta or slab bacon, cut into small dice
¼ pound all-purpose potato (1 potato)
2 tablespoons olive oil
6 clean, dry littleneck, Manila, or other small clamshells

1. Fill a large bowl with cool water. Gently submerge the gelatin sheets in the water. Let soften and bloom for about 10 minutes.

2. Meanwhile, strain the clam juice through a chinois or fine-mesh sieve lined with a paper coffee filter into a medium bowl.

3. Using your hands, lift the gelatin sheets from the water and squeeze them gently between your fingers. Transfer the sheets to the clam juice. Stir gently until dissolved. Season to taste with salt and pepper.

4. Pour into a chilled iSi Gourmet Whip canister. Charge with 1 or 2 N_2O cream chargers. Chill for at least 1 hour.

5. Cook the bacon in a small sauté pan over low heat until the fat is rendered. Raise the heat to medium and cook until crisp and brown. Remove with a slotted spoon and drain on paper towels.

6. Peel and cut the potato into tiny cubes.

7. Heat the olive oil in a small sauté pan over medium heat. Add the potato cubes and cook for 5 to 8 minutes or until crispy and cooked through, tossing occasionally. Season to taste with salt and pepper.

8. To serve, shake the clam foam vigorously and pour a little into each of the clamshells. Garnish the foam with the bacon and potatoes.

CHILLED PURPLE PERUVIAN POTATO SOUP WITH CHIVES

Serves 6

I love the drama of this deep-blue-to-purple soup, as well as its subtle flavor. It's no longer unusual to find purple Peruvian potatoes in the markets, but it's not easy to keep their color when you make soup. The trick is to use larger potatoes, which have the best color, and to keep the soup cold, cold, cold. I begin by soaking the potatoes overnight in ice water, which sets the color. Refrigerate the soup overnight before serving it. Some kind of alchemy happens in the cold environment and the color actually deepens.

I still recall the first time I saw a blue potato. Gale and I had opened the restaurant Trio in Evanston, Illinois, in the early 1990s. Tom Cornille of Cornille and Sons, who is our produce expert in Chicago, and I would walk around his warehouse at the South Water Street Market, where vendors sell wholesale produce, fish, and meat. I was working hard to come up with interesting vegetable dishes for the winter menu, when fresh produce was scarce. When I said I wanted to make a potato soup, Tom pointed out purple potatoes— and I was hooked.

1 pound purple potatoes, peeled, white inner layer
removed, and left whole
1 tablespoon vegetable oil
1 leek, white part only, well washed and coarsely
chopped
1 white onion, thinly sliced
4 cups cold Vegetable Stock (see page 266)
Kosher salt and freshly ground white pepper
Juice of 1 orange
Finely chopped chives, for garnish

1. Soak the potatoes in a bowl of ice water overnight in the refrigerator.
2. Heat the oil in a medium saucepan over low heat. Add the leek and onion and cook, stirring occasionally, for about 5 minutes or until softened but not browned.
3. Add the potatoes and enough cold stock to cover. Bring to a simmer for about 20 minutes or until the potatoes are fork-tender.
4. Transfer the soup to a blender and puree until smooth. You may need to cut the potatoes to fit, but if possible keep them whole so they do not bleed. Strain through a chinois or fine-mesh sieve into a large metal bowl. Add enough of the remaining cold stock to achieve the consistency of soup. Season to taste with salt and white pepper. Stir in the orange juice. Submerge the bowl in an ice-water bath to keep cold.
5. Serve the chilled soup in Asian ceramic spoons or demitasse cups, garnished with chopped chives.

CARROT PARFAIT WITH CARROT PAINT

Serves 25

At any given time, I offer several collections, or tasting menus, at Tru. They may concentrate on fish, seafood, meat, or vegetables. When I was coming up with an idea for a wonderful *amuse-bouche* for a vegetable collection, I thought of a perfect organic carrot that morphs into this light, pretty parfait. I made a carrot reduction to go with it, reduced the reduction a little further, and called it carrot paint. When it's "painted" on a plate, it makes a dramatic presentation. The carrot parfait was just the first in a series of vegetable parfaits, a never-ending selection of mini-explosions of pure flavors and colors. This serves twenty-five, which sounds like a lot, but it's difficult to make this any smaller and it's lovely, light, and easy to eat.

3 cups plus 2 tablespoons organic carrot juice
　　(see page 281)
1 1/2 cups plus 2 tablespoons heavy cream
Salt and freshly ground white pepper
7 sheets gelatin
Carrot Paint (recipe follows)

1. In a medium-sized saucepan over medium-high heat, bring the carrot juice to a simmer. Stirring constantly, simmer the juice for about 15 minutes or until reduced to 1 scant cup.

2. In the bowl of an electric mixer fitted with the whisk attachment, whip the heavy cream until soft peaks form. Season to taste with salt and white pepper.

3. Meanwhile, fill a large bowl with cool water. Gently submerge the gelatin sheets in the water. Let soften and bloom for about 10 minutes. Using your hands, lift the gelatin sheets from the water and squeeze them gently between your fingers.

4. Transfer the sheets to a blender along with the reduced carrot juice. Blend until smooth.

5. Gently fold the carrot mixture into the whipped cream. Season to taste with more salt and pepper.

6. Pour the mixture onto a rimmed 9-by-13-inch baking pan or half-sheet pan. The pan should be large enough so that the mixture is not more than 1/4 inch deep. Chill for 2 hours or until set.

7. To serve, using a 1/2-inch-wide paintbrush, brush a stroke of carrot paint across the plate. Cut the parfait into small teardrops or rectangles with a cookie cutter and arrange on small plates on top of the paint.

CARROT PAINT

Makes 1 cup

4 cups carrot juice (see page 281)
1/2 cup grapeseed oil
Kosher salt

1. In a medium-sized saucepan over low heat, slowly simmer the carrot juice, whisking frequently, for about 30 minutes or until the juice is reduced to 1/2 cup.

2. Strain the juice through a chinois or fine mesh sieve into a small bowl. Set aside at room temperature to cool.

3. Transfer the juice to a blender. With the motor running, slowly pour in the oil. Process until emulsified. Season to taste with salt.

4. Transfer the paint to a small glass or ceramic bowl. Use immediately or cover and refrigerate for up to 3 days.

THAI SNAPPER WITH HIJIKI SEAWEED, LEMON BALM SALAD, AND YUZU SOY DRESSING

Serves 4 to 6

When I lived in New York's West Village in the early 1980s, I discovered good sushi. I ate it all the time and developed a great fondness for it, which has only grown over the years. These days, I eat at Nobu in New York whenever I can and am always inspired by chef Nobu Matsuhisa. I developed this dish to satisfy my love of sashimi, although the fish is lightly cured with the yuzu soy dressing. Make sure the snapper or whatever fish you are using is super-fresh and of the highest quality before you make this light and simple dish.

1 very fresh snapper fillet with skin (about 8 ounces)
¼ cup hijiki seaweed
½ lotus root, thinly sliced
½ red bell pepper, seeded, ribbed, and thinly sliced
¼ cup micro cress or micro-greens mix
4 to 6 tablespoons Yuzu Soy Dressing (recipe follows)
¼ cup chopped fresh lemon balm, for garnish

1. Slice the snapper into paper-thin pieces, each weighing about ¼ ounce. Cover with plastic wrap and refrigerate.

2. Mix the seaweed with the lotus root, red bell pepper, and micro cress. Cover with plastic wrap and refrigerate.

3. To serve, toss the seaweed mixture with about 3 tablespoons of yuzu soy dressing. Spoon equal amounts of seaweed salad onto the center of each plate. Place a few pieces of snapper on top of the salad. Drizzle the fish with about 1 tablespoon of the dressing. The acid in the dressing will cure the fish slightly. Garnish with lemon balm.

YUZU SOY DRESSING

Makes about ¾ cup

¼ cup soy sauce
2 tablespoons toasted sesame oil
2 tablespoons yuzu or lemon juice
Juice from 1 orange
1 tablespoon finely chopped fresh cilantro
1 tablespoon finely sliced scallion, sliced on the diagonal

1. Whisk together the soy sauce, sesame oil, yuzu juice, and orange juice until thoroughly blended.

2. Stir in the cilantro and scallion. Use immediately or cover and refrigerate for up to 3 days. Stir before serving.

KUMAMOTO OYSTERS WITH PASSION FRUIT GELÉE ON AROMATIC ROCK SALT

Serves 6

As much as I like any ice-cold, fresh oyster, just shucked and still tasting a little metallic from the seawater, I prefer small slurps to large gulps. This is one reason why I adore small, sweet Kumamoto oysters, generally classified as a Pacific oyster. Oysters traditionally are served with cocktail sauce or mignonette, both of which are slightly acidic. I prefer to add a little acid with a passion fruit vinaigrette and gelée. Use any oysters you like—Belon, Olympia, bluepoint, Hama Hama—but make sure they are in season and very fresh. To ensure this, shuck them yourself just before serving.

2 cups rock salt
2 tablespoons star anise
2 tablespoons pink peppercorns
2 tablespoons black peppercorns
12 cinnamon sticks, broken into 1-inch pieces
12 Kumamoto oysters, shucked
¼ cup Passion Fruit Vinaigrette (recipe follows)
¼ cup Passion Fruit Gelée cubes, about ¼ inch square (recipe follows)
¼ cup extra-virgin olive oil

1. Mix the rock salt, star anise, pink and black peppercorns, and cinnamon sticks in a small bowl to make the aromatic rock salt.
2. To serve, spread some of the rock-salt mixture in a shallow bowl to create a bed for the oysters. Put 2 of the oysters on the rock salt.
3. Drizzle a small amount of the passion fruit vinaigrette over the oysters and top them with passion fruit gelée cubes. Drizzle the oysters with olive oil. Repeat to make 5 more servings.

ABOUT THE WINE: *Silky-textured Kumamoto oysters are playfully served with various exotic flavors of gelée that offer an interesting counterpoint to the briny, sweet bivalve. A clean, fruity wine is best here. The pure stone-fruit flavors of Pinot Gris Beblenheim from Alsace's Marcel Deiss will pull together all the opposing elements.*

PASSION FRUIT VINAIGRETTE

Makes 1 cup

6 tablespoons passion fruit puree (see Note)
Juice of ½ lemon
1 tablespoon honey
1 tablespoon champagne vinegar
6 tablespoons olive oil
Kosher salt and freshly ground white pepper

1. In a blender, combine the passion fruit puree, lemon juice, honey, and vinegar. Puree for 30 seconds or until smooth.
2. With the motor running, slowly pour in the oil and blend until emulsified. Transfer to a small glass or ceramic bowl and season to taste with salt and pepper.
3. Use immediately or refrigerate the vinaigrette in a tightly lidded nonreactive container for up to 1 week. Whisk well before using.

NOTE: *Passion fruit puree is sold frozen in specialty stores and many natural food stores.*

PASSION FRUIT GELÉE

Makes 2 cups

1 ½ cups passion fruit puree (see Note, page 26)
1 cup spring or tap water
7 sheets gelatin

1. In a medium saucepan, bring the puree and water to a boil over medium-high heat and cook for 2 to 3 minutes. Remove the pan from the heat and set aside to cool slightly.

2. Meanwhile, fill a bowl with cool water. Gently drop the gelatin sheets into the water, several at a time, until all are submerged. Let soften and bloom for about 5 minutes.

3. Using your hands, lift the gelatin sheets from the water and squeeze them gently between your fingers. Transfer the sheets to the passion fruit mixture. Stir gently until dissolved. Strain through a fine-mesh sieve into another bowl.

4. Pour the mixture onto a clean, rimmed 9-by-13-inch baking sheet. The pan should be large enough so that the mixture is not more than ¼ inch deep. Chill for 30 minutes to 1 hour or until set.

5. Cut the gelée into ¼-inch-square cubes. Use immediately or refrigerate until needed.

RED AND YELLOW TEARDROP TOMATOES STUFFED WITH GOAT CHEESE WITH 100-YEAR-OLD BALSAMIC

Serves 6

When tomatoes are in season, I go full tilt. There's no stopping me, and as much as I experiment, I always come back to the combinations I know and love. For instance, is there anything better than ripe, sweet tomatoes with a fantastic farmers' market goat cheese? The small, colorful tomatoes are pretty, too, on a plate, and when you bite into them, the flavors explode in your mouth, as an *amuse-bouche* should. If you don't have goat cheese, serve these tasty little tomatoes with great extra-virgin olive oil and kosher salt and pepper. You don't need anything more. I know, because I still remember snatching sun-warmed cherry tomatoes from my father's garden when I was a kid and popping them in my mouth like candy!

½ cup fresh goat cheese
1 tablespoon heavy cream
1 tablespoon half-and-half
Kosher salt and freshly ground white pepper
6 red teardrop, cherry, or grape tomatoes
6 yellow teardrop, cherry, or grape tomatoes
2 tablespoons aged balsamic vinegar
    (preferably 100-year-old vinegar)

1. In a small mixing bowl, combine the goat cheese, cream, and half-and-half. Mix until smooth and season to taste with salt and white pepper.

2. Slice a sliver off the bottom of each tomato so that they can stand on their own. Cut the top half off the tomatoes to reveal the seeds. Using tiny tweezers, remove the seeds to hollow out the tomatoes.

3. Using a pastry bag fitted with a small, plain tip, pipe the goat cheese mixture into the hollowed-out tomatoes. You might not use all the filling.

4. To serve, garnish the tomatoes with a drizzle of balsamic vinegar.

DECONSTRUCTED INSALATA CAPRESE WITH OLIVE OIL SORBET

Serves 4 to 6

The last time I traveled in Spain I was struck with how the chefs were "deconstructing" classic dishes: keeping the same flavor minglings but presenting them in unusual ways. I was traveling with my friend chef Jose Andres from Jaleo restaurant in Washington, D.C., and we visited his mentor, chef Ferran Adrià, co-owner with his brother, Albert, of the world-acclaimed restaurant El Bulli outside Barcelona. Ferran and Albert have since become major influences in my culinary life and good friends. On that evening Ferran made an olive oil sorbet that intrigued me. I went home and started to work with it, pairing it with a classic caprese salad. But instead of drizzling rich, fruity olive oil over the tomatoes and mozzarella cheese, I serve a mound of ice-cold olive oil sorbet amid the vegetables. As it melts, the olive oil pools on the plate and mingles with the tomatoes, basil, and cheese in the most tantalizing way.

3 cups extra-virgin olive oil
Kosher salt and freshly ground black pepper
3 medium vine-ripened yellow tomatoes (about 1 pound)
3 medium vine-ripened red tomatoes (about 1 pound)
1 10-ounce ball fresh mozzarella or mozzarella di bufala
6 leaves fresh basil

1. To make the olive oil sorbet using a conventional ice-cream machine, cover and refrigerate the olive oil for at least 2 hours or until thoroughly chilled. Season to taste with salt and pepper. Freeze in an ice-cream machine according to the manufacturer's directions. Put the frozen sorbet in a chilled container, press plastic wrap against the surface, and cover. Freeze until ready to serve. Or, if using a Pacojet, pour the olive oil into a Pacojet container and freeze completely. About 30 minutes before serving, place the container in a Pacojet machine and spin according to the manufacturer's directions. Freeze until ready to serve.

2. Peel and seed the tomatoes. Cut them into ¼-inch-thick slices.

3. Cut the mozzarella into small dice.

4. Stack the basil leaves on top of one another and roll into a thin cylinder. Slice into thin strips.

5. To serve, arrange a slice of yellow tomato in the center of each plate. Lay a slice of red tomato on top of the yellow tomato.

6. Scoop a small mound of sorbet, measuring about 1 tablespoon, onto the center of the tomatoes.

7. Sprinkle diced mozzarella around the tomatoes. Season to taste with salt and pepper. Sprinkle the sliced basil around the mozzarella.

MARINATED WHITE ANCHOVIES WITH GREEN OLIVES AND TOMATOES

Serves 6

In the spring of 2003, when I cooked at the James Beard House in New York City, I took my crew out for lunch at Otto Enoteca and Pizzeria in the West Village, owned by my friend chef Mario Batali. We tasted a salad made with white anchovies, Sicilian green olives, tomatoes, and extra-virgin olive oil that we literally couldn't stop talking about. When I got back to Tru, I developed my own recipe as an *amuse-bouche,* put it on the menu, and it has been one of the customers' favorites ever since. If you have the best ingredients, you won't go wrong here: a ripe, sweet tomato, great green olives, the best extra-virgin olive oil, and excellent anchovy fillets.

Olive oil is one of my favorite cooking tools and intrinsic to my cooking. I can't emphasize how important it is to use great olive oil. Italy, France, Spain, and Greece all produce terrific olive oil and you will want to sample various oils from these countries. Tasting it is like tasting wine—it has almost as much to do with aroma, texture, and color as with taste. Depending on the strength and intensity of the oil, some are better for finishing a dish while others are better for marinating, cooking, or flavoring food. I recommend Terre Bormane olive oils, which are Italian oils available at health food stores, gourmet shops, and some supermarkets. Opalino and Albis are the two Terre Bormane oils I use most often for marinating, finishing, and even cooking—although I usually cook with a pure olive oil rather than an extra-virgin oil. Don't hold back; it's essential.

1 plum tomato, peeled, seeded, and chopped
2 tablespoons finely chopped fresh green olives (brunoise)
1 teaspoon finely grated lemon zest
2 tablespoons extra-virgin olive oil
Kosher salt and freshly ground black pepper
12 canned white anchovy fillets

1. In a small bowl, toss together the tomato, olives, and zest. Add the olive oil and toss again. Season to taste with salt and pepper.

2. Lay 2 fillets on each of 6 small plates. Spoon the tomato-olive mixture evenly over the anchovies and serve.

BLACK GARBANZO BEAN AND CELERY SALAD

Serves 6

This is a cool salad. Several years ago, I ate at Felidia in New York City, where chef-owner Lidia Matticchio Bastianich served a black and white garbanzo bean salad. Until then, I had never seen black garbanzo beans. They are about the size of large peas and their texture is a little firmer and crunchier than that of white garbanzos.

As a kid growing up, I always loved salads made with white, or buff-colored, garbanzo beans (also called chickpeas and ceci beans), celery, and olive oil—the sort of oil-based salad Italians make so well. While I updated it for Tru's customers, this remains a salad in the tradition of Old World Italian cooking.

1 tablespoon peeled and thinly sliced rib celery
1 cup cooked Black Garbanzo Beans (recipe follows)
1 tablespoon extra-virgin olive oil
1 tablespoon sherry vinegar
½ teaspoon minced shallot
½ teaspoon chopped chives
Kosher salt and freshly ground black pepper
Celery leaves, for garnish

1. In a small saucepan of boiling water, blanch the sliced celery just until bright green. Drain, plunge into ice water to shock, and drain again.
2. In a mixing bowl, toss together the beans, olive oil, vinegar, shallot, and chives. Season to taste with salt and pepper.
3. Spoon the salad into 6 small bowls and garnish each with celery leaves.

BLACK GARBANZO BEANS

Makes about 1 cup

2 tablespoons unsalted butter
2 ribs celery, coarsely chopped
1 medium carrot, peeled and coarsely chopped
1 fennel bulb, coarsely chopped
1 onion, halved
2 tablespoons fennel seeds
1 tablespoon coriander seeds
1 tablespoon mustard seeds
1 tablespoon black peppercorns
2 bay leaves
2 to 3 tablespoons fresh thyme
½ bunch flat-leaf parsley stems
1 quart Vegetable Stock (see page 266)
1 cup dried black garbanzo beans
¼ cup sherry vinegar
Kosher salt and freshly ground white pepper

1. In a large stockpot, heat the butter over medium-high heat. Add the celery, carrot, and fennel and cook for 8 to 10 minutes or until translucent. Add the onion and cook for 2 or 3 minutes until it begins to soften.
2. Lay a piece of cheesecloth on the countertop and pile the seeds, peppercorns, bay leaves, thyme, and parsley stems in the center. Gather the corners and tie with kitchen string to make a sachet.
3. Pour the stock into the pot and add the sachet. Bring to a boil, reduce the heat, and simmer for about 1 hour. Cool by submerging the pot in a large bowl or sink filled with ice and water. Refrigerate until completely cold.
4. Return the cold stock to the stove and add the beans. Bring to a simmer and cook for about 1½ hours, or until the beans are tender. Do not let the liquid boil.
5. Add the sherry vinegar and season to taste with salt and pepper. Let the beans cool in the liquid. Scoop out the beans and discard any vegetables. If not using immediately, store the beans and cooking liquid together, covered and refrigerated, for up to 2 days.

PROSCIUTTO DI PARMA WITH TRICOLOR MELON AND MASCARPONE

Serves 6

If this classic is done right, it's nothing short of superb. If executed poorly, it's boring at best. Start with really good prosciutto and really ripe melon. Otherwise, why bother? I had the good fortune to spend time in Parma, Italy, and gained an understanding of why their ham is so good. It's moist, lightly salted, and perfectly cured. It's also sliced by hand, which I think is very important. Electric slicers generate just enough heat to melt the fat and dry out the prosciutto. I suggest you use a very sharp knife or make sure your slicer is extremely sharp so it works quickly.

I love the salty sweetness of good prosciutto. One taste of the real thing is all you need to understand why food lovers the world over revere it. Prosciutto di Parma is luxuriously streaked with fat, lightly fragrant, and tastes pleasing.

I had the privilege a few years ago of representing the United States at the International Prosciutto di Parma Festival in Parma. This region of Italy is home to Parma ham, Parmigiano-Reggiano cheese, and a third luxury: the Ferrari! It's a mountainous area where the pigs are fastidiously raised. Once the meat is butchered, it's cured for ten or twelve months in a way that results in moist, delicious ham unlike any from any other part of the world.

1 cup mascarpone cheese
¼ cup Homemade Crème Fraîche (see page 280)
2 tablespoons white wine vinegar
Kosher salt and freshly ground black pepper
¼ pound Crenshaw melon, peeled and thinly sliced
¼ pound honeydew melon, peeled and thinly sliced
¼ pound red watermelon, peeled and thinly sliced
6 paper-thin slices of prosciutto di Parma
2 tablespoons extra-virgin olive oil
2 tablespoons aged balsamic vinegar

1. In a small bowl, whisk the mascarpone with the crème fraîche and white wine vinegar. Season to taste with salt and pepper.

2. Put the Crenshaw, honeydew, and watermelon slices in a bowl and toss with 10 to 12 tablespoons of the mascarpone mixture. Season to taste with salt and pepper.

3. To serve, put a slice of prosciutto on each of 6 plates. Spoon melon salad in the center of each slice of prosciutto. Drizzle with olive oil and balsamic vinegar. Top each with about 1 tablespoon of the mascarpone mixture.

CHAPTER THREE

Cold Appetizers

BY THE TIME A TRU GUEST gets to the cold appetizer on the menu, he is ready for some serious food and presentation. The hors d'oeuvres and *amuse-bouche* that preceded are charming, but, let's face it, they are teasers for bigger things to come.

I love these cold appetizers. Not only are they a showcase for luxurious caviar, smoked salmon, and sweet Peekytoe crabmeat, they allow me enormous room for creativity—and nothing stimulates me more than the appetizers centered around fish and seafood. Working with fish is where I shine in the kitchen, and where I like to be. When I create these gems, I can go all out with gorgeous presentations, too. Nothing makes me happier!

These dishes call out for vinaigrettes, foams, gelées, and small, boldly flavored salads. They joyfully ease you into the main part of a meal, while generating their own excitement. You'll never be left out in the cold!

37   *Tramonto's Caviar Staircase with Homemade Crème Fraîche*

38   *Live Japanese Fish and Chips*

42   *Mosaic of Seafood with Saffron Foam*

45   *Peekytoe Crab Salad with Crispy Sawagani Crab and Micro Greens*

49   *Octopus Carpaccio with Niçoise Vinaigrette*

51   *Beef Tartar with Quail Egg and Beef Gelée*

TRAMONTO'S CAVIAR STAIRCASE WITH HOMEMADE CRÈME FRAÎCHE

Serves 6

Since I began serving caviar as a chef in 1987, I've had enormous respect for it. But my passion for the salty little sturgeon roe is beyond words! I can hardly get enough, although all you need is a small bite to satisfy a yearning. When you taste the different varieties, your palate becomes sensitive to their nuances and subtleties, such as nuttiness, brininess, or fruity overtones, which makes tasting this luxury a never-ending culinary adventure.

At Trio, the restaurant I opened in the early 1990s with Gale, I came up with the idea of serving caviar on an artist's palette. When I opened Tru, I wanted an even more dramatic presentation and so created my famous glass caviar staircase (available at tramontocuisine.com) as a way to elevate the caviar, both literally and figuratively. My friend Howard Harris of H-3 Architectural Systems in Chicago, Illinois, manufactured the idea for me. It was Howard's idea to etch my signature in the staircase as a play on the concept of a signature dish. Today, about 85 percent of our customers order the caviar staircase, which means the restaurant's forty-five staircases are in constant use.

True caviar is the roe of three types of sturgeon that swim in the Caspian Sea: beluga, osetra, and sevruga. Iran, which borders the Caspian, is known for selling some of the best caviar in the world and I try to serve Iranian caviar exclusively. I like other caviar, but I revere Iranian caviar.

The big gray to ink-black grains of beluga caviar are considered the finest. Osetra, with its vaguely nutty flavor and smaller grains, is preferred by some, while others like sevruga's bolder taste—and slightly lower price tag. All are magnificent. Farmed American and Chinese sturgeon produce admirable caviar, too. Roe from salmon, whitefish, lumpfish, and trout are also marketed as "caviar," but, while tasty, they are not the real deal. I rely on color and flavor to round out a caviar presentation.

Buy caviar from a reputable dealer and make sure it has been stored in a cold place where the temperature hovers around the freezing mark and where the tins are rotated. The eggs should be whole and full and smell pleasingly of the sea when the tin is opened.

Store unopened tins or jars of caviar in the coldest part of the refrigerator, pushed to the back of the box. They keep for about three weeks, but once opened, the caviar should be consumed within forty-eight hours. Rarely a hardship!

6 large hard-cooked eggs
1 loaf Brioche (see page 280), cut into
    24 ¼-inch-thick slices
¼ cup Homemade Crème Fraîche (see page 280)
3 tablespoons beluga or golden osetra caviar
3 tablespoons salmon roe
3 tablespoons smoked whitefish roe
3 tablespoons wasabi roe
½ cup capers, rinsed and coarsely chopped
½ cup finely chopped red onion

1. Separate the egg yolks and egg whites. Finely chop each separately. You may choose to press the yolks through a tamis instead of chopping with a knife.

2. To serve, arrange 4 slices of brioche on a small plate. Put a dollop of crème fraîche next to the brioche, or offer the crème fraîche in a small serving dish.

3. Put ½ tablespoon of beluga caviar alongside the brioche. Put ½ tablespoon of the salmon roe below the beluga, followed by the same amount of whitefish and wasabi roe. Arrange some chopped egg yolk, egg white, capers, and, finally, red onion next to the caviar. Repeat to make 5 more servings.

ABOUT THE WINE: *Balance the rich texture and briny flavor of caviar by serving an off-dry Riesling Kabinett from Germany or ice-cold Russian vodka. If you are seduced by the romance of sparkling wine, a glass of blanc de blancs from Schramsberg of Napa Valley or vintage champagne from Salon will work beautifully.*

LIVE JAPANESE FISH AND CHIPS

Serves 6

Wow! Is this a fun dish to play with. When I serve this at Tru, I spoon the marinated fish and salad into a small bowl that is placed over a larger bowl filled with water and graced with a living, colorful beta fish, or, as they are sometimes known, Japanese fighting fish. Our customers love the dramatic presentation, which has garnered the restaurant a lot of press. I was inspired by a visit to my friend Alan Wong's Honolulu restaurant of the same name. Alan served martinis in double-glass martini glasses with a beta fish swimming in the outside portion, and I was blown away.

We keep twenty beta fish at the restaurant. Each lives in its own bowl filled with spring water, which we change regularly. We put only ten fish to work on a given night. This way, they get lots of time off, and never work Sundays or holidays! They have a great life.

You can serve marinated snapper and bass for this dish, as I sometimes do, but I especially like the marriage of tuna, salmon, and hamachi with octopus. Anyone who likes sashimi and sushi will appreciate the Asian flavors mingling with one another.

GRILLED OCTOPUS:

1 tablespoon cayenne pepper
1 tablespoon ground cinnamon
1 tablespoon dry mustard powder
1 tablespoon crushed coriander
1 tablespoon lemon zest
1 teaspoon kosher salt
1 teaspoon finely ground black pepper
1 baby octopus (about 8 to 10 ounces), cleaned
About 2½ cups diced Marinated Tuna, Salmon,
   and Hamachi (recipe follows)
Kosher salt and freshly ground black pepper
½ cup Avocado Puree (recipe follows)
1½ cups Cucumber-Mango Salad (recipe follows)
1 tablespoon toasted black sesame seeds
1 tablespoon toasted white sesame seeds
30 Fried Vegetable Chips (recipe follows)

1. To prepare the octopus, mix the cayenne, cinnamon, dry mustard, coriander, zest, salt, and pepper in a small bowl.

2. Prepare a charcoal or gas grill. The coals should be medium-hot.

3. Rub the octopus with the spice mixture, working it gently into the flesh.

4. Put the octopus in a fine-mesh grill basket and grill for 4 to 6 minutes or until lightly browned.

5. Let the octopus cool slightly and then dice into small cubes. Transfer to a small bowl and refrigerate for at least 1 hour or until chilled. Serve within 3 or 4 hours of grilling.

6. Toss the tuna, salmon, hamachi, and octopus in a small bowl. Season to taste with salt and pepper.

7. To serve, spoon the fish onto a small plate. Arrange avocado puree and cucumber-mango salad next to the fish. Sprinkle the sesame seeds over the fish. Serve with vegetable chips. Repeat to make 5 more servings.

ABOUT THE WINE: *The assertive Asian elements of soy, sesame, rice wine vinegar, and cilantro combined with the rich, oily texture of fish require a wine with refreshing acidity, exotic aromatics, and forward fruit flavors. A medium-dry Alsatian gewürztraminer such as Domaine Zind-Humbrecht* Herrenweg de Turckheim *will tame the richness of the fish and complement the dish with its bold, spicy-floral character.*

MARINATED TUNA, SALMON, AND HAMACHI

Makes about 2½ cups

Juice of 1 lemon
Juice of 3 limes
½ cup rice wine vinegar
2 tablespoons fish sauce
2 tablespoons soy sauce
2 tablespoons extra-virgin olive oil
1 tablespoon toasted sesame oil
2 teaspoons yuzu or fresh lemon juice
2 tablespoons honey
Kosher salt and freshly cracked black pepper
½ cup minced scallions
½ bunch fresh cilantro, chopped
*6 ounces very fresh sushi-grade tuna, cut into
    medium-small dice*
*6 ounces very fresh Norwegian or wild salmon,
    cut into medium-small dice*
*6 ounces very fresh hamachi (yellowfin tuna),
    cut into medium-small dice*

1.   In a glass or ceramic bowl, stir together the lemon juice, lime juice, rice wine vinegar, fish sauce, soy sauce, olive oil, sesame oil, yuzu juice, and honey. Season to taste with salt and pepper and then stir in the scallions and cilantro.

2.   Add the tuna, salmon, and hamachi and turn gently to coat. Cover with plastic wrap and refrigerate for no longer than 30 minutes before serving.

AVOCADO PUREE

Makes about 1 cup

2 avocados
1 tablespoon Homemade Crème Fraîche (see page 280)
Juice of 1 lemon
1 Roma or plum tomato, peeled, seeded, and diced
¼ jalapeño pepper, seeded and finely diced
1 tablespoon minced fresh, peeled ginger
Pinch of cayenne pepper
Kosher salt and freshly ground black pepper

1.   Halve the avocados and remove the pits. Carefully peel and chop the flesh coarsely.

2.   Transfer to the bowl of a food processor fitted with a metal blade. Add the crème fraîche and lemon juice. Process until smooth.

3.   Scrape the puree into a small bowl and stir in the tomato, jalapeño, ginger, and cayenne. Season to taste with salt and pepper. Cover with plastic wrap and refrigerate for no longer than 3 or 4 hours before serving.

CUCUMBER-MANGO SALAD

Makes about 1½ cups

*1 seedless cucumber, peeled and sliced into thin
    matchsticks*
*1 firm, ripe mango, peeled and sliced into thin
    matchsticks*
1 tablespoon finely chopped fresh cilantro
Kosher salt and freshly ground black pepper

Just before serving, toss the cucumber, mango, and cilantro in a small bowl. Season to taste with salt and pepper.

FRIED VEGETABLE CHIPS

Makes about 32 chips

8 to 10 thin latticed white potato slices (also called
   gaufrettes pommes de terre)
4 cups vegetable oil
8 to 10 paper-thin sweet potato slices
8 to 10 paper-thin taro root slices
8 to 10 paper-thin lotus root slices
Kosher or sea salt

1. Soak the white potato slices in cold water for 10 minutes.

2. Meanwhile, in a deep, heavy saucepan, heat the vegetable oil over high heat until a deep-frying thermometer registers 350 degrees.

3. Drain the potato slices and gently pat dry with paper towels. Drop the white potato, sweet potato, taro root, and lotus root slices into the hot oil and fry for 3 to 5 minutes or until golden brown and crispy. Remove from the oil with a slotted spoon and drain on a double thickness of paper towels. Sprinkle with salt while still hot. Transfer the chips to a wire rack to cool.

MOSAIC OF SEAFOOD WITH SAFFRON FOAM

Serves 6

I define this as a deconstructed version of traditional bouillabaisse. About fifteen years ago, I sampled bouillabaisse at my friend chef Raymond Blanc's restaurant and country-house hotel, Le Manoir aux Quat' Saisons in Oxford, England, where I had *staged.* The chef poached the fish and seafood separately and then combined them in the terrine and it looked like a lovely mosaic piece of art.

I poach the fish and seafood separately as well, and serve them in small bowls bound by a light aspic and topped with saffron foam. (Saffron is the classic herb found in the Mediterranean-style stew called bouillabaisse.) This is a light, refreshing, and stunningly beautiful dish that brilliantly shows off the lobster, shrimp, monkfish, and other fish and seafood.

1 gallon Court Bouillon (see page 267), or water
1½-pound live lobster
3 jumbo shrimp
3 tablespoons Clarified Butter (see page 279)
8 ounces monkfish
8 ounces sashimi-grade tuna, cut into a 1-inch-thick log
10 bay or sea scallops
13 mussels, preferably Prince Edward Island mussels
4 cups Madeira Aspic (recipe follows)
¼ cup Fish Stock (see page 266)
¾ cup marinated wakame or hijiki seaweed salad
    (see Note), or fresh microgreens
2 cups Saffron Foam (recipe follows)
6 sprigs fresh chervil, for garnish
Confetti flowers (mixed petals of nasturtiums,
    geraniums, and violets), for garnish
¼ cup peeled, seeded, and diced tomato, for garnish
1 tablespoon sesame seeds, for garnish
6 2½- to 3-inch-long fresh chives, for garnish

1. Bring the court bouillon to a boil in a large stockpot over medium-high heat. Add the lobster, headfirst, reduce the heat slightly, and cook for 12 to 14 minutes or until the lobster is bright red. Remove with tongs and plunge into a bowl of ice water to cool. Do not turn the heat off from under the pot.

2. When the lobster is cool enough to handle, remove the meat from the claws and tail. Slice the tail meat into ¼-inch-thick medallions.

3. Add the shrimp to the simmering court bouillon and cook for 3 to 4 minutes or until pink. Drain and immediately submerge in ice water. Drain again. Remove the shells, cut the shrimp in half lengthwise, remove the veins, and set aside.

4. In a medium nonstick sauté pan, heat 1 tablespoon of the clarified butter over medium-high heat. Sear the monkfish for 3 to 4 minutes, turning once or twice to sear both sides. Transfer to a cutting board to cool slightly. Slice the monkfish into ¼-inch-thick medallions and set aside.

5. Wipe out the sauté pan. Heat 1 tablespoon of the clarified butter over medium-high heat. Sear the tuna for 2 to 3 minutes, turning once or twice to sear all sides. Transfer to a cutting board to cool slightly. Slice into ¼-inch-thick slices and set aside.

6. Wipe out the sauté pan again. Heat the remaining tablespoon of clarified butter over medium-high heat. Sear the scallops for 3 to 4 minutes, turning to sear on all sides. Transfer to a cutting board to cool slightly. Slice in half and set aside.

7. Put the mussels in a saucepan and add enough cold water to cover. Cover the pan and bring to a boil over high heat. Shaking the pan occasionally, cook for 3 to 5 minutes or until the mussels open. Using a slotted spoon, lift the mussels from the pan. Discard any that have not opened. Set aside the opened ones to cool. When cool, remove the mussels from the shells.

8. To prepare the mosaics, arrange the sliced seafood in a pretty pattern in each of 6 bowls with wide rims. Fill in the gaps with the warm aspic and chill.

9. Drizzle the fish stock over the mosaics and spoon about 2 tablespoons of the seaweed salad onto the right-hand side of the rim of each bowl.

10. Shake the saffron foam vigorously and squeeze a little onto the left side of the rim of each bowl. Garnish the salad with a sprig of chervil. Garnish each mosaic with the confetti flowers, tomatoes, sesame seeds, and a

chive. As you eat the mosaic, dip it into the foam and eat the salad.

NOTE: *You can buy seaweed salad at specialty stores, natural food markets, and Asian markets.*

ABOUT THE WINE: *Bright, mouth-tingling sauvignon blanc, particularly from cool-climate regions in South Africa and New Zealand, exhibits aromas and flavors of citrus and tropical fruit while offering an intriguing herbal edge. Seresin Estate of Marlborough, New Zealand, and Mulderbosch Vineyards of Stellenbosch, South Africa, produce wines that will elevate the flavors of the sea and marry well with the saffron foam.*

MADEIRA ASPIC

Makes 4 cups

1 350-ml bottle Madeira wine
1 350-ml bottle white wine
Granulated sugar
1 cup cold water
Kosher salt and freshly ground black pepper
9 sheets gelatin

1. Put the Madeira, white wine, and sugar to taste in a medium-sized saucepan over medium-high heat. Bring to a boil. Reduce the heat and simmer the wine mixture for about 30 minutes or until reduced by half.
2. Add the water to the wine reduction and bring to a simmer. Remove from the heat, and then season to taste with salt and pepper.
3. Meanwhile, fill a large bowl with cool water. Gently drop the gelatin sheets into the water, several at a time, until all are submerged. Let soften and bloom for 5 minutes.
4. Using your hands, lift the gelatin sheets from the water and squeeze them gently between your fingers. Transfer them to the Madeira reduction. Stir gently until dissolved.

5. Strain through a chinois or fine-mesh sieve into a bowl, and allow to cool at room temperature. Cover and refrigerate for up to 2 weeks.
6. Reheat the aspic in small saucepan over low heat before serving.

SAFFRON FOAM

Makes 2 cups

⅛ teaspoon saffron threads
2 tablespoons white wine
2 tablespoons Fish Stock (see page 266)
1½ cups half-and-half
½ cup heavy cream
2 sprigs fresh thyme
Kosher salt and freshly ground black pepper
2½ sheets gelatin
2 N₂O cream chargers

1. Toast the saffron in a dry saucepan over medium heat for about 20 seconds or until fragrant. Pour in the white wine and increase the heat to medium-high. Bring to a boil and boil for about 1 minute or until reduced to a syrup.
2. Add the fish stock, half-and-half, heavy cream, and thyme and bring to a simmer. As soon as the cream simmers, remove the pan from the heat. Let stand for 30 minutes. Season to taste with salt and pepper.
3. Fill a large bowl with cool water. Gently submerge the gelatin sheets in the water. Let soften and bloom for about 5 minutes.
4. Using your hands, lift the gelatin sheets from the water and squeeze them gently between your fingers. Transfer the sheets to the saffron mixture. Stir gently until dissolved.
5. Strain through a chinois or fine-mesh sieve into a bowl.
6. Pour into a chilled iSi Gourmet Whip canister. Charge with 1 or 2 N₂O cream chargers. Chill for at least 1 hour.

PEEKYTOE CRAB SALAD WITH CRISPY SAWAGANI CRAB AND MICRO GREENS

Serves 6

Take my word for it, crabmeat tastes great with tart Granny Smith apples and lemon in this dish, which combines some of my favorite flavors. I use sweet, tender Peekytoe crabmeat, from the waters off the coast of Maine, but another high-quality crabmeat will work. The organic soy reduction gives the dish Asian flair, and the gelée and Tramonto's Lemon Dust enhance the already welcome dose of acid. At Tru, we garnish this with tiny, fried Sawagani crabs, which are sold live and require no cleaning. They are not easy to find, but if you can locate them, try them; they make a delicious and cute garnish.

2 cups Peekytoe or other high-quality cooked crabmeat, picked over to remove any shells

1 cup finely diced Granny Smith or other tart apple

1 tablespoon freshly grated lemon zest

4 teaspoons fresh lemon juice

2 tablespoons extra-virgin olive oil

Kosher salt and freshly ground black pepper

1 cup Micro Green Salad (recipe follows)

3 tablespoons Homemade Crème Fraîche (see page 280)

About 6 tablespoons Organic Soy Reduction (recipe follows)

1 tablespoon Tramonto's Lemon Dust (see page 272), for garnish

Citrus Gelée cubes (recipe follows), for garnish

¼ cup confetti flowers (mixed petals of nasturtiums, geraniums, and violets), for garnish

6 2½- to 3-inch-long fresh chives, for garnish

6 Crispy Sawagani Crabs (recipe follows), for garnish, optional

1. Mix the crabmeat, apple, lemon zest, lemon juice, and olive oil in a small bowl. Season to taste with salt and pepper.

2. To serve, place a 1½-inch ring mold in the center of a plate and fill it with some of the crab salad. Press down on the crab with a spoon to make sure the mold is tightly packed. Gently remove the mold.

3. Top the crab with micro green salad. Dot the plate with crème fraîche and drizzle with soy reduction. Sprinkle lemon dust over the dish and garnish with citrus gelée cubes and flowers. Place a chive on top of the salad and place a crispy crab next to or on top of the salad. Repeat to make 5 more servings.

ABOUT THE WINE: *The natural sweetness and delicate flavor of the crab take center stage when paired with the dry, mineral-laced Rudi Pichler Weissburgunder Smaragd from Austria's terraced Wachau Valley, or with the white-peach-scented Pinot Gris Reserve from Chehalem Winery, Willamette Valley, Oregon.*

MICRO GREEN SALAD

Makes about 1 cup

1 cup micro cress or tatsoi

¼ cup edible flowers, such as nasturtiums, pansies, or roses

1 teaspoon extra-virgin olive oil

Kosher salt and freshly ground black pepper

Mix the micro cress and flowers in a small bowl. Toss with the olive oil. Season to taste with salt and pepper. Serve at once.

ORGANIC SOY REDUCTION

Makes about 1 cup

5 cups organic soy sauce
½ cup honey

1. Put the soy sauce and honey in a medium saucepan and bring to a simmer over medium-high heat. Stir constantly to dissolve the honey. Reduce the heat to medium-low and simmer the mixture for 15 to 20 minutes or until syrupy and reduced to about 1 cup.
2. Strain through a chinois or fine-mesh sieve into a bowl. Cover with plastic wrap and refrigerate until chilled.

CITRUS GELÉE

Makes about 2 cups

3 cups fresh orange juice
1 cup champagne
14 sheets gelatin

1. In a medium saucepan, bring the orange juice and champagne to a boil over medium-high heat and cook for 2 to 3 minutes. Remove the pan from the heat and set aside to cool slightly.
2. Meanwhile, fill a bowl with cool water. Gently drop the gelatin sheets into the water, several at a time, until all are submerged. Let soften and bloom for about 5 minutes.
3. Using your hands, lift the gelatin sheets from the water and squeeze them gently between your fingers. Transfer the sheets to the orange mixture. Stir gently until dissolved. Strain through a fine-mesh sieve into another bowl.
4. Pour the mixture into a clean, rimmed 9-by-13-inch baking sheet. The pan should be large enough so that

the mixture is not more than ¼ inch deep. Chill for 30 minutes to 1 hour or until set.
5. Cut the gelée into ¼-inch-square cubes. Use immediately or refrigerate until needed.

CRISPY SAWAGANI CRABS

About 2 cups canola oil or olive oil
6 live Sawagani crabs
Kosher salt

1. In a shallow skillet, heat the oil over medium-high heat until very hot. Using a slotted spoon or tongs, gently lower the crabs into the hot oil. Fry for 1 minute or until the crabs are bright red, turning once.
2. Remove with a slotted spoon and drain on paper towels. Sprinkle lightly with salt and use for garnish.

OCTOPUS CARPACCIO WITH NIÇOISE VINAIGRETTE

Serves 6

At Tru, we grill, poach, braise, and sauté octopus—we love it and will take it any way we can get it! But it's always a challenge to make it look beautiful because the tentacles flop all over the plate. I worked to make this dish eye-appealing and the results are nothing short of impressive. I cook the octopus, pack it in a cylinder, freeze it, and then slice it crosswise. I add the olive vinaigrette to pick up on the Mediterranean origins of many octopus dishes, as well as to provide great flavor! Believe me, your guests will ask you how you did this and they will be wowed! All in all, this is just another brick in my culinary wall.

Use any freezer-safe metal canisters, or even a stainless steel bain-marie. It should be three to six inches tall and three to five inches in diameter.

6 1-inch slices Octopus Terrine (recipe follows)
½ cup extra-virgin olive oil
2 tablespoons fresh lemon juice
Cracked black pepper
1 tablespoon Fleur de Sel or other high-quality sea salt
6 pitted and diced Peloponnese olives
6 pitted and diced Niçoise olives
6 red teardrop tomatoes, quartered
6 yellow teardrop tomatoes, quartered
½ cup micro arugula

1. Place a slice of octopus terrine in the center of a white plate.
2. Drizzle a little olive oil around the terrine and spread a little over the top. Sprinkle with a few drops of lemon juice, cracked black pepper, and salt.
3. Sprinkle some of the diced olives onto the olive oil.
4. Place 4 quarters of the red tomato and 4 quarters of the yellow tomato around the terrine in the olive oil, alternating colors. Finish the plate by garnishing the tomatoes with a little micro arugula. Repeat to make 5 more servings.

ABOUT THE WINE: *This dish is essentially a deconstructed octopus salad. The sweet, acidic tomatoes and briny olives could use a bright, clean dry white wine to balance things. Maria Gomes is a grape that produces lemony-fresh white wines. Portuguese star winemaker Luis Pato offers a flavorful, quaffable version that is perfect for this dish.*

OCTOPUS TERRINE

*Makes about
30 ¼-inch-thick slices*

6 pounds Braised Octopus (recipe follows)

1. Allow the braised octopus to come to room temperature.
2. Using a wet towel, rub the skin off the tentacles. Discard the head. Pull the tentacles apart and remove and discard some of the suction cups in the center of the tentacles. Cut the tentacles into 3-inch-long pieces.
3. Wet the inside of a 1 quart stainless steel bain-marie (3 inches wide and 7 inches high). Line with plastic wrap, leaving a 2- to 3-inch overhang of plastic. Place 1 piece of a tentacle of the octopus in the center of the bain-marie, standing up. Continue to fill the bain-marie with the remaining pieces of octopus until the mold is full. If possible, add 1 more tentacle to the bain-marie. Continue to add pieces of octopus until it is tightly packed. (It might be easier to place the bain-marie on its side, and then fill it with the final octopus pieces.)
4. Fold the overhanging ends of the plastic wrap over the top of the bain-marie. Place a second bain-marie on top of the plastic wrap. Weight the second bain-marie with sugar, salt, water, marbles, dried beans, rice, or similar items and freeze overnight.
5. Remove from the freezer and let sit at room temperature for 10 minutes. Remove the top bain-marie. Tap the outside of the bottom bain-marie, and then turn it upside

down on a towel. If the terrine doesn't come out of the mold, let it sit at room temperature for an additional 5 minutes and run a little warm water over the bottom and sides of the bain-marie to loosen it.

6. Wrap the terrine in plastic wrap and freeze until needed.

BRAISED OCTOPUS

Makes 6 pounds

1 whole 6-pound octopus
2 cups dry white wine
1 medium onion, chopped
1 medium carrot, chopped
1 leek, chopped
3 cloves garlic, halved
5 fresh thyme sprigs
2 bay leaves
2 tablespoons sea salt
2 to 3 wine corks, for tenderizing the octopus
       (ancient Italian grandmother's secret)

1. Rinse the octopus 3 to 4 times in cold water.
2. Combine all the ingredients in a large pot. Add enough cold water to cover all the ingredients.
3. Put the pot over medium heat and bring the water to a boil. Once the water starts boiling, reduce the heat and slowly simmer for 2½ to 3 hours. Test the octopus for doneness by piercing with a small knife. The knife should slide in and out easily. If the octopus is not tender, continue to simmer for 30 to 40 minutes or until it is fork-tender.
4. Remove the octopus from the cooking liquid. Discard the liquid, vegetables, and corks. Set the octopus aside at room temperature to cool for about 30 minutes.

BEEF TARTAR WITH QUAIL EGG AND BEEF GELÉE

Serves 6

When I lived in England, I once stayed at the fabulous Gleneagles Hotel in Perthshire, Scotland. Perched in the highlands, the hotel is surrounded by dramatic, wild countryside. As impressed as I was with the natural beauty, I was equally impressed with the old-fashioned beef tartar prepared tableside in the hotel dining room under the auspices of my friend, the executive chef at the time, Alan Hill. A waiter arrived at the table with Scottish beef resting on a slab of ice. He chopped the beef and mixed it with the usual ingredients in a big glass bowl. It was stunning—fresh-tasting and delicious. At Tru, I developed a more contemporary beef tartar, and so I add beef consommé gelée to boost the concentrated beef flavor and to preserve the art of making consommé, which is so easy! I serve it with a fried quail egg, white anchovies, caper berries, and a frisée salad with truffle vinaigrette.

12 ounces beef tenderloin or sirloin, finely diced
3 tablespoons finely diced shallots
3 tablespoons Lemon Oil (see page 277)
2 tablespoons snipped fresh chives
1 tablespoon Dijon mustard
Salt and freshly ground black pepper
1 cup frisée lettuce
½ cup micro arugula
2 tablespoons olive oil
¼ cup Clarified Butter (see page 279)
6 quail eggs
6 white anchovy fillets
¼ cup Truffle Vinaigrette (see page 105)
Beef Consommé Gelée, cut into ½-inch cubes
*   (recipe follows)*
Horseradish Foam (recipe follows)
6 caper berries

1. In a small bowl, combine the beef, shallots, lemon oil, chives, and mustard. Season to taste with salt and pepper. Gently toss to combine the ingredients. Cover and refrigerate for up to 2 hours.

2. Fill each of 6 2-inch-wide collars with about ¼ cup of the beef tartar. Level off the tartar to make a flat top.

3. In a small bowl, toss the frisée and arugula with the olive oil. Season to taste with salt and pepper. Set aside.

4. Heat the clarified butter in a small nonstick skillet or sauté pan over medium heat. One at a time, break the eggs into a small cup and slide into the skillet. Cook for 1 to 2 minutes or until the whites are set. Remove the eggs from the skillet and place on a cutting surface.

5. Using a small ring cutter, cut out the eggs just beyond the yolk.

6. Remove the collars from the beef tartar. Top the tartar with an anchovy fillet, some of the frisée salad, and then put an egg on top of the salad.

7. Garnish each plate with dots of truffle vinaigrette, 6 to 8 cubes of the beef gelée, a squirt of horseradish foam, and a caper berry.

ABOUT THE WINE: *Sparkling rosé is a very elegant accompaniment that will match the flavorful beef and handle the richness of the quail egg. Predominantly Pinot Noir, Bruno Paillard Rosé is a powerful sparkler with deep red fruit, cream, and mushroom flavors that reflect the bold elements of this dish.*

BEEF CONSOMMÉ GELÉE

*Makes 1 thin layer in a
9-by-12-inch jelly-roll pan*

2 cups Beef Consommé (recipe follows)
Kosher salt and freshly ground white pepper
6 sheets gelatin

1. In a small saucepan, heat the consommé over medium heat until hot. Season aggressively with salt and white pepper. (The flavors diminish when the gelée is chilled.) Remove from the heat.
2. Meanwhile, fill a large bowl with cool water. Gently drop the gelatin sheets into the water until all are submerged. Let soften and bloom for 5 minutes.
3. Using your hands, lift the gelatin sheets from the water and squeeze them gently between your fingers. Transfer to the warm consommé. Stir gently until dissolved.
4. Strain through a chinois or fine-mesh sieve into a small jelly-roll pan or other rimmed metal pan measuring about 9 inches by 12 inches, and allow to cool at room temperature. Refrigerate, uncovered, for about 30 minutes or until set. When the jelly is set, cover with plastic wrap and keep refrigerated until needed.

BEEF CONSOMMÉ

Makes 6 cups

½ cup coarsely chopped onion
¼ cup coarsely chopped carrots
¼ cup coarsely chopped celery
¼ cup tomato paste
8 large egg whites
4 ounces ground beef
4 sprigs fresh thyme
1 tablespoon distilled white vinegar
8 cups cold Beef Stock (see page 261)

1. Put the onion, carrots, celery, and tomato paste in a food processor fitted with a metal chopping blade. Process until the vegetables are chopped into small pieces.
2. In a medium-sized bowl, whisk together the egg whites, ground beef, chopped vegetables, and thyme. Transfer to a stockpot.
3. Whisk in the vinegar and beef stock.
4. Whisking constantly, bring the liquid to a simmer over low heat. As soon as a coagulated froth (called a raft) forms on the surface of the liquid, stop whisking. Use the handle of a wooden spoon to poke a hole through the raft (large enough to accommodate a ladle) so that the stock can bubble through the hole without breaking the raft. Cook at a bare simmer, undisturbed, for 30 minutes.
5. Line a chinois or fine-mesh sieve with several layers of moistened cheesecloth or a large coffee filter and set over a large pot. Ladle the consommé up through the hole in the raft into the lined sieve, being careful not to break up the raft more than necessary so that very little of it mixes with the consommé, and strain. Allow the consommé to cool, then cover and refrigerate until needed. Discard the raft.
6. When cold, strain the consommé one more time through a chinois or fine-mesh sieve to ensure that it's crystal clear.

Makes 2 cups

2 cups heavy cream
½ cup grated fresh horseradish
Kosher salt and freshly ground white pepper
1 sheet gelatin
2 N$_2$O cream chargers

1. Put the cream and horseradish in a medium saucepan. Season to taste with salt and white pepper. Bring to a boil over medium-high heat. Remove from the heat and allow to steep for 20 minutes.

2. Meanwhile, fill a large bowl with cool water. Gently drop the gelatin sheet in the water. Let it soften and bloom for about 5 minutes.

3. Using your hands, lift the gelatin sheet from the water and squeeze gently between your fingers. Transfer the sheet to the cream mixture. Stir gently until dissolved. Let it cool slightly and then strain through a chinois or fine-mesh sieve into a bowl.

4. Pour into a chilled iSi Gourmet Whip canister. Charge with 1 or 2 charges. Chill for at least 1 hour.

CHAPTER FOUR

Hot Appetizers

LIKE THEIR COUSINS, COLD APPETIZERS, hot appetizers are epicenters of creativity. I love to take vegetables, cheeses, seafood, pasta, and lovely but underutilized meats such as tongue and beef cheeks and build glorious small dishes that, with only a little urging, could be main courses. But they're most definitely not; they are the first act, meant to set the stage. The *amuse-bouche* may have warmed up the audience, but the appetizer gets the first wave of wild applause.

For these dishes, you must begin with flawless ingredients. Most of all, my hot appetizers will inspire you to consider pairing lobster with mashed potatoes, or to serve ten, twenty, or more vegetables on one platter! You may never have thought of cooking frog legs, but as an appetizer it suddenly makes perfect sense. You could make a feast of several of these dishes, or make just one to precede a more substantial dish. Whatever you decide, don't hold back. When you're hot, you're hot!

58   *Swan Creek Ricotta Gnocchi with Parmigiano-Reggiano*
     Cream and Shaved White Truffles

61   *Braised 31-Vegetable Ragout with Chervil Butter*

64   *Oozy Quail Egg Ravioli with Porcini Mushrooms*

68   *Braised Veal Tongue and Artichoke Napoleon with*
     Asian Pear and Fennel Pollen

73   *Roasted Sweetbread Salad with Walnut Vinaigrette*
     and Beet Paint

77   *Frog Leg Risotto with Parsley and Lots and Lots of Garlic*

80   *Butter-poached Maine Lobster and Truffle*
     Mashed Potato "Martini"

82   *Langoustine Ravioli with Buttered Leeks, Foie Gras Sauce,*
     and Blood Orange Reduction

84   *Black Truffle Risotto with Lobster, French Beans,*
     and Lobster Emulsion

SWAN CREEK RICOTTA GNOCCHI WITH PARMIGIANO-REGGIANO CREAM AND SHAVED WHITE TRUFFLES

Serves 6

This gnocchi is one of the best recipes I have ever created. It's light and feathery, which may sound counterintuitive to anyone who has never tasted really, really good gnocchi, an Italian word that literally means "dumpling." Gnocchi often are made from potatoes, but I make mine with ricotta. When people hear *dumpling* they think "heavy." Not at all! I have revised my gnocchi recipe over the years and this version is my very favorite.

As is traditional, the gnocchi dough incorporates ricotta cheese and I like to use Swan Creek ricotta, which is handmade, organic cheese. Swan Creek Farm in North Adams, Michigan, is a wonderful, family-run, grass-based farm with chickens, geese, ducks, cows, sheep, goats, and hogs—all carefully and humanely raised. George Rasmussen, who owns the farm with his wife, Deborah, makes a weekly trip to Chicago with eggs, cheese, and meat in the back of his truck—very rural products brought directly to a very urban setting. Our business relationship is a good example of how chefs and farmers can work together to benefit one another. I rely on him for the highest-quality meat, poultry, cheese, and eggs; he depends on me to help keep his business thriving. Simple, straightforward, and how it should be!

GNOCCHI:

1 pound whole-milk ricotta cheese
Kosher salt and freshly ground white pepper
Pinch of ground nutmeg
1 tablespoon truffle flour (see Note)
1 large egg
1 cup all-purpose flour

SAUCE:

1 cup Homemade Crème Fraîche (see page 280),
   or store-bought
½ cup heavy cream
¼ cup grated Parmigiano-Reggiano cheese
Kosher salt and freshly ground white pepper
2 tablespoons chopped chives
Shaved white truffles, for garnish

1. Line a sieve with cheesecloth and set the sieve over a large bowl. Put the ricotta cheese in the sieve, cover with plastic wrap, and refrigerate for at least 6 hours or overnight to drain.

2. Transfer the drained ricotta to a clean, large bowl. Season with salt and white pepper to taste, nutmeg, and truffle flour; add the egg, and stir to mix.

3. Using a rubber spatula, stir in the all-purpose flour, ⅓ cup at a time. When all the flour is incorporated, form the dough into a ball. Wrap the dough in plastic wrap and refrigerate for about 30 minutes or up to 24 hours. It also freezes very well for up to 1 month.

4. Turn out the chilled dough onto a lightly floured work surface and flatten slightly with the palm of your hand. Divide the dough into 6 pieces and roll into 1-inch-thick logs. Cut the logs into teaspoon-sized chunks. Roll the chunks into balls and press one side of the balls onto the backside of a fork to form the gnocchi.

5. Lay the gnocchi on lightly floured baking sheets in single layers. Cover loosely with plastic wrap or clean dish towels and refrigerate until ready to cook. The gnocchi will keep for about 24 hours before cooking.

6. To make the sauce, in a large sauté pan, heat the crème fraîche and cream over medium heat for 3 to 5 minutes or until slightly thick. Stir in the cheese and season lightly with salt and pepper. Keep the sauce warm.

7. Meanwhile, in a large pot of lightly salted boiling water, cook the gnocchi for 3 to 4 minutes or until they bob to the surface. Scoop them from the water with a slotted spoon or spider (do not drain through a colander or they will break). Add the gnocchi to the cream sauce. Toss gently, add the chives, and toss again. Spoon into small bowls and garnish with shaved truffles.

NOTE: *Truffle flour is wheat flour infused with the aroma of white truffles. Surprisingly potent, it's used as a flavoring or a thickener for sauces. A little goes a long way. Truffle flour is sold in specialty markets in small glass jars and keeps for about a month stored in a cool, dark place. It freezes for several months.*

ABOUT THE WINE: *This sinfully decadent dish becomes heavenly when served with mature Nebbiolo-based wine. One of the most layered and complex wines served with this dish at the restaurant is the stunning Barbaresco Riserva* Santo Stefano *Bruno Giacosa 1978. The natural affinity of hypnotic white truffles and the dusky-rose-and-earth-flavored wine is never more ethereal.*

BRAISED 31-VEGETABLE RAGOUT WITH CHERVIL BUTTER

Serves 4 to 6

On a trip to France, I had the pleasure of eating at Michel Bras's Michelin three-star restaurant in Laguiole, France. He is a master with vegetables, and after trying some of his combinations I was inspired to create this pure vegetable ragout. I love spring and summer vegetables, and so in an effort to showcase them for my vegetable collection at Tru, I walked into the cooler and picked every one I saw. I don't expect you to have all of these vegetables in your own kitchen, but the point is to gather as many as you can, prepare them lovingly, and then wow your guests. I promise, they will be amazed by the wild array of taste and color.

Visit the farmers' market, the green grocer, your own vegetable garden. Take full advantage of the season. Go crazy! How can you have too many tender, full-flavored vegetables or too many delicate, subtle ones? You can't! I pull them together with a simple compound butter—in this case, a chervil butter—which elevates the flavor, although you don't have to use it. The vegetables are delicious on their own. But you must take care to cook each one separately and carefully before you merge them on the same plate. That's what makes this incredible. Remember: Support your local green market and farmers' market! They are so important.

1 cup dried cocoa, black, or white beans

6 tablespoons unsalted butter, divided

2 ounces black trumpet mushrooms, sliced

2 ounces chanterelle mushrooms, sliced

2 ounces oyster mushrooms, sliced

2 ounces morel mushrooms, sliced

½ cup white wine

1 cup Vegetable Stock, divided (see page 266)

¼ cup Clarified Butter (see page 279)

6 baby carrots (preferably Thumbelina)

6 baby red beets, roasted and peeled (see Note)

6 baby yellow beets, roasted and peeled (see Note)

6 baby turnips, roasted and peeled (see Note)

6 baby artichokes, cleaned, halved or quartered

6 fingerling potatoes, roasted and sliced (see Note)

6 Brussels sprouts, blanched (see Note)

4 baby fennel, blanched (see Note)

24 haricots verts, blanched (see Note)

24 yellow wax beans, blanched (see Note)

1 small leek, white and light-green parts only, julienned and blanched (see Note)

6 stalks pencil-thin green asparagus, blanched (see Note)

6 stalks thin white asparagus, blanched (see Note)

6 baby radishes, blanched (see Note)

6 cloves garlic, blanched (see Note)

6 baby ramps, blanched (see Note)

6 scallions, blanched and sliced (see Note)

6 red pearl onions, blanched (see Note)

6 white pearl onions, blanched (see Note)

6 sugar snap peas, blanched (see Note)

6 pods English peas, shelled and blanched (see Note)

6 ears baby corn, blanched (see Note)

1 large purple potato, diced and blanched (see Note)

2 cups bias-cut celery, blanched (see Note)

6 edamame beans (fresh soybeans), halved

6 cherry or currant tomatoes

1 cup Chervil Butter (recipe follows)

About 1 teaspoon fresh thyme leaves

Kosher salt and freshly cracked black pepper

2 tablespoons Tramonto's Ruby Red Grapefruit Dust, for garnish (see page 272)

1. Soak the dried beans in cold water to cover at room temperature for at least 6 hours or overnight. Change the water several times during soaking.

2. Drain and transfer the beans to a pot. Add enough water to cover by at least 2 inches. Bring to a boil over medium-high heat, reduce the heat, and simmer for 40 minutes to 1½ hours (cooking time depends on the type of beans) or until the beans are tender but not mushy. Drain and set aside to cool.

3. Melt 4 tablespoons of the butter in a large sauté pan over medium-high heat. Add the mushrooms and sauté for 2 to 3 minutes or until the mushrooms are browned and softened. Add 3 tablespoons of white wine and 3 tablespoons of vegetable stock and cook for an addi-

tional 1 to 2 minutes while stirring the bottom of the pan with a wooden spoon to dissolve any browned solids into the liquid.

4. Heat the clarified butter in a large sauté pan over medium-high heat. Add the carrots, roasted beets, and roasted turnips. Cook for 3 to 5 minutes or until browned and tender. Add 3 tablespoons of white wine and 3 tablespoons of vegetable stock. Cook for 2 to 3 minutes while stirring the bottom of the pan with a wooden spoon to dissolve any browned solids into the liquid.

5. In a skillet, heat the remaining 2 tablespoons of butter over medium heat. Add the artichokes and cook, stirring, for 8 to 10 minutes or until tender.

6. Put the remaining 2 tablespoons of white wine and the remaining vegetable stock in a large pot over medium heat. Add all the vegetables, including the edamame and tomatoes, and stir. Cook for 5 minutes or until heated through and the liquid is nearly evaporated. Add the chervil butter and the thyme leaves to the pot and toss until the vegetables are coated and hot. Season to taste with salt and pepper.

7. To serve, spoon a portion of vegetables onto a plate and arrange in a random pattern, taking their colors into account and dispersing all 31 vegetables evenly on the plate. Sprinkle with about 1 teaspoon of grapefruit dust. Repeat to make 4 to 6 servings.

NOTE: *To roast vegetables, put them, unpeeled, in the center of a large sheet of aluminum foil. Add 2 to 3 cloves of garlic, ½ teaspoon of sugar, 2 to 3 sprigs of fresh thyme, and about ¼ cup of olive oil. Sprinkle with salt and cracked black pepper. Fold the foil into a packet, set it on a bed of kosher salt in a baking pan, and roast at 350 degrees for 20 to 30 minutes or until the vegetables are tender.*

To blanch vegetables, bring a large shallow pan of vegetable stock or lightly salted water to a boil over high heat. Add the vegetables and simmer rapidly for 2 to 8 minutes, depending on the vegetables, until they are just tender. Drain immediately and refresh with ice-cold water to stop the cooking. Set aside to cool.

ABOUT THE WINE: *A Piemontese wine such as the black-cherry- and truffle-scented Barbera d'Asti Costamiole Prunotto offers pronounced acidity, low tannin, sweet oak, and copious, earthy fruit that mingle well with the various vegetables in this dish.*

CHERVIL BUTTER

Makes about 2 cups

2 cups unsalted butter, softened
1 cup chopped chervil leaves
Juice of 1 lemon
Kosher salt and freshly ground black pepper
1 tablespoon crushed fennel seeds, optional
1 teaspoon fennel pollen (see Note), optional

1. In the bowl of a standing mixer fitted with the paddle attachment, combine the ingredients, including the optional fennel seeds and pollen. Mix on medium speed until blended.

2. Lay a sheet of plastic wrap on the work surface. Spoon the butter in a mound in the center. Using the plastic wrap as a guide, roll the butter into a cylinder. Secure the ends of the plastic wrap and then overwrap with more plastic wrap. Chill, or freeze for up to 2 months.

NOTE: *Fennel pollen is available in some gourmet stores and shops specializing in spices.*

OOZY QUAIL EGG RAVIOLI
WITH PORCINI MUSHROOMS

Serves 6

When I hear that age-old question, which came first, the chicken or the egg? I say, Who cares? Eggs are so good, what's the point debating the issue? Just enjoy eggs any way you can, whenever you can. For this dish, I nestle them in a large ravioli. Although this recipe is in the hot appetizer chapter, I also recommend serving this between a fish and a meat course because it's so compatible with red wine. I remember an earthy ravioli course I ate in the late 1980s at chef Gualtiero Marchesi's three-Michelin-star restaurant, which was in Milan. (He now owns Ristorante Gualtiero Marchesi in Erbusco and Hostaria dell'Orso in Rome.)

The ravioli packs a powerful flavor punch, filled as it is with cauliflower puree and rich truffle butter and served alongside softened, warmed porcini slices and the porcini puree. I love the quail egg inside the ravioli, especially if it's correctly cooked so that the egg is nice and runny—the best way to eat an egg!

6 Quail Egg Ravioli (recipe follows)
2 tablespoons unsalted butter
¼ cup Vegetable Stock (see page 266)
1 medium-to-large porcini mushroom,
*   cleaned and trimmed*
3 tablespoons extra-virgin olive oil
Sea salt
¼ cup sliced chives
1 cup warm Porcini Puree (recipe follows)
1 cup Porcini Emulsion (recipe follows)
Black truffles, grated, for garnish (as much as
*   you can afford)*
Parmigiano-Reggiano, grated, for garnish
Minced chives, for garnish

1. Preheat the oven to 350 degrees.
2. In a large pot, bring lightly salted water to a boil. Add the ravioli, still on the parchment paper, which will release from the ravioli during boiling. When the water re-turns to a boil, cook for about 1 minute or just until the ravioli barely bob to the surface. Do not overcook or the egg will overcook. Remove the ravioli and drain in a colander.
3. In a small sauté pan, heat the butter and the vegetable stock over medium heat. Cook for 1 minute and then remove from the heat and baste the ravioli with the liquid to keep them moist and make them shiny.
4. Slice the mushroom into paper-thin slices using a mandolin or very sharp knife. You will need 12 perfect slices.
5. Lay the slices on an ovenproof ceramic plate. Drizzle with olive oil, sea salt, and the chives. Transfer to the oven for about 2 minutes or until the mushrooms soften.
6. Spoon warm porcini puree in the center of a small plate. Top with a ravioli and 2 slices of porcini mushrooms, with some of the chives. Repeat to make 5 more servings.
7. Meanwhile, in a deep saucepan, bring the porcini emulsion to a simmer over medium-high heat. Tilt the pan and, using a handheld immersion blender or hand mixer, beat the emulsion so that bubbles form. For the best results, submerge the blender only halfway into the emulsion.
8. Skim the bubbles off the top of the emulsion and use to garnish the ravioli. If no bubbles form, add 1 tablespoon of cold butter and about ½ cup of vegetable stock to the pot and bring it back to a simmer and start again.
9. Spoon the emulsion around the ravioli. Garnish with grated truffles and cheese on top and sprinkle with minced chives.

ABOUT THE WINE: *Winemaker Ted Lemon produces distinctive Sonoma County Chardonnay under his Littorai label. Perfectly balanced, with lush tree-fruit flavors, pinpoint acidity, and a restrained sweet oak presence, the wine pairs beautifully with a broad range of food flavors. The Mays Canyon Chardonnay from the cool Russian River Valley handles the richness of the egg and complements the delicately earthy porcini puree.*

QUAIL EGG RAVIOLI

Makes 8

2 10-by-4-inch sheets Pasta Dough (recipe follows),
    lightly floured on both sides
2 cups Cauliflower Puree (recipe follows)
8 quail eggs
Kosher or sea salt
2 tablespoons Truffle Butter (see page 106)
1 cup Clarified Butter (see page 279)

1.   Lay 1 of the pasta sheets over a ravioli mold and press it into it to make 6 cups.

2.   Spoon cauliflower puree into each cup, forming nests to cushion the quail eggs.

3.   Cut the quail eggs open with a paring knife or quail egg scissors, drain and reserve excess egg white from the yolks. Nestle the yolks on top of the puree and sprinkle with salt. Put a dab of truffle butter in the corner of each ravioli.

4.   Brush the remaining sheet of pasta with the reserved egg whites and lay over the top of the raviolis. Seal by pressing gently with a rolling pin. Use dampened fingers to secure the seals. Flip the sealed ravioli onto a parchment-paper-lined pan. Brush with clarified butter.

PASTA DOUGH

Makes 2 10-by-4-inch sheets

2 cups all-purpose flour
½ cup semolina flour
1 teaspoon kosher salt
3 large eggs
4 large egg yolks
1 tablespoon olive oil, plus more for oiling the bowl

1.   In a large mixing bowl, mix the flour, semolina, and salt. Make a large well in the center and add the eggs,

egg yolks, and olive oil to the well. Place 2 fingers in the egg mixture and blend the eggs and oil together. Gradually incorporate the surrounding flour into the eggs, moving clockwise around the bowl, to form a soft dough. Turn the dough out onto a lightly floured surface and continue to knead for about 8 to 10 minutes or until the dough is smooth and elastic.

2.   Oil a large bowl and transfer the dough to the bowl. Turn it to coat with oil. Cover with plastic wrap and set aside to rest in a warm, draft-free place for 2 hours.

3.   Turn the dough out onto a lightly floured surface and knead a few times. Divide in half and keep 1 half covered with plastic wrap.

4.   Turn the pasta machine to its widest setting. Run the piece of dough through the pasta machine 3 times. Turn the machine to its next setting and run the dough through the machine 3 times at this setting. Continue to adjust the machine to its next narrowest setting and run the pasta through the machine until the pasta sheet is $\frac{1}{16}$ inch thick and 10 inches long. Cover with plastic wrap and repeat to make the other sheet of pasta. Keep both sheets covered with plastic wrap until ready to use or wrap well and freeze for up to 1 month.

CAULIFLOWER PUREE

Makes about 2 cups

1½ pounds fresh cauliflower florets
2 cups heavy cream
4 sprigs fresh thyme
1 bay leaf
Kosher salt and freshly ground black pepper

1.   In a large saucepan, combine the cauliflower florets with the cream, thyme, and bay leaf. Season to taste with salt and pepper. Bring to a boil over medium-high heat, immediately reduce the heat, and simmer for about 25 minutes or until the cauliflower is tender.

2. Remove the thyme sprigs and bay leaf from the pan. Pour off the cream and reserve. Transfer the cauliflower to a blender and process, adding as much of the reserved cream as necessary to make the puree smooth.

3. Press the softened cauliflower through a chinois or fine-mesh sieve. Season to taste with salt and pepper. Refrigerate until cold. This can be refrigerated for up to 24 hours.

PORCINI PUREE

Makes about 1 cup

4 porcini mushrooms (about ½ pound), sliced
3 shallots, sliced
2 cloves garlic, sliced
6 sprigs thyme
¼ cup olive oil
2 cups Vegetable Stock (see page 266)
2 tablespoons white truffle oil
Kosher salt and freshly ground white pepper

1. Preheat the oven to 350 degrees.

2. Put the mushrooms, shallots, garlic, thyme, and olive oil in a roasting pan and toss to mix well. Cover with aluminum foil and roast for about 45 minutes or until the mushrooms are very tender.

3. Meanwhile, in a saucepan, heat the vegetable stock until warm.

4. Transfer the ingredients from the roasting pan to a blender. Add the warm stock and process until smooth. With the motor running, add the truffle oil until emulsified.

5. Pass the puree through a chinois or fine-mesh sieve. Season to taste with salt and white pepper.

PORCINI EMULSION

Makes about 2 cups

1 tablespoon unsalted butter
¼ pound porcini mushrooms, trimmed and sliced
2 shallots, sliced
3 tablespoons porcini powder (see Note)
Kosher salt and freshly ground black pepper
1 cup dry vermouth
2 cups heavy cream

1. In a sauté pan, melt the butter over medium heat. Add the mushrooms and shallots and sauté for 3 to 4 minutes or until lightly browned. Add the porcini powder and season to taste with salt and pepper.

2. Pour the vermouth into the pan and cook, stirring with a wooden spoon to scrape up the browned bits sticking to the pan, until nearly all the vermouth evaporates. Add the cream and bring to a simmer over medium heat.

3. Transfer to a blender and puree until smooth. Pass through a chinois or fine-mesh sieve and use immediately or cover and refrigerate for up to 24 hours.

NOTE: *Porcini powder is sold in specialty stores. It is a natural byproduct of mushroom production and adds good flavor.*

BRAISED VEAL TONGUE AND ARTICHOKE NAPOLEON WITH ASIAN PEAR AND FENNEL POLLEN

Serves 6

As a very young cook in the 1980s, I ordered a veal tongue salad at New York's legendary Lutece, when the great André Soltner was there. I was terrified when I ordered it, because I had never had tongue before and, as much as I wanted to try it, I was afraid I might not like it. But one bite convinced me it was heaven in my mouth. Years later, I tried a warm braised veal tongue dish at Troisgros, the famed French restaurant in Lyon, and I loved it even more. It was perfectly cooked and forever changed my opinion about eating tongue.

Since then I have discovered I prefer tongue that is lightly pickled and meant to be served sliced and cold, not unlike the tongue you find in New York delis. In this recipe, the Niçoise flavors of artichokes, asparagus, lemon, and truffles come together in a glorious appetizer. Try it. Like me, you will love it!

4 tablespoons unsalted butter

3 onions, julienned

1 tablespoon sugar

3 cups Duck Fat Confit Potatoes (recipe follows)

½ cup Oven-dried Tomato Rings (recipe follows)

1 cup sliced Artichoke Hearts (recipe follows)

2 cups sliced Veal Tongue (recipe follows)

9 spears asparagus, blanched (see Note on page 63)
      and cut to fit ring molds, as necessary

½ cup micro greens or other baby greens

1 Asian pear, peeled, cored, and julienned

2 tablespoons Lemon Vinaigrette (recipe follows)

1 cup Veal Sauce (recipe follows)

2 cups White Truffle Emulsion (recipe follows)

¼ cup chopped toasted hazelnuts

About 1 tablespoon fennel pollen (see Note on page 63),
      for garnish

1. In a large sauté pan, heat the butter over medium-low heat. When melted, add the onions and sugar. Reduce the heat to low and cook, stirring occasionally, for about 45 minutes or until the onions are soft and turn caramel color. Use immediately or cover and refrigerate until needed.

2. Preheat the oven to 350 degrees. Put 6 3-inch ring molds on a baking sheet.

3. To make the napoleons, start by laying slices of the duck fat confit potatoes in the bottom of the ring molds. They should be as flat as possible. Next, add a layer of caramelized onions, followed by a layer of tomato rings. Add a layer of sliced artichoke hearts and then a layer of sliced veal tongue. Top with 3 pieces of asparagus spears.

4. Transfer to the oven and bake for 3 to 4 minutes or until hot.

5. Transfer each ring mold to the center of a serving plate and carefully remove the molds.

6. Toss the micro greens with the julienned pear and the vinaigrette and spoon some on top of each napoleon. Spoon the veal sauce and the truffle emulsion around the napoleons. Sprinkle the tops with the chopped hazelnuts. Dust the plates with fennel pollen.

ABOUT THE WINE: *The tomatoes, artichokes, and asparagus require a wine with high acidity and, most important, no oak flavors. I often pair a dry-style German Riesling with this dish. Consider Muller-Catoir Riesling Spätlese Trocken Gaisböhl, with its elegant structure and sturdy fruit concentration.*

DUCK FAT CONFIT POTATOES

Makes 3 cups

15 medium-sized fingerling potatoes
(about 1½ pounds), scrubbed
2 cups duck fat
6 black peppercorns
2 cloves garlic
2 sprigs fresh thyme

1. Put the potatoes, duck fat, peppercorns, garlic, and thyme in a large pot.
2. Bring to a simmer over low heat. Insert a thermometer into the liquid fat to make sure it maintains a simmering temperature of 180 degrees and does not exceed it. Simmer for 2 to 3 hours. Alternatively, put the pot containing the fat and other ingredients in a preheated 300-degree oven and cook, uncovered, for about 3 hours or until the potatoes are tender.
3. Remove the potatoes from the fat and transfer to a bowl. Set aside at room temperature to cool.
4. Cut the potatoes into ¼-inch slices. Transfer to a bowl. Cover and refrigerate until needed.

OVEN-DRIED TOMATO RINGS

Makes 1 cup

3 large vine-ripened tomatoes (about 1 pound)
¼ cup olive oil
2 tablespoons granulated sugar
2 sprigs fresh thyme

1. Preheat the oven to 200 degrees.
2. Cut the tomatoes into ½-inch-thick slices. Toss with the olive oil, sugar, and thyme.
3. Place the tomatoes in a single layer on a baking sheet. Transfer to the oven and bake for 5 hours or until dry. Cool to room temperature. Store in a small bowl or glass container until needed.

ARTICHOKE HEARTS

Makes 2 cups

1 teaspoon fresh lemon juice
2 globe artichokes
1 cup white wine
½ cup extra-virgin olive oil
Juice of 1 lemon
1 shallot, thinly sliced
2 cloves garlic
2 sprigs fresh thyme
2 teaspoons kosher salt
2 teaspoons freshly ground black pepper

1. Fill a medium glass, ceramic, or other noncorrosive bowl with water and add 1 teaspoon lemon juice.
2. To cut out the artichoke hearts (or centers), trim the stem flush with the base and cut off the pointed top. Remove the outer leaves until only the tender ones remain. Scoop out the prickly choke and discard. As you work, drop the trimmed artichokes into the acidulated water.
3. Put the white wine, olive oil, lemon juice, shallot, garlic, thyme, salt, and pepper in a medium-sized saucepan. Drain the artichoke hearts and add them to the pan.
4. Bring to a low simmer over low heat and cook for about 30 minutes or until tender.
5. Remove the artichoke hearts from the liquid and set aside at room temperature to cool. Thinly slice the artichoke hearts.

VEAL TONGUE

Makes 2 cups

1 1-pound veal tongue, outer membrane removed
½ cup chopped white onion
¼ cup chopped carrots
1 leek, white and light-green parts only, chopped
2 cloves garlic
1 bay leaf
3 teaspoons kosher salt
2 tablespoons freshly ground black pepper
1 cup white wine
3 cups Veal Stock (see page 261)

1. Put the veal tongue, onion, carrots, leek, garlic, bay leaf, salt, pepper, white wine, and veal stock in a large pot. Bring to a simmer over medium-high heat. Reduce the heat and simmer for about 2 hours or until the tongue is tender.

2. Remove the tongue from the pot and transfer to a plate. Set aside at room temperature to cool. Cut the tongue into ¼-inch slices. Cover and refrigerate until needed.

LEMON VINAIGRETTE

Makes about 1 cup

½ cup extra-virgin olive oil
⅓ cup fresh lemon juice
¼ cup white wine vinegar
2 teaspoons Dijon mustard
½ shallot, minced
Kosher salt and freshly ground white pepper

1. In a blender, combine the olive oil, lemon juice, white wine vinegar, mustard, and minced shallot. Blend until thoroughly emulsified. Season to taste with salt and white pepper.

2. Use immediately or cover and refrigerate for up to 1 week. Whisk well before using.

VEAL SAUCE

Makes 2 cups

¼ cup olive oil
½ to 1 pound veal tenderloin tips or other pieces of veal
1 cup chopped onion
½ cup chopped carrots
½ cup chopped celery
2 cups dry red wine
4 cups Veal Demi-glace (see page 268)
Kosher salt and freshly ground black pepper
4 tablespoons chopped black truffles, optional

1. Place a medium-sized saucepan over high heat until hot and smoking. Add 1 tablespoon of the oil and the veal tips and sear on both sides until golden and a crust forms.

2. Add the remaining oil and then add the onion, carrots, and celery. Reduce the heat to medium and cook, stirring from time to time, for about 8 minutes or until the vegetables are tender and golden.

3. Add the wine, raise the heat to high, and cook, stirring the bottom of the pan with a wooden spoon to deglaze, until simmering. Simmer for about 10 minutes or until most of the wine has evaporated and the bottom of the pan is almost dry.

4. Reduce the heat to low, add the veal demi-glace, and simmer over low heat for about 30 minutes. Strain through a chinois or fine-mesh sieve, return to the saucepan, and bring to a simmer over low heat. Simmer for 30 minutes longer, or until reduced to 1 cup with a saucelike consistency. Season to taste with salt and pepper. Stir in the truffles. Set aside and keep warm until needed.

WHITE TRUFFLE EMULSION

Makes 2 cups

½ cup heavy cream
1 cup Vegetable Stock (see page 266)
¼ cup white truffle oil
3 tablespoons unsalted butter
Kosher salt and freshly ground black pepper

1. Heat the cream and stock in a medium-sized saucepan over medium-high heat. Bring to a boil, and as soon as it starts to boil, immediately remove the pan from the heat.

2. Add the truffle oil and let sit for 1 minute. Return to the heat and bring to a boil again.

3. Remove the pan from the heat and add the butter. Using a handheld immersion blender, whip the mixture until foamy. Season to taste with salt and pepper. Use the truffle emulsion while still foamy.

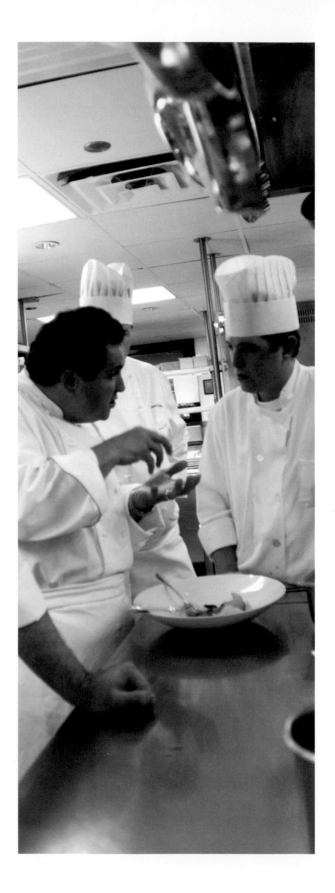

ROASTED SWEETBREAD SALAD WITH WALNUT VINAIGRETTE AND BEET PAINT

Serves 6

I can barely remember when I didn't appreciate sweetbreads. I remember eating them in the 1980s at Bouley in New York and falling in love with them. About five years ago, David Bouley, who was then just opening Danube, his restaurant in Manhattan's Tribeca neighborhood, came to Tru to cook with me as a guest chef for an event. Tru had only been open for about a year, and both David and I were pretty stressed out about our fledgling restaurants. But cooking together was an exhilarating, refreshing experience for us both.

Sweetbreads are rich, creamy, subtly flavored—a luxury worth enjoying. When they are crispy on the outside and moist on the inside, they have no equal. Serving them in a salad enhances them, while providing a gentle introduction for the first-timer. The earthiness of the beets and walnut vinaigrette and the intensity of the bacon and roasted garlic are great with the sweetbreads.

Be sure to buy plump, high-quality veal sweetbreads, covered with a shiny membrane, from a reliable butcher. The thymus gland of a calf, sweetbreads are composed of two lobes, one more elongated than the other. (There are lamb sweetbreads, too, but I think veal are superior.) For tenderness, these are poached and pressed before they are sautéed. Soaking the sweetbreads first in milk overnight pulls out the blood and turns them white. Don't neglect this important step.

½ cup all-purpose flour
Kosher salt and freshly ground black pepper
6 2-ounce portions Poached and Pressed Sweetbreads
  (recipe follows)
2 tablespoons Clarified Butter (see page 279)
3 porcini mushrooms, trimmed and thinly sliced
4 ounces slab or thick-cut bacon, cut into ⅛-inch
  cubes and cooked until crispy
12 cloves roasted garlic (see Note)

12 spears pencil-thin green asparagus, blanched and
  chilled (see Note)
12 haricots verts, blanched and chilled (see Note)
12 baby red beets, roasted and halved (see Note)
12 baby yellow beets, roasted and halved (see Note)
8 cups mesclun salad mix
¾ cup Walnut Vinaigrette, plus more for drizzling
  (recipe follows)
Beet Paint, for garnish (recipe follows)

1. Season the flour with salt and pepper to taste. Dredge the sweetbreads with the flour, shaking off any excess.

2. Heat the butter in a large sauté pan over medium-high heat. Add the sweetbreads and cook for 2 to 3 minutes or until golden brown and crispy. Turn over and cook the other side for 2 to 3 minutes until golden brown and crispy. Slice thinly.

3. In a large bowl, mix together the mushrooms, bacon, garlic, asparagus, haricots verts, beets, and mesclun. Toss with the walnut vinaigrette.

4. To serve, using a dry 1- to 1½-inch paintbrush, paint a line of beet paint on a plate. Mound some of the salad in the center of the plate. Arrange the sliced sweetbreads on top of the salad. Drizzle the walnut vinaigrette around the plate. Repeat to make 5 more servings.

NOTE: *To roast garlic, slice the top off the head of garlic and put in a shallow baking dish. Add ¼ teaspoon of sugar, 2 sprigs of fresh thyme, and 1 tablespoon of olive oil. Cover the dish with foil and roast at 350 degrees for about 15 minutes or until the cloves are golden brown. When cool enough to handle, separate the cloves from the head. Squeeze the pulp from the skins.*

To blanch vegetables, bring a large shallow pan of vegetable stock or lightly salted water to a boil over high heat. Add the vegetables and simmer rapidly for 2 to 8 minutes, depending on the vegetables, until they are just tender. Drain immediately and refresh with ice-cold water to stop the cooking. Set aside to cool.

To roast vegetables, put them, unpeeled, in the

center of a large sheet of aluminum foil. Add 2 to 3 cloves of garlic, ½ teaspoon of sugar, 2 to 3 sprigs of fresh thyme, and about ¼ cup of olive oil. Sprinkle with salt and cracked black pepper. Fold the foil into a packet, set it on a bed of kosher salt in a baking pan, and roast at 350 degrees for 20 to 30 minutes or until the vegetables are tender.

ABOUT THE WINE: *The dominant herbal, earthy, and smoky elements of this dish can mesh with either white or red wine. The hazelnut and ripe pear flavors of Domaine d'Auvenay Meursault Les Clous envelop the velvety-textured sweetbreads. Robust and spicy, the black-fruit-dominated Crozes-Hermitage Cuvée Albéric Bouvet Gilles Robin from the southern Rhône Valley handles the bold bacon flavors.*

POACHED AND PRESSED SWEETBREADS

Makes about 1 pound

1 pound veal sweetbreads
Whole milk
2 tablespoons Clarified Butter (see page 279)
½ cup sliced leeks, white and light-green parts only
½ cup chopped onions
½ cup chopped celery
¼ cup black peppercorns
4 bay leaves
2 tablespoons chopped fresh thyme
1 cup white wine
6 quarts Vegetable Stock (see page 266)

1. Rinse the sweetbreads for 15 or 20 minutes under cold, running water. Transfer to a large dish, add enough whole milk to cover, cover with plastic wrap, and refrigerate for 12 hours or overnight. This draws out the blood and turns the sweetbreads white and creamy.

2. In a large stockpot, heat the butter over medium-low heat. Add the leeks, onions, and celery and cook, cov-

ered, for 3 to 4 minutes or until translucent. Add the peppercorns, bay leaves, and thyme and stir to combine.

3. Add the wine, raise the heat to medium, and cook, stirring with a wooden spoon to scrape up any browned bits from the bottom of the pan, until nearly all the wine evaporates.

4. Add the stock and bring to a simmer. Lift the sweetbreads from the milk, and rinse to remove excess milk. Add to the stockpot and poach for 10 to 15 minutes or until an instant-read thermometer inserted in the thickest part of a sweetbread registers 140 degrees.

5. Remove the sweetbreads from the poaching liquid. Lay them in a large jelly-roll or half-sheet pan (you may need to use 2 pans) and pour as much of the poaching liquid over the sweetbreads as is needed to cover. Top with another pan of the same size so that the top pan sits directly on the sweetbreads. Transfer to the refrigerator. Weight with a gallon milk jug filled with milk or water.

6. After 2 hours, remove the pan and lift the sweetbreads from the liquid. Discard the liquid. Trim the sweetbreads of fat, sinews, and membranes.

WALNUT VINAIGRETTE

Makes about 2 cups

¼ cup toasted walnuts
½ cup white wine vinegar
1 teaspoon maple syrup
1 shallot, minced
1 teaspoon finely chopped fresh thyme
Kosher salt and freshly ground white pepper
1 ¼ cups walnut oil

1. Put the walnuts, white wine vinegar, maple syrup, shallot, and thyme in a blender. Season to taste with salt and white pepper. Blend until smooth.

2. With the motor running, slowly add the walnut oil and blend until emulsified.

3. Use immediately or cover and refrigerate for up to 1 week. Whisk well before using.

BEET PAINT

Makes about ¼ cup

10 large red beets
½ cup honey
1 tablespoon extra-virgin olive oil
Kosher salt and freshly ground black pepper

1. Juice the beets in a juicer. Strain through a chinois or fine-mesh sieve into a medium saucepan and add the honey. Bring to a simmer over medium heat, reduce the heat to medium-low, and simmer very gently for about 1 hour or until syrupy and reduced to about ¼ cup. While the juice is simmering, skim off any foam that rises to the top.

2. Strain the beet paint through a chinois or fine-mesh sieve into a small bowl. Cover and set aside to cool.

3. When cool, whisk in the oil until smooth. Season to taste with salt and pepper. Use right away or cover and refrigerate for up to 3 days.

FROG LEG RISOTTO WITH PARSLEY AND LOTS AND LOTS OF GARLIC

Serves 4 to 6

These frog legs, with all the bold garlic flavor, bring to mind classic French escargot, such as those I ate in France at Roger Vergé's restaurant, Le Moulin de Mougins, in Mougins, France. I co-opted those lovely flavors, substituted frog legs for snails, worked them into a risotto—and it was magic.

I encourage you to buy good Italian rice for the risotto, since it really makes a difference in the final texture and taste. The best known and most popular is Arborio rice, but even better are other medium-grain rices such as Carnaroli and Vialone Nano. These rices have a high-starch surface content, which contributes to the risotto's final creaminess without reducing the rice to mush. In a good risotto, the grains should remain a little chewy.

As a child, there was no fear when it came to eating frog legs regularly. My Italian grandmother breaded and sautéed them in olive oil, garlic, and parsley and served them with sautéed cardoons. I lightened up the preparation here, but the spirit of the dish is true to my grandmother's. If you haven't tasted frog legs, this is a good introduction to them. And if you already share my fondness for them, you will love this. By the way, they really do taste a little like chicken!

6 cups Vegetable Stock (see page 266)
2 tablespoons unsalted butter
4 cups Arborio, Carnaroli, or Vialone Nano rice
1 shallot, finely chopped
1 ½ cups white wine
1 cup coarsely chopped black trumpet or chanterelle
   mushrooms
2 cups Frog Leg Braise (recipe follows)
1 cup haricots verts, blanched
½ cup peeled, seeded, and chopped tomato
½ cup freshly grated Parmigiano-Reggiano cheese
1 cup Garlic-Parsley Butter (recipe follows)
1 cup heavy cream, whipped to stiff peaks

Kosher salt and freshly ground white pepper
6 frog legs (about 1 pound), for garnish, optional
All-purpose flour
3 tablespoons olive oil
¼ cup snipped fresh chives, for garnish
Grated Parmigiano-Reggiano cheese, for garnish
1 tablespoon chopped fresh tarragon, for garnish
Sprigs of tarragon, for garnish

1. Heat the vegetable stock in a medium saucepan over medium heat until it simmers. Reduce the heat and keep at a low simmer.

2. Heat a large saucepan over medium heat until very hot, then add the butter and let it melt. Add the rice and stir until the rice is coated with butter. Add the shallot and stir for 3 to 4 minutes or until translucent. Add the wine and, stirring constantly, cook for another 3 to 4 minutes or until the wine is reduced by half. Add the stock, 1 cup at a time, stirring before each addition, until the rice is almost covered by the stock. Stirring frequently, cook for 15 minutes or until the rice has softened but is still firm.

3. Add the mushrooms and frog leg braise and any liquid. Stir for 3 to 4 minutes or until the mushrooms and frog leg braise are heated through. Add the haricots verts, tomato, cheese, and garlic-parsley butter and stir until the butter melts and the vegetables soften. Add the whipped cream and stir until the rice is smooth and creamy. Season to taste with salt and white pepper.

4. Season the frog legs with salt and pepper and dust lightly with flour.

5. In a sauté pan, heat the olive oil over medium-high heat and cook the frog legs for about 1 ½ minutes, turning several times, until golden brown. Lift the frog legs from the pan and drain on paper towels.

6. Spoon about ½ cup of the risotto into each serving bowl and garnish with chives, grated Parmigiano-Reggiano cheese, chopped tarragon, a sprig of tarragon, and a frog leg.

ABOUT THE WINE: *A clean, fresh, light-bodied Tocai Friulano with aromas of flowers, tropical fruit, and*

almonds offers textural contrast to the silky risotto and tames the assertive garlic. Ronco delle Mele from Venica and Venica in Collio, Italy, is a very fine choice with this dish.

FROG LEG BRAISE

Makes 2 cups

6 frog legs (about 1 pound)
⅓ cup all-purpose flour
2 tablespoons salt, plus more for seasoning
2 tablespoons freshly ground black pepper, plus more
*   for seasoning*
¼ cup olive oil
1½ cups white wine, divided
½ cup chopped carrots
1 leek, white and light-green parts only, coarsely
*   chopped*
8 cloves garlic
2 sprigs fresh tarragon
3 sprigs fresh thyme
¾ cup fresh lemon juice
4 cups Chicken Stock (see page 265)

1. Rinse the frog legs and pat dry. Slice the meat from the bones and reserve the bones. Mix the flour with 2 tablespoons of salt and 2 tablespoons of pepper.

2. Spread the flour on a plate and then dredge the frog leg meat with it so that they are well coated. Shake off any excess flour.

3. Heat a large sauté pan over high heat until hot but not smoking. Reduce the heat to medium-high, add the olive oil, and cook the meat for 3 to 4 minutes, turning several times, until golden brown. Remove the meat from the pan and set aside until cool enough to handle.

4. Add ½ cup of the white wine and cook, scraping the bottom of the pan with a wooden spoon, until the liquid has evaporated.

5. Add the reserved bones, the carrots, leek, garlic, tarragon, and thyme and cook for 15 minutes, stirring occasionally, until the vegetables are soft and golden brown.

6. Add the remaining cup of white wine and the lemon juice, and season to taste with salt and pepper. Cook for 8 to 10 minutes or until the liquid is reduced by three-fourths. Add the chicken stock and simmer slowly for about 1 hour to reduce the liquid. Strain through a chinois or fine-mesh sieve into a bowl. You will have about ½ cup of liquid. Adjust the seasonings, return the meat to the pan, cover, and refrigerate until needed.

GARLIC-PARSLEY BUTTER

Makes 1 cup

½ pound unsalted butter, cut into small pieces
Grated zest of ½ lemon, very finely chopped
1 shallot, finely chopped
Leaves of 2 bunches of fresh flat-leaf parsley
½ head garlic, separated into individual cloves
*   and peeled*

1. Put the butter, lemon zest, and shallot in the bowl of an electric mixer fitted with a paddle attachment and blend on medium speed until smooth.

2. Put the parsley, garlic, and about ¼ cup of the butter mixture into the bowl of a food processor fitted with a metal blade. Process until smooth.

3. Transfer the parsley-butter mixture to the electric mixer and blend with the remaining butter until smooth and green. Transfer to a bowl, cover with plastic wrap, and refrigerate until needed.

BUTTER-POACHED MAINE LOBSTER AND TRUFFLE MASHED POTATO "MARTINI"

Serves 6

This has been a signature dish of mine for at least ten years—it was one of the recipes that earned me the 1994 *Food & Wine* magazine Best Chef in America Award, and to this day customers still ask me to make this for them. I love the marriage of lobster and mashed potatoes. To me, it's a tempting juxtaposition of rich man's food meeting poor man's food. I layer the two in a handblown martini glass, dramatically garnished with a long lobster tentacle and fresh chives. I collect handblown glasses, but any large, stemmed piece of glassware makes a sensational presentation—or use a pretty shallow bowl. Just don't miss this one! When you reheat lobster in butter, the meat sucks up the fat and any trace of toughness disappears, leaving behind moist, succulent lobster.

3 cups warm Yukon Gold Potato Puree (recipe follows)
12 ounces warm, chopped lobster meat (from the tail and knuckles of 3 1-pound lobsters) from Poached Lobster Tails and Claws (recipe follows)
Juice of ½ orange
1 tablespoon chopped black truffles
2 tablespoons white truffle oil
Kosher salt and freshly ground black pepper
6 lobster claws from Poached Lobster Tails and Claws
1 teaspoon Tramonto's Orange Dust (see page 272), for garnish
6 lobster tentacles, for garnish
6 fresh chive sticks, for garnish
¼ cup confetti flowers (mixed petals of nasturtiums, geraniums, and violets), for garnish

1. Mix the warm potato puree, warm lobster meat, orange juice, chopped truffles, and truffle oil in a mixing bowl. Season with salt and pepper to taste.
2. To serve, put ½ cup of the potato puree mixture in a large, dramatic martini glass. Place a poached lobster claw on top.

3. Garnish with a pinch of orange dust, a lobster tentacle, and a chive. Finally, complete the garnish with a sprinkling of confetti flowers. Repeat to make 5 more servings.

ABOUT THE WINE: *The butter and cream in this dish lead one to a big, full-flavored white wine with sufficient acidity to deal with the rich ingredients. A Corton-Charlemagne Grand Cru from Vincent Girardin is a worthy foil.*

YUKON GOLD POTATO PUREE

Makes about 3 cups

8 Yukon Gold potatoes, or other all-purpose potatoes (about 2 pounds)
1 cup heavy cream
½ pound unsalted butter, cut into small pieces
Kosher salt and freshly ground white pepper

1. Peel the potatoes and cut them into medium-sized cubes.
2. Put the potatoes in a medium-sized saucepan, add enough cold water to cover, and lightly salt the water. Bring to a boil over medium-high heat. Reduce the heat and simmer for about 15 minutes or until just tender. Drain the potatoes.
3. In a small saucepan, heat the cream and butter over medium heat until the butter melts.
4. Force the potatoes through a ricer and then press through a tamis or fine-mesh sieve into a bowl. Add the cream-and-butter mixture and stir until smooth. Season to taste with salt and white pepper. Cover and set aside to keep warm.

POACHED LOBSTER TAILS AND CLAWS

Serves 6

½ cup chopped leeks, white and light-green parts only
½ cup chopped onion
½ cup chopped carrot
4 sprigs fresh thyme
4 bay leaves
10 cups of water
3 1-pound live Maine lobsters
4 cups Beurre Monté (see page 278)

1. Put the leeks, onion, carrot, thyme, bay leaves, and water in a large stockpot. Bring to a boil over medium-high heat. Reduce the heat and simmer.

2. Meanwhile, kill the lobsters by inserting a large, sharp knife in the back of the head where it meets the lobster body. This will kill it instantly. Remove the claws and tails from the lobsters. Reserve 6 tentacles for garnish.

3. Add the claws to the simmering court bouillon and simmer for 4 minutes. Add the tails and simmer for 4 minutes longer.

4. Drain the claws and tails and immediately submerge in cold water. Drain again.

5. Remove the meat from the claws and tails. Transfer to a bowl and set aside at room temperature to cool Cover and refrigerate until needed.

6. Heat the *beurre monté* over medium heat until bubbling. Add the lobster tails and claws so that they are completely submerged and "poach" for about 10 minutes or until the lobster is heated through. Take care that the *beurre monté* does not get too hot or it will separate.

LANGOUSTINE RAVIOLI WITH BUTTERED LEEKS, FOIE GRAS SAUCE, AND BLOOD ORANGE REDUCTION

Serves 4 to 6

The first time I tasted lobster and foie gras together, I was dining at Restaurant Jacques Maximin, chef Jacques Maximin's restaurant in Vence, France, near Nice. As part of a quest to discover the source of some of my favorite dishes, I had sought out chef Maximin and here's why: When in New York, I had worked for chef Alfred Portale at the Gotham Bar and Grill. Alfred, who was one of my mentors, had worked for chef Maximin in France, and because I admired Alfred and his food so much, I was sure I would find inspiration from chef Maximin's, too. I was not disappointed! The way he combined and layered flavors was amazing to me.

I put my own twist on this recipe by using langoustines and blood oranges; citrus, langoustines, and foie gras work fantastically together. You can use large shrimp in place of langoustines for the ravioli and on the dish. That, too, works beautifully.

6 langoustines
1 tablespoon unsalted butter
¼ cup chopped leeks, white and light-green parts only
12 Langoustine Ravioli (recipe follows)
2 cups Foie Gras Sauce (recipe follows)
¼ cup Blood Orange Reduction (recipe follows)
2 tablespoons lobster roe

1. With sharp kitchen shears or a knife, cut the tails from the langoustines and reserve them.
2. Bring a large pot of lightly salted water to a boil over medium-high heat. Drop the langoustine bodies into the boiling water, cover, and cook for 2 to 3 minutes or until the langoustines turn bright red. Put the tails in the water with the bodies and cook for 1 minute. Drain both the bodies and the tails. Set aside, covered, to keep warm.
3. Melt the butter in a small sauté pan over medium heat. Add the leeks and cook, stirring occasionally, for

5 minutes or until the leeks have softened without browning.
4. Meanwhile, bring a large pot of lightly salted water to a boil. Add the langoustine ravioli and cook for 3 to 5 minutes or until cooked through and the ravioli bob to the surface. Drain.
5. Place 2 to 3 ravioli in the center of a small bowl. Place a langoustine body and tail on top of the ravioli. Spoon about ⅓ to ½ cup of foie gras sauce into the bowl. Garnish the sauce with leeks and a drizzle of the blood orange reduction. Sprinkle lobster roe over the langoustine. Repeat to make 5 more servings.

ABOUT THE WINE: *The components of briny, sweet langoustines, zippy blood orange juice, and ultrarich foie gras sauce call for an intensely fruit-driven wine with palate-cleansing acidity. Etude Pinot Gris from the cool Carneros zone of southern Napa and Sonoma counties functions well and adds another layer of flavor to the lushly textured ravioli.*

LANGOUSTINE RAVIOLI

Makes 12

TARRAGON-CHERVIL BUTTER:
½ pound unsalted butter, cut into small pieces and softened
1 tablespoon chopped fresh tarragon
1 tablespoon chopped fresh chervil
Kosher salt and freshly ground black pepper

RAVIOLI:
12 langoustines
12 3-inch-square wonton wrappers
1 large egg mixed with 1 teaspoon water, for egg wash
12 ½-inch sprigs fresh chervil
2 tablespoons extra-virgin olive oil

1. To make the tarragon-chervil butter, put the butter in a small bowl. Add the tarragon and chervil and mash

with a fork or small spatula until the herbs are evenly incorporated. Season to taste with salt and pepper. Cover and refrigerate until needed.

2. With sharp kitchen shears or a knife, cut the tails from the langoustines and reserve them.

3. To prepare the ravioli, bring a large pot of lightly salted water to a boil over medium-high heat. Drop the langoustine bodies into the boiling water, cover, and cook for about 5 minutes or until the langoustines turn bright red. Put the tails in the water with the bodies and cook for 1 minute. Drain both the bodies and the tails. Set aside, covered, to keep warm. Reserve the bodies for garnish.

4. Remove the meat from the langoustine tails and cut into ½-by-¼-inch pieces.

5. Lay the wonton wrappers out on a work surface. Brush them with the egg wash.

6. Place about ½ teaspoon of the tarragon-chervil butter in the center of each wrapper. Place a piece of langoustine on top of the butter. Top with a sprig of chervil.

7. Fold over the wrappers to form triangles. Fold in the corners to create squares.

8. Bring a large pot of lightly salted water to a boil over high heat. Add the ravioli and cook for 3 minutes. Drain and rinse with cold water. Toss the ravioli with olive oil to coat. Lay the ravioli on a baking sheet. Cover with plastic wrap and refrigerate until needed.

FOIE GRAS SAUCE

Makes 2 cups

3 ounces grade A foie gras, coarsely chopped
Kosher salt and freshly ground black pepper
2 tablespoons brandy or Madeira wine
1 pound unsalted butter, cut into small pieces
½ cup white wine
½ cup Fish Stock (see page 266)

1. Season the foie gras with salt and pepper to taste.

2. Heat a dry cast-iron skillet or sauté pan over high heat until very hot. Sear the foie gras on all sides for 1 minute or until partially cooked. Add the brandy and cook, scraping the bottom of the skillet with a wooden spoon, until the brandy has been almost completely absorbed. Remove the pan from the heat and set aside at room temperature to cool.

3. Put the butter in the bowl of a food processor fitted with a metal blade. Add the foie gras and process until smooth.

4. Transfer to a bowl. Cover and refrigerate until needed.

5. Put the wine and fish stock in a small saucepan and bring to a boil over medium-high heat. As soon as the liquid comes to a boil, remove the pan from the heat and whisk in the foie gras butter until smooth. Season to taste with salt and pepper.

BLOOD ORANGE REDUCTION

Makes about ¼ cup

Juice of 10 blood oranges
1 tablespoon granulated sugar

1. Strain the juice through a chinois or fine-mesh sieve into a medium-sized saucepan.

2. Bring to a boil over medium-high heat. Reduce the heat and simmer for 20 to 25 minutes or until the juice is reduced to ¼ cup. Stir in the sugar until dissolved.

3. Transfer to a small bowl and set aside at room temperature to cool. Cover and refrigerate until needed. Pour into a squirt bottle for garnishing.

BLACK TRUFFLE RISOTTO WITH LOBSTER, FRENCH BEANS, AND LOBSTER EMULSION

Serves 4 to 6

Whenever I attempt to give this recipe some time off, my customers clamor for it; consequently it has not been off the menu at Tru since we opened in 1999. The key is to fold the whipped cream into the risotto at the very end, which smoothes and enriches it even as it lightens it up. The great Swiss chef and my good friend Anton Mosimann, whom I *staged* with in London in 1990, taught me this trick, as well as many others. The risotto, laced with haricot verts and lobster and garnished with truffles, is an elegant dish, which I serve in individual copper or silver pots for the wow effect. Even a dish as simple as risotto can stand a little dressing up!

6 cups Vegetable Stock (see page 270)
2 tablespoons unsalted butter
4 cups Arborio, Carnaroli, or Vialone Nano rice
1 shallot, minced
1½ cups white wine
1 cup haricots verts, cut into 1-inch lengths
Meat from 4 cooked lobster tails, chopped (see Note)
½ cup freshly grated Parmigiano-Reggiano cheese
1 cup heavy cream, whipped until stiff peaks form
Kosher salt and freshly ground white pepper
2 cups Lobster Emulsion (recipe follows)
¼ cup sliced black truffles, for garnish
3 tablespoons white truffle oil, for garnish
Grated Parmigiano-Reggiano cheese, for garnish
1 tablespoon Tramonto's Orange Dust, for garnish
    (see page 272)

1. Heat the vegetable stock in a medium-sized saucepan over low heat to a simmer.

2. Melt the butter in a large saucepan over medium heat. Add the rice and stir continuously for 2 minutes or until the rice is completely coated. Add the shallot and cook for 2 to 3 minutes or until the shallot is translucent. Add the white wine and simmer until the wine is reduced by half. Add the vegetable stock, 1 cup at a time, stirring before each addition, until the rice is almost completely covered. Stirring constantly, cook the rice for 10 minutes or until it is still a little firm in the center.

3. Meanwhile, bring a large shallow pan of lightly salted water to a boil over high heat. Add the haricots verts and simmer rapidly for 2 to 3 minutes or until tender. Drain immediately and refresh with ice-cold water to stop the cooking.

4. Add the blanched haricots verts and lobster meat to the risotto and cook for 3 to 4 minutes or until heated through. Add the ½ cup grated Parmigiano-Reggiano cheese and stir until melted. Fold in the whipped cream and stir until the rice is smooth and creamy. Season to taste with salt and white pepper.

5. Put ½ cup of risotto in each bowl and spoon the lobster emulsion over the risotto. Garnish with sliced black truffles, a drizzle of white truffle oil, freshly grated Parmigiano-Reggiano cheese, and Tramonto's orange dust.

NOTE: *To cook the lobster tails, plunge 4 whole lobsters headfirst into a large pot of rapidly boiling salted water. Cover and boil for 8 to 12 minutes or until bright red and cooked through. Using a pair of long-handled tongs, remove the lobsters from the pot and immediately submerge in cold water. Drain the lobsters and allow to cool. Chop or break off the tails and remove the meat. Use the claw meat for another use.*

ABOUT THE WINE: *The decadent combination of heavy cream, cheese, and pungent white truffles begs for a structured wine with refreshing acidity and an earthy, mineral presence. St. Aubin Le Chatenière Marc Colin exhibits flavors of preserved lemons, ripe apples, wet stones, and subtle new oak.*

LOBSTER EMULSION

Makes 2 cups

1 cup heavy cream
¾ cup Vegetable Stock (see page 266)
¼ cup Lobster Glace (see page 268)
2 tablespoons unsalted butter

Put the cream, vegetable stock, and lobster glace in a medium-sized saucepan over medium-high heat. Bring to a boil. As soon as the cream mixture starts to boil, remove the pan from the heat. Add the butter. Using a handheld immersion blender, whip the mixture until foamy. Use the foamy top immediately as desired.

CHAPTER FIVE

Foie Gras

AMERICANS MAY NOT HAVE EMBRACED foie gras to the extent that Europeans have, but, happily, my customers are the lucky exceptions. I absolutely love foie gras and serve it at every meal and in as many fresh and exciting ways as I can. This is not hard work! Foie gras is a universal ingredient that melds as exquisitely with savory as with sweet flavors. The first time I paired it with chocolate, for instance, I was blown away!

The livers of specially fattened geese and ducks have been savored for centuries. Evidence points to the Egyptians appreciating it, and we know the Romans fed their geese a diet rich in figs to sweeten the meat. No doubt the Greek gods perched high on Mount Olympus indulged in this ultimate luxury.

Goose foie gras is richer than duck, but both are sublime. The foie gras of southwest France is best known, but other countries produce very good examples, too. I buy much of my foie gras from domestic farms, the two primary ones being Hudson Valley Foie Gras in New York State and Sonoma Valley Foie Gras in northern California.

Always buy grade A livers. Clean them by removing all veins, blood clots, and sinews (use needle-nose pliers or tweezers, if necessary). They should be pale beige and firm to the touch, and when cooked have a silken texture that cannot be mistaken for anything else. Don't wait to eat foie gras only in restaurants. It's surprisingly easy to cook and always disarmingly delectable, and, in the culinary world, beyond reproach. *Bon appétit!*

89   *Seared Foie Gras with Caramelized White Peaches and Maine Blueberries*

91   *Seared Foie Gras with Rhubarb Ice Cream, Pickled Rhubarb,
and Pomegranate Molasses*

94   *Sautéed Foie Gras with Honeydew Melon Soup and Muscat Reduction*

97   *Caramel Taffy Apple Foie Gras with Lavender Salad and Green Apple Chips*

100   *Macadamia Nut—crusted Foie Gras with Banana French Toast
and Chocolate Sauce*

103   *Cured Foie Gras au Torchon with Peppered Pineapple Relish and Fun Buns*

SEARED FOIE GRAS WITH CARAMELIZED WHITE PEACHES AND MAINE BLUEBERRIES

Serves 6

When you caramelize peaches and serve them with foie gras, the results are pretty dreamy. I created this when a crate of supersweet, juicy white Georgia peaches arrived at the kitchen door, delivered by Lee Jones of Chef's Garden, one of the farmers we rely on. Lee is a good friend, too, with an incredible farm in Huron, Ohio, where I sometimes escape for a little R & R and good company. He is the founder and creator of the Culinary Vegetable Institute, of which Gale and I are board members, dedicated to educating chefs and the public alike about the agriculture of cultivating fruits and vegetables. If you are ever in the area, it's worth making time to visit. Lee will be happy to show you around and I guarantee you will never again look at fruits and vegetables the same way.

White peaches are one of my favorite fruits, and as I eagerly bit into one from the crate that morning, I recalled a caramelized orange and peach cobbler that chef Nico Ladenis had made with foie gras. Nico, a good friend, is the brilliant chef-owner of the Michelin three-star restaurant Chez Nico in London, and his cobbler truly was out of this world. So is this foie gras when paired with the peaches and with sauce made from tiny, sweet Maine blueberries. Pretty luscious, to be sure!

1 ¼ pounds grade A foie gras
3 ripe white or yellow peaches
1 cup coarse sugar
½ cup Maine Blueberry Sauce (recipe follows)
½ cup Homemade Crème Fraîche (see page 280)

1. Preheat the oven to 400 degrees.
2. With a sharp knife, cut the foie gras into 6 slices.
3. Heat a dry cast-iron skillet over medium-high heat. When hot, sauté the foie gras for about 1½ minutes on each side or until dark golden brown. Transfer to a baking sheet.

4. Meanwhile, cut each peach in half and remove the pit. Cut each half into 3 wedges.
5. Spread the sugar on a flat plate or sheet of wax paper. Gently roll the peaches in the sugar and transfer to a baking sheet. Using a small blowtorch, caramelize the sugar.
6. Bake the foie gras for 2 minutes or until heated through and nicely browned.
7. To serve, place a slice of foie gras on a plate. Arrange 3 caramelized peach wedges around the foie gras. Spoon some blueberry sauce around the foie gras and garnish with a dollop of crème fraîche. Repeat to make 5 more servings.

ABOUT THE WINE: *The summery peach, apricot, and honeysuckle scents and flavors of late-picked Viognier work perfectly with this preparation. The northern Rhône Valley appellation of Condrieu is the source of the best version of this sweet style: Condrieu Les Ayguets Yves Cuilleron 1999.*

MAINE BLUEBERRY SAUCE

Makes about 1½ cups

½ cup white verjuice (see Note on page 19)
2 tablespoons sugar
1 tablespoon honey
Grated zest and juice of ½ lemon
½ vanilla bean
2 cups small Maine blueberries, stems removed and rinsed
⅓ cup Red Wine Sauce (see page 271)
Kosher salt and freshly ground white pepper

1. Combine the verjuice, sugar, honey, lemon zest, lemon juice, and vanilla bean in a large skillet. Bring to a boil over medium-high heat. As soon as it comes to a boil, reduce the heat and simmer for 2 minutes. Add the blueberries and cook over medium heat for 8 to 10 min-

utes or until the mixture has thickened. Set aside to cool at room temperature.

2. Transfer the mixture to a bowl, cover, and set aside at room temperature for 8 hours or overnight to steep.

3. In a small saucepan over low heat, stir together the red wine sauce and steeped blueberry mixture until heated through. Season with salt and white pepper. Cover to keep warm until ready to serve.

SEARED FOIE GRAS WITH RHUBARB
ICE CREAM, PICKLED RHUBARB,
AND POMEGRANATE MOLASSES

Serves 6

When I was inspired to develop a dish combining foie gras and rhubarb, I relied on a system I often use: I asked my sous-chefs to come up with recipe ideas along with me. We brainstormed for several weeks and finally tried using hot and cold elements by marrying a rhubarb ice cream with foie gras. I thought to myself: This is not going to happen! But it worked. The tartness and creaminess of the ice cream mingles with the fat in the foie gras, further offset by the pickled rhubarb and small dab of pomegranate molasses. It comes together like ambrosia, the food of the gods!

1 pound grade A foie gras
18 pieces Pickled Rhubarb (recipe follows)
1 cup Savory Anglaise (recipe follows)
¼ cup Red Wine Sauce (see page 275)
1 cup toasted slivered almonds
1 cup Rhubarb Ice Cream (recipe follows)
Pomegranate molasses, for garnish (see Note)

1. With a sharp knife, cut the foie gras into 6 slices.
2. Heat a dry cast-iron skillet over medium-high heat. When hot, sauté the foie gras for about 1½ minutes on each side or until golden brown and soft.
3. Place 3 pieces of the pickled rhubarb in the center of a round plate. Spoon a circle of the savory anglaise around the rhubarb. Spoon the red wine sauce in the space between the rhubarb and the anglaise. Place a slice of foie gras on top of the rhubarb. Sprinkle the almonds over the foie gras. Scoop a quenelle (oval-shaped mound) of the rhubarb ice cream and place on top of the foie gras. Using a squeeze bottle, garnish each plate with a line of pomegranate molasses. Repeat to make 5 more servings.

ABOUT THE WINE: Tart rhubarb presented in two forms, pickled and creamy, determines the wine choice. Chehalem Vineyards Cerise, a blend of fruity Gamay and cherry- and rose-petal-scented Pinot Noir from Oregon's Willamette Valley, offers high-pitched flavors, silky texture, and rhubarb-level acidity.

NOTE: Pomegranate molasses is sold at specialty stores.

PICKLED RHUBARB
Makes about 18 pieces

9 stalks rhubarb
1 cup red wine vinegar
1 cup red verjuice (see Note on page 19)
1 cup grenadine
¼ cup raspberry vinegar

1. Using a vegetable peeler, peel the rhubarb to remove the fibrous outer part of the stalks. Cut the rhubarb into 1-by-3-inch pieces. Transfer the pieces to a bowl.
2. Put the red wine vinegar, verjuice, grenadine, and raspberry vinegar in a medium-sized saucepan. Place over medium-high heat and bring to a boil. Reduce the heat and simmer for about 10 minutes, or until reduced by half.
3. Pour the hot liquid over the rhubarb. Cover the bowl with plastic wrap and set aside at room temperature to steep for 6 to 8 hours or until the rhubarb is soft and red. Use immediately or refrigerate for up to 1 week.

SAVORY ANGLAISE

Makes 2 cups

2 cups heavy cream
2 sprigs fresh thyme
7 large egg yolks, at room temperature

1. In a medium-sized saucepan, combine the cream and thyme and bring to a simmer over medium-high heat.

2. Meanwhile, whisk the egg yolks in a small bowl. Pour a few tablespoons of the hot cream into the eggs and whisk to temper the yolks so that they won't scramble in the hot cream. Slowly whisk the tempered yolks into the cream in the saucepan until smooth and blended.

3. Return the cream to a low heat and whisk for 3 to 5 minutes or until thick. Strain through a chinois or fine-mesh sieve into a bowl. Press a piece of plastic wrap directly on the surface to prevent a skin from forming. Chill in an ice-water bath until cool and then refrigerate until needed or for up to 24 hours.

RHUBARB ICE CREAM

Makes about 2 cups

1 cup Savory Anglaise (see recipe at left)
1 cup Pickled Rhubarb (see page 91)
¼ cup Simple Syrup (see page 279)

1. Stir together the anglaise, rhubarb, and syrup in a metal bowl.

2. If using a conventional ice-cream machine, puree all ingredients until smooth in a blender or food processor and then strain through a chinois or fine-mesh sieve. Cover and refrigerate the mixture for at least 2 hours or until thoroughly chilled. Freeze in the ice-cream machine according to the manufacturer's directions. Put the ice cream in a chilled container and cover with plastic wrap. Freeze for at least 3 hours or until ready to serve.

If using a Pacojet, pour the mixture into a Pacojet canister and freeze completely. Place the canister in the machine and spin according to the manufacturer's directions.

SAUTÉED FOIE GRAS WITH HONEYDEW MELON SOUP AND MUSCAT REDUCTION

Serves 6

Because I hold Alain Ducasse in such high esteem, I wanted to include a recipe in this book that reflects the influence he has had on my cooking style. This dish, with its Mediterranean flavors, does just that.

Alain is one of my heroes and I eat his food as often as I can. Between his restaurants in Monaco, Paris, and New York, I have indulged myself eight to ten times and always return to Tru fired up, raring to go—and vaguely depressed. Depressed because I realize how far I still have to travel before I will be satisfied with my own cooking. Recently, I saw Alain at a benefit for Meals on Wheels at New York's Rockefeller Center and he complimented me on *Amuse-Bouche,* the book I published in 2002. I was absolutely thrilled that a guy of that stature took notice of my work. It was a defining moment of my career!

Foie gras is so rich and luxurious, it's tricky to serve during the summer when everyone wants light, easy food, and so I came up with the idea of matching it with a cool melon soup. The secret is to use the best, ripest melon you can find for a soup that is nothing more complicated than juiced melon with mint leaves. How refreshing! I think of this, too, as a play on the classic pairing of prosciutto di Parma and honeydew, with the foie gras standing in for the ham. Okay, okay, it's a stretch, but it tastes great!

1 pound grade A foie gras
1½ cups Honeydew Melon Soup (recipe follows)
1 Charantais or cantaloupe melon (about 1 pound),
    peeled and cut into ½-inch cubes
½ cup Muscat Reduction (recipe follows)
2 generous tablespoons fresh micro mint or mint tops,
    for garnish

1. With a sharp knife, cut the foie gras into 6 slices and then halve each, for a total of 12 pieces.
2. Heat a dry cast-iron skillet over medium-high heat.

When hot, sauté the foie gras for about 1½ minutes on each side or until golden brown.
3. Meanwhile, heat the honeydew melon soup in a small saucepan over very low heat for about 2 minutes or until just barely warm.
4. Put the diced melon in a saucepan and add the muscat reduction. Cook over low heat for 2 to 3 minutes or until the melon is warm.
5. To serve, place 8 to 10 melon cubes in the center of a bowl. Spoon in only enough soup to barely cover the bottom of the bowl. Top the melon with 2 chunks of barely overlapping foie gras. Garnish with mint. Repeat to make 5 more servings.

ABOUT THE WINE: *The mint-scented melon soup lightens this dish, so keep the wine choice light as well. A Chardonnay-based sparkling wine such as Pierre Peters Blanc de Blancs with its honey and hazelnut notes or a fruity demi-sec from Schramsberg of Napa Valley satisfies. For a sweet alternative, serve a glass of the muscat used in the melon-soup recipe. Bonny Doon Vineyard's Muscat Vin de Glaciere Santa Cruz is an excellent New World choice.*

HONEYDEW MELON SOUP

Makes about 2 cups

2 honeydew melons
¼ cup fresh mint leaves

1. Cut the melon flesh from the rinds. Juice the melons with the mint leaves.
2. Strain through a chinois or fine-mesh sieve into a bowl. You should have about 2 cups of juice.
3. Transfer to a pitcher, cover, and refrigerate until needed or for up to 8 hours.

MUSCAT REDUCTION

Makes ½ cup

1 375-ml bottle muscat wine
½ cup white verjuice (see Note on page 19)
¼ cup honey

1. In a medium-sized saucepan, combine the wine, verjuice, and honey and bring to a boil over medium-high heat. Reduce the heat and simmer for 20 to 30 minutes or until syrupy and reduced to about ½ cup.

2. Set aside and allow to cool. Transfer to a bowl, cover, and refrigerate until needed or for up to 2 days.

CARAMEL TAFFY APPLE FOIE GRAS WITH LAVENDER SALAD AND GREEN APPLE CHIPS

Serves 6

A few years ago I participated in the Masters of Food and Wine in Carmel, California, and while there I wandered into a taffy-apple shop in nearby Monterey. The candy apples were amazing, and so I bought a box and brought them back to the guys in the kitchen. We cut them up for sampling and I immediately thought of pairing them with foie gras, which classically is served with apples. The resulting dish illustrates another of my favorite culinary philosophies of letting worlds collide. Here is the elegance of foie gras with the down-to-earth qualities of taffy apples, mirrored again by the elegance of the lavender salad and the earthiness of the green apple chips.

CARAMEL SAUCE:

1 cup superfine sugar
¼ cup water
¼ cup heavy cream

LAVENDER SALAD:

1 Fuji or other firm, sweet apple
1 fresh lavender sprig, leaves and flower finely chopped
2 tablespoons Lemon Oil (see page 277)
Fine sea salt

1 pound grade A foie gras
6 Green Apple Chips (recipe follows), for garnish
6 fresh lavender sprigs, for garnish
6 tablespoons toasted, chopped salted peanuts,
*   for garnish*

1. To make the caramel sauce, in a small, heavy-bottomed saucepan, stir together the sugar and water and bring to a simmer over medium heat. Without stirring, simmer for 8 to 10 minutes or until the sugar is a deep brown color. Tilt the pan to promote even cooking.

2. Remove the pan from the heat and very carefully add the cream. Swirl the pan until the cream is incorporated.

Transfer the caramel sauce to a bowl and set aside to cool to room temperature. Cover and refrigerate until needed.

3. To make the salad, halve and core the apple, but do not peel it. Using a Japanese mandolin or a very sharp knife, cut the apple, with its skin on, into matchsticks.

4. In a small bowl, gently toss the apples with the chopped lavender and the lemon oil. Season with sea salt.

5. Meanwhile, preheat the oven to 400 degrees.

6. Using a sharp knife, cut the foie gras into 6 slices.

7. Heat a dry cast-iron skillet or ovenproof sauté pan over medium-high heat. When hot, sauté the foie gras for about 1½ minutes on each side or until a deep golden brown. Transfer the skillet to the oven and roast for 2 to 3 minutes or until cooked through.

8. Garnish a plate with streaks of caramel sauce. Mound some of the lavender salad in the center of the plate. Lean a slice of foie gras against the salad. Garnish the plate with an apple chip and a lavender sprig. Sprinkle with chopped peanuts. Repeat to make 5 more servings.

ABOUT THE WINE: *The foie gras preparations that incorporate tree fruit such as apples or pears often have an affinity with Chenin Blanc–based wines. Huet's exquisite Vouvray Cuvée Constance is Loire Valley sweet wine at its pinnacle. A glass of this unctuous, golden wine elevates this dish to dizzying heights.*

GREEN APPLE CHIPS

Makes 6 to 8 slices

1 Granny Smith or other large tart apple
1 cup Simple Syrup (see page 279)

1. Preheat the oven to 200 degrees. Line a jelly-roll pan with a silpat (silicone baking mat) or parchment paper.

2. Core the apple but do not peel it. Using a Japanese mandolin or a very sharp knife, cut the apple into paper-thin slices. Dip each slice of apple into the syrup to coat completely. Arrange in a single layer in the pan. Bake the apple slices for 1½ to 2 hours or until they are dry and starting to color to a light golden brown. Transfer to a wire rack to cool to room temperature. Store in an airtight container until needed.

MACADAMIA NUT–CRUSTED FOIE GRAS WITH BANANA FRENCH TOAST AND CHOCOLATE SAUCE

Serves 6

One of my favorite childhood taste memories is of my mother's killer banana French toast, which we ate with crispy bacon. Years later, I did a *stage* at the acclaimed Paris restaurant Apicius with my friend chef Jean-Pierre Vigato, where I learned a lot about chocolate. For the first time I saw it paired with foie gras, which at first sounds odd but it tastes amazing. When I came back to Chicago and tried it myself, people thought I was crazy—until they tried it.

At first I simply served this seared foie gras on top of the French toast, but when I added chocolate it became the most popular foie gras dish on our menu! This is the true meaning of our logo, which illustrates the importance of thinking outside the box. This is that sort of thinking in action!

CHOCOLATE SAUCE:

2 cups crème de cassis
½ cup brandy
½ cup Veal Demi-glace (see page 268)
1 cup Red Wine Sauce (see page 271)
3 ounces semisweet chocolate, finely chopped
½ cup heavy cream
1 tablespoon unsalted butter

BANANA CHUTNEY:

¼ cup currants
2 cups golden raisins
½ cup brandy
3 tablespoons unsalted butter
2 bananas, cut into medium dice
¼ cup brown sugar
1 vanilla bean, rinsed, dried, and split in half lengthwise
1½ tablespoons molasses
Kosher salt and freshly ground pepper

FRENCH TOAST:

6 large eggs
¼ cup heavy cream
6 to 7 tablespoons unsalted butter
6 ¾-inch-thick slices homemade Brioche (see page 280), or from a good bakery

—

1¼ pounds grade A foie gras
6 slices caramelized bananas (see Note)
¼ cup toasted and coarsely chopped macadamia nuts, for garnish
1 tablespoon Mint Syrup (recipe follows)

1. To make the chocolate sauce, put the crème de cassis and brandy in a saucepan and bring to a simmer over medium-high heat. Cook gently for about 10 minutes or until the sauce reduces by half.

2. Add the veal demi-glace and the red wine sauce and continue to simmer for about 15 minutes or until the sauce is further reduced by half again. Remove the sauce from the heat and add the chocolate. Let stand for a few seconds and then whisk until the chocolate is completely melted. Add the cream and butter. Return to medium heat and whisk until smooth. Set aside.

3. To make the banana chutney, put the currants and golden raisins in a small bowl and add the brandy. Toss gently and set aside to macerate for about 20 minutes.

4. Melt the butter in a sauté pan over medium heat, add the bananas, brown sugar, and vanilla bean, and cook for 6 to 8 minutes or until the bananas are lightly browned and caramelized. Add the molasses and the currants and raisins along with any brandy that has not been absorbed. Season to taste with salt and pepper. Set aside.

5. Before preparing the French toast, reheat the chocolate sauce and the banana chutney.

6. To make the French toast, whisk the eggs and cream in a shallow dish.

7. Melt the butter in a skillet over medium heat.

8. Dip 1 or 2 slices of the brioche at a time in the egg batter. Turn once until moistened but not saturated.

9. Cook for 1 to 2 minutes on each side until golden brown. Transfer the French toast to a plate and cover to keep warm. Repeat with the remaining slices of brioche.

10. Heat a dry cast-iron skillet or sauté pan over high heat until very hot. Sear the foie gras on each side for 1 to 2 minutes or until lightly browned. Slice into 6 2½-ounce portions. Set aside and keep warm.

11. To serve, put a slice of French toast on a plate. Top with 2½ tablespoons of the banana chutney and a slice of the foie gras. Top with caramelized banana slices and then drizzle chocolate sauce around the plate. Garnish with macadamia nuts and, using a squeeze bottle, dot the plate with 4 or 5 dots of mint syrup. Repeat to make 5 more servings.

NOTE: *To caramelize banana slices, heat 2 tablespoons of unsalted butter over medium-high heat. Add the banana slices and cook for 6 to 8 minutes or until lightly browned and caramelized. Set aside to cool in the pan until needed.*

ABOUT THE WINE: *Madeira, an island off the coast of Morocco, produces amber-colored wines of varying sweetness that are traditionally enjoyed as an aperitif or digestif. Often, the food-matching properties of fine Madeira are overlooked. Impress your friends by serving a slightly sweet, nutty, and smoky Madeira such as Cossart Gordon fifteen-year-old Bual as a counterpoint to the mouthwatering, bittersweet chocolate sauce.*

MINT SYRUP

Makes 2 cups

2 cups fresh mint leaves
1 cup fresh spinach leaves
1½ cups light corn syrup
Kosher salt and freshly ground black pepper, optional

1. In a large pot of boiling water, blanch the mint leaves for about 30 seconds. Remove with a slotted spoon and immediately submerge in ice-cold water. Drain. Pat dry with paper towels.

2. In the same pot of boiling water, blanch the spinach leaves for about 1 minute. Drain and immediately submerge in ice-cold water. Drain again. Pat dry with paper towels.

3. Transfer the mint and spinach to a blender. Add the corn syrup. Puree until smooth. Strain through a chinois or fine-mesh sieve. Transfer the puree to a bowl. Taste and season with salt and pepper, if necessary. Chill in an ice bath. Cover and refrigerate for up to 3 days.

CURED FOIE GRAS AU TORCHON WITH PEPPERED PINEAPPLE RELISH AND FUN BUNS

Serves 8

When you master this foie gras terrine, you will have completed Foie Gras 101 and will have earned an A+! This is a basic foie gras terrine, which, while time-consuming, is extremely easy. It can stay in the refrigerator for up to two weeks, so can be made well in advance. Because these travel so well and slice so smoothly, we make two, three, or more *torchons* for upcoming special events.

Begin with grade A foie gras, which is the best: finely grained, flawless, and just-firm to the touch—never mushy. *Torchon* means "torch," and while its shape resembles one, I also think of this as one of the shining lights of the culinary universe. It's made with foie gras cured in salt and sugar. Don't let the term *cure* turn you off; curing is just another kitchen technique and, while it demands long resting periods, there's nothing to it.

Because it's so rich and fatty, foie gras is usually served with an acidic accompaniment to cut the richness. Here I rely on a peppered pineapple relish and lentil salad and serve the *torchon* with small brioche rolls that we call Pull-apart Fun Buns. I spread them with truffle butter. After all, truffles and foie gras have a long history of happy reunions.

⅓ cup brandy
⅓ cup Madeira wine
⅓ cup port wine
1 pound grade A foie gras
1 teaspoon kosher salt
⅛ teaspoon ground white pepper
⅓ teaspoon superfine sugar
⅓ teaspoon pink salt (sodium nitrate)
Kosher salt (see step 6 below)
1 cup Lentil Salad (recipe follows)
4 bunches mâche
1 cup Kracher Gelée cubes (recipe follows)

½ cup Peppered Pineapple Relish (recipe follows)
½ cup Truffle Vinaigrette (recipe follows)
8 homemade Pull-apart Brioche Fun Buns (see page 280), or from a good bakery, warmed
1 cup Truffle Butter (recipe follows)
Fleur de Sel sea salt
Cracked black pepper

1. In a small saucepan, bring the brandy, Madeira, and port to a boil over medium-high heat. Immediately reduce the heat and simmer for 15 to 20 minutes or until the liquid is reduced to ⅓ cup. Remove from the heat and set aside to cool to room temperature.

2. Gently pull the 2 lobes of foie gras apart. They should be approximately the same size.

3. In a small bowl, mix together the salt, white pepper, sugar, and pink salt.

4. Using your fingers, gently spread the salt mixture over the foie gras until it's lightly coated. Transfer to a bowl and pour the reduced brandy over the foie gras. Cover with plastic wrap and refrigerate for approximately 3 hours.

5. Dampen a 3-foot square of cheesecloth and spread it out on a clean work surface. Put the foie gras at one end and roll up into a cylinder about 3 inches in diameter. Twist the ends in opposite directions to secure tightly (this forms a *torchon*). Tie the ends with kitchen string.

6. Spread a generous layer of kosher salt in a small pan, such as an 8-inch-square pan. Lay the *torchon* in the pan and then cover with more kosher salt until the *torchon* is completely buried in the salt. Refrigerate for 16 to 18 hours.

7. Remove the *torchon* from the salt, brushing off the excess. Unwrap the cheesecloth and then wrap the foie gras in plastic wrap. Refrigerate for 24 hours or until very cold and firm.

8. To serve, unwrap the foie gras and slice it into ½-inch-thick slices with a hot knife. (To heat the knife, run it under very hot water and then wipe dry.) Place a slice on a plate and put small mounds of lentil salad and mâche next to it. Garnish with cubes of Kracher gelée, a

teaspoon of peppered pineapple relish, and drops of truffle vinaigrette. Repeat with the 7 remaining plates.

9. Serve with warm brioche and truffle butter on the side. Sprinkle the foie gras with Fleur de Sel and cracked black pepper.

ABOUT THE WINE: *The delicate gelée provides the wine-pairing link for this decadent dish. We use Austrian genius Alois Kracher's* Grande Cuvée Trockenbeerenauslese #9 *1995 as the base for the gelée. A glass of this tropically accented nectar is the logical and delectable accompaniment.*

LENTIL SALAD

Makes about 1 cup

3 tablespoons unsalted butter
2 shallots, minced
1 carrot, finely diced
1 rib celery, finely diced
⅓ cup Beluga black lentils, rinsed and drained
⅓ cup Crimson red lentils, rinsed and drained
⅓ cup French green lentils (Puy), rinsed and drained
6 sprigs fresh thyme
¼ cup snipped fresh chives
½ cup Truffle Vinaigrette (recipe follows)
Kosher salt and freshly ground black pepper

1. Set 3 small saucepans over low heat. Melt 1 tablespoon of butter in each one. Divide the shallots, carrot, and celery evenly among the pans and cook, stirring occasionally, for about 5 minutes or until the vegetables begin to soften without coloring. Add the Beluga lentils to one pan, the Crimson lentils to another, and the French lentils to the third. Pour enough cold water into each pan to cover the lentils. Add 2 sprigs of thyme to each pan.

2. Raise the heat under each and bring to a boil. Reduce the heat and simmer, partially covered, for 12 to 15 minutes or until the lentils are very tender and most

of the water has evaporated. Remove the pans from the heat and set aside to cool just slightly.

3. Drain through a chinois or fine-mesh sieve and put all the lentils in one bowl. Remove the thyme. Toss the lentils with the chives and truffle vinaigrette. Season to taste with salt and pepper. Cover with plastic wrap and refrigerate until needed but for no longer than 24 hours.

TRUFFLE VINAIGRETTE

Makes about 1 cup

1 2-ounce can sliced black truffles, rinsed and drained
2 tablespoons warm water
2 teaspoons Dijon mustard
½ cup truffle oil
Kosher salt and freshly ground black pepper

1. Combine the truffles, water, and mustard in a blender and puree until smooth.

2. With the motor running, slowly add the truffle oil until emulsified.

3. Transfer to a small glass or ceramic bowl and season to taste with salt and pepper. Use immediately or refrigerate the vinaigrette in a nonreactive container with a tight-fitting lid for up to 2 weeks. Whisk well before using.

KRACHER GELÉE

Makes about 1½ cups

1 375-ml bottle Kracher Cuvée Beerenauslese or other
sweet wine, such as Sauternes or muscat
9 sheets gelatin

1. Bring the wine to a simmer in a medium-sized saucepan over medium-high heat. As soon as the wine simmers, remove from the heat.

2. Meanwhile, fill a large bowl with cool water. Gently drop the gelatin sheets into the water until all are submerged. Let soften and bloom for about 5 minutes.

3. Using your hands, lift the gelatin sheets from the water and squeeze them gently between your fingers. Transfer the sheets to the warm wine. Stir gently until dissolved. Let cool at room temperature.

4. Pour the wine into a small jelly-roll or other rimmed metal pan measuring about 9 inches by 13 inches. Refrigerate, uncovered, for about 2 hours or until set. When the gelée is set, cut into ¼-inch cubes. Cover with plastic wrap and refrigerate until needed but for no longer than 12 hours.

PEPPERED PINEAPPLE RELISH

Makes about ½ cup

½ fresh pineapple
1 tablespoon unsalted butter
2 tablespoons Grand Marnier or other orange-flavored
liqueur
1 tablespoon brown sugar
Cracked black pepper

1. Peel, core, and remove the brown "eyes" from the pineapple. Cut the flesh into very fine dice. Transfer to a fine-mesh sieve set over a small bowl to drain. Reserve the diced pineapple and the juice.

2. In a small sauté pan set over medium-high heat, melt the butter. Add the pineapple and sauté for about 4 minutes or until lightly browned. Add the Grand Marnier, brown sugar, and strained pineapple juice and simmer for about 10 minutes or until the juice is reduced by half.

3. Transfer to a small bowl and set aside to cool to room temperature. Season with cracked black pepper. Cover with plastic wrap and refrigerate until needed.

TRUFFLE BUTTER

Makes 1 cup

1 cup unsalted butter, softened
1 2-ounce can sliced black truffles, rinsed, drained,
and finely chopped
1 tablespoon white truffle oil
Kosher salt and freshly ground white pepper

1. In a small bowl, cream the butter with a wooden spoon. Add the truffles and truffle oil and blend until smooth. Season with salt and white pepper.

2. Fit a pastry bag with a plain tip and fill the bag about halfway with the butter. Pipe the butter into 8 small ramekins. Cover with plastic wrap and refrigerate until needed but for no longer than 1 week.

Soups

WHAT MAY SOUND LIKE A CLICHÉ is nonetheless true: Soup feeds the soul. It's comforting, homey, and lends itself to big, simmering batches and many, many flavors. I associate good homemade soup with my childhood, and to this day I love making it, smelling it, and eating it.

Since my days at Trio, soup has always been part of my degustation menus, and customers are fascinated to find something so familiar served in elegant Versace cups. They love it! Soup needs to be contained, but can be served in many things other than ordinary soup bowls. You don't have to turn to Versace cups. Try hollowed-out baby pumpkins, ice bowls, or two-handled antique cups. Be playful and add the element of surprise.

From satiny-smooth lobster bisque to clear tomato water to curried cauliflower soup, the soups I serve at Tru run the gamut from the sublime to the supreme. For instance, I make a soup with truffles, one of the most precious and treasured ingredients in the world. I also make a soup with lowly sauerkraut and earthy sunchokes, but these are no less delicious for being humble. The act of making soup is rife with possibilities, and I take full advantage of them all. After all, if you can boil water, you can make soup! But it's not just soup, it's art.

110   *Lobster Bisque with a Spoon of Lobster Ceviche*

113   *Walla Walla Onion Soup with Orange-kissed Beignets*

116   *Curried Cauliflower Soup with Cumin Cracker*

118   *Chilled Sunchoke Velouté, Pickled Sunchokes, and Sevruga Caviar*

121   *Chilled Tomato Water with Baby Heirloom Tomatoes and Olive Oil*

122   *Carrot and Hawaiian Ginger Soup with Carrot Salad*

125   *Tramonto's Totally Insane Black and White Truffle Soup*

LOBSTER BISQUE WITH A SPOON
OF LOBSTER CEVICHE

Serves 4 to 6

Lobster bisque is everything a classic French soup should be: smooth, indulgent, rich, and creamy. My bisque is all this but with a difference: I add a spoon of lobster ceviche. I knew I had to have a lobster bisque on Tru's menu after tasting the incredible bisque chef Gordon Ramsey made for us at his three-Michelin-star restaurant in London, called Gordon Ramsey. Rich Melman, my partner, and I were traveling through Europe before opening Tru, researching food, style, and culinary trends. One taste of Gordon's soup convinced us to include a bisque on my menu! It's a signature soup at Tru, which we serve every night—and have since day one.

When you stir the chilled spoon of ceviche into the hot soup at Tru, you fall into the realm of cooking at the table, and experience small chunks of lobster and vegetables in the smooth soup. Because I serve six to eight soups nightly at Tru, it's important to present a balance of textures and flavors.

LOBSTER CEVICHE:

Meat from 3 cooked lobster tails (see step 3 below),
*   finely diced (about ½ to ¾ cup)*
¼ cup finely chopped red onion
¼ cup finely diced red pepper
¼ cup finely diced yellow pepper
1 tablespoon finely diced jalapeño pepper
2 tablespoons chopped fresh cilantro
Juice of 1 lemon
Juice of 1 orange
Juice of 2 limes
2 tablespoons extra-virgin olive oil
Kosher salt and freshly ground white pepper

BISQUE:

4 to 6 1½- to 2-pound lobsters, cooked and cooled
*   (see Note)*
3 tablespoons olive oil
1 cup tomato paste

1 cup brandy
1 cup chopped white onion
1 cup chopped celery
1 cup chopped carrots
2 tablespoons chopped fresh thyme
2 tablespoons chopped fresh tarragon
½ cup dry white wine
½ cup dry sherry
4 cups water
6 cups heavy cream
½ cup unsalted butter
Kosher salt and freshly ground white pepper

—

1 tablespoon lobster roe, for garnish
Lobster tentacles, for garnish
½ cup steamed milk, for garnish, optional (see Note)

1.   To make the ceviche, combine the diced lobster meat, red onion, red and yellow peppers, jalapeño pepper, and cilantro in a glass or ceramic bowl. Gently toss to combine. Add the citrus juices and olive oil and mix well. Season to taste with salt and white pepper.

2.   Cover with plastic wrap and refrigerate until needed.

3.   To make the bisque, remove the heads, tails, and claws from the lobsters. Discard the heads and save the claws and their meat for another use. (Reserve 3 tails for the ceviche and the tentacles for garnishing.) Chop each lobster body into 4 pieces.

4.   Heat a large stockpot over medium-high heat. When hot, add the oil, and when the oil is hot, add the lobster bodies and sear for 4 to 5 minutes, turning the pieces until golden brown on all sides.

5.   Reduce the heat to medium, add the tomato paste, and stir until the lobster pieces are coated. Add the brandy and cook for 2 to 3 minutes or until the liquid evaporates, stirring the bottom of the pan with a wooden spoon to deglaze.

6.   Add the onion, celery, and carrots and reduce the heat to medium. Cook for 5 minutes, stirring occasionally, until the vegetables soften. Add the thyme and tarragon.

7.   Add the wine and sherry, raise the heat to medium-high, and cook for 4 to 5 minutes or until the liquid

nearly evaporates. As the soup cooks, stir the bottom of the pan with a wooden spoon to deglaze.

8.   Add the water, making sure it covers the lobster pieces. If not, add more water until it does. Bring to a boil and cook until the liquid reduces by three-fourths. Add the cream, bring to a simmer, reduce the heat, and simmer gently, uncovered, for about 30 minutes or until the soup is reduced to 4 cups.

9.   Strain the soup through a chinois or fine-mesh sieve into a large, clean saucepan. Discard the lobster pieces and vegetables. Add the butter to finish the soup and cook over medium heat until the butter melts. Stir gently and season to taste with salt and white pepper.

10.   To serve, ladle the soup into small bowls or demitasse cups. Garnish each serving with a spoonful of ceviche, lobster roe, reserved lobster tentacles, and steamed milk, if using.

NOTE: *To cook live lobsters, plunge the lobsters headfirst into a large pot of rapidly boiling salted water. Cover and boil for 8 to 12 minutes or until bright red and cooked through. Using tongs, remove the lobsters from the pot and immediately submerge in ice-cold water. Drain the lobsters and allow to cool.*

To steam milk, use a home cappuccino maker. One cup of milk yields about ½ cup of steamed milk.

ABOUT THE WINE: *The fragrant mirabelle-plum aroma and citrus notes of Châteauneuf-du-Pape Blanc Château La Nerthe complement the inherent sweetness of the lobster. The moderate acidity of the wine is sufficient in taming the richness of the bisque while the ceviche offers a pleasing tanginess.*

WALLA WALLA ONION SOUP WITH ORANGE-KISSED BEIGNETS

Serves 6 to 8

If you have never thought of putting orange and onion together, you're missing out on a great flavor pairing. It's a winner that I exploit in this mild onion soup served with hot, light, orange-scented beignets. I remember a trip to New Orleans in search of beignets, which are a magnificent tradition among the many great culinary traditions in that city. My friend chef Emeril Lagasse was cooking for me at Emeril's restaurant one night and he brought some orange beignets to the table. Just one bite told me they would taste great with onion soup.

I make the soup with mild, sweet Walla Walla onions, which come from Washington State and are in season in the spring. I serve it with a few drips of rich aged balsamic vinegar. The best is aged for many years, for which you pay a price, but you need only a little for impact. Whatever you do, use aged balsamic, the oldest you can afford—don't settle for the cheap supermarket balsamics. They taste nothing like the real thing.

3 pounds Walla Walla or other sweet onions
½ pound unsalted butter, cut into large slices
2 cups Vegetable Stock (see page 266)
1 cup heavy cream
Kosher salt and freshly ground black pepper
1 tablespoon finely crushed pink peppercorns,
*   for garnish*
6 chive sticks, for garnish
18 Orange-kissed Beignets (recipe follows)
4 teaspoons 25-, 50-, or 100-year-old balsamic vinegar,
*   depending on your budget, for garnish*

1. Cut the onions into very fine julienne slices.
2. Put ¼ pound of the butter in the bottom of a large, heavy-bottomed saucepan. Scatter the onions over the butter. Lay the remaining slices of butter over the onions. Cover the pan with a tight-fitting lid or plastic wrap.
3. Put the saucepan over low heat and cook, stirring every 20 minutes, for about 1½ hours or until the onions are softened by not colored. Remove from the heat and set aside to cool slightly.
4. Transfer the onions to a blender and process until smooth. Strain through a chinois or fine-mesh sieve back into the saucepan. Add the vegetable stock and cream and bring to a simmer, uncovered, over medium-high heat. Reduce the heat and simmer gently, partially covered, for about 30 minutes, until the flavors meld. Season with salt and pepper.
5. Ladle the soup into bowls and garnish each bowl with pink peppercorns and a long chive. Serve with the beignets and about ½ teaspoon balsamic vinegar per serving for dipping.

ABOUT THE WINE: *Choose a Pacific Northwest theme by pairing a Washington State wine with this dish. Semillon excels in this region. The Matthews Cellars bottling exhibits citrus, pear, and fig flavors that marry well with the sweet onions, fruity pink peppercorns, and buttery, rich beignets.*

113

SOUPS

ORANGE-KISSED BEIGNETS

Makes 18

3 cups all-purpose flour
3 tablespoons baking powder
2 large eggs
¼ cup fresh orange juice
1 teaspoon olive oil
4 large egg whites
1½ teaspoons kosher salt
4 cups canola oil
Kosher salt
1 tablespoon Tramonto's Orange Dust (see page 272)

1. In a large mixing bowl, whisk together the flour and baking powder.
2. In a small mixing bowl, whisk together the eggs, orange juice, and olive oil.

3. Make a well in the center of the flour. Slowly pour in the egg mixture and stir the flour with it until smooth and lump-free. Cover and set aside to rest for 20 minutes.

4. In the bowl of an electric mixer fitted with the whisk and set on medium-high speed, beat the egg whites and salt until soft peaks form. Fold into the batter and set aside to rest for 30 minutes.

5. Heat the canola oil in a deep, heavy saucepan over high heat until a deep-frying thermometer reads 350 degrees. Spoon about 1 tablespoon of the batter into the oil and fry for 1 to 3 minutes or until golden brown. Remove with a slotted spoon and drain on paper towels. Season with salt and orange dust. Repeat with the remaining batter, frying only several beignets at a time so you don't crowd the pan.

CURRIED CAULIFLOWER SOUP
WITH CUMIN CRACKER

Serves 6 to 8

The brilliant, vibrant color and intense flavor of this soup will thrill anyone who loves curries—and I count myself among them. I honed my appreciation for curries when I lived in London years ago and tasted a lot of them with my old partner in crime Bob Payton. My favorite place for curry in the city was called Chutney Mary's.

Later I had the pleasure of meeting Madhur Jaffrey, a critically acclaimed Indian chef and author I have long admired, who totally inspired me to incorporate Indian and Malaysian flavors into my cooking. This soup is based on a curried cauliflower and vegetable dish she made. It underscored the magical combination of cauliflower and curry, and the crunch of the cumin crackers brings everything into balance.

4 tablespoons unsalted butter
1 cup chopped white onion
2 Granny Smith or other large tart apples, peeled, cored, and chopped
1 head white cauliflower (about 2½ pounds), outer leaves removed, cored, and broken into florets
2 tablespoons curry powder
1 cup dry white wine
4 cups Vegetable Stock (see page 266)
Kosher salt and freshly ground black pepper
6 to 8 Cumin Crackers (recipe follows)

1. In a large saucepan set over low heat, melt 2 tablespoons of the butter. Add the onion and apples and cook, stirring occasionally, for about 15 minutes or until the onion softens.

2. Add the cauliflower and curry powder and stir to combine. Add the wine, raise the heat to medium, and simmer for about 10 minutes or until the wine evaporates.

3. Pour the stock over the vegetables and raise the heat to medium-high. Bring to a simmer, reduce the heat to medium, and simmer gently, partially covered, for about 20 minutes or until the cauliflower is tender.

4. Transfer the soup to a blender and process until smooth. You will have to do this in batches. Strain through a chinois or fine-mesh sieve into a bowl and season to taste with salt and pepper.

5. Serve the soup immediately or let it cool to room temperature, cover with plastic wrap, and refrigerate for at least 1 hour or until chilled.

6. To serve, reheat the soup over low heat for 7 to 10 minutes or until heated through. Whisk in the remaining 2 tablespoons of butter and adjust the seasonings. Ladle the soup into bowls and serve each with a cumin cracker.

ABOUT THE WINE: *The warm Indian spice flavors of curry and cumin sing when paired with a perfumed dry or off-dry gewürztraminer. The wine, however, must offer sufficient firm acidity, which can sometimes be a shortcoming for this grape variety. Gewürztraminer Herrenweg de Turckheim Domaine Zind-Humbrecht, with its characteristic musky rose and lychee aromas and flavors, is an excellent choice. A fine American option comes from Navarro Vineyards in Mendocino County's Anderson Valley.*

TRU

CUMIN CRACKERS

Makes 25 to 30

3 ½ cups all-purpose flour
10 tablespoons unsalted butter
1 tablespoon sugar
½ teaspoon ground cumin
¾ teaspoon kosher salt
1 ¼ cups cold buttermilk
2 large egg whites, lightly beaten
Kosher salt and freshly ground black pepper
½ teaspoon cumin seeds, plus more for sprinkling

1. Preheat the oven to 350 degrees. Position a rack in the center of the oven. Line a jelly-roll pan or large baking sheet with parchment paper.

2. In the bowl of an electric mixer fitted with a paddle attachment, combine the flour, butter, sugar, ground cumin, and ¾ teaspoon of salt. Mix at low speed just until combined. With the mixer running, add the buttermilk in a slow, steady stream until absorbed and the dough starts to come together. Turn the dough out onto a lightly floured work surface and shape into a disk. Set aside to rest for about 15 minutes, or cover with plastic wrap and refrigerate for up to 24 hours if you are not ready to bake the crackers right away.

3. To make the crackers in a pasta machine, generously flour the work surface, the dough, and the pasta machine. Break about 4 ounces of dough from the disk and roll this through the pasta machine, beginning with the thickest setting and rolling the dough through every setting down to number 1. Dust the dough and machine with flour as necessary. Cut the dough as necessary to fit through the machine. (Alternatively, roll out the dough into a paper-thin sheet, dusting the work surface and the rolling pin with additional flour as needed.) Carefully transfer the dough to the prepared pan.

4. Brush the dough lightly with the beaten egg whites. Sprinkle with salt, pepper, and cumin seeds.

5. Repeat with the remaining dough to make 6 sheets.

6. Bake on the center rack for 6 to 10 minutes or until lightly browned and crisp. Transfer to a wire rack to cool completely. Break into irregular-shaped pieces to serve.

This soup demonstrates the joy I get from integrating the world of peasant cooking with that of haute cuisine, like Levi's meets Versace! In this case, I marry a chilled sunchoke soup with caviar. I love how the sweetness of the lowly sunchokes is complemented by the saltiness of the upscale caviar. Sunchokes are also known as Jerusalem artichokes, although they are not artichokes but the tubers of a sunflower plant native to North America. They show up in Native American cooking, and when they were carried from the New World to the Old World, Italians enthusiastically embraced them, too. I like to balance the soup with sevruga caviar, with its small, slightly less potent grains. But you can use beluga or osetra caviar instead. It's a matter of personal taste and personal budget. Regardless of the caviar you use, be sure to serve this soup very, very cold. Best of all, serve the chilled soup on a bed of crushed ice or in an ice bowl.

1 teaspoon fresh lemon juice

About 1¼ pounds sunchokes

8 cups heavy cream

2 sprigs fresh thyme

1 bay leaf

Kosher salt and freshly ground white pepper

½ cup white wine vinegar

¼ cup white verjuice (see Note on page 19)

¼ cup honey

10 coriander seeds

5 mustard seeds

1 to 2 ounces sevruga (or beluga or osetra) caviar,
*   for garnish*

1 tablespoon Coriander-Orange Oil (see page 273),
*   for garnish*

8 Chervil sprigs, for garnish

1. Fill a large, nonreactive bowl with water and stir in the lemon juice to make acidulated water. Peel the sun-chokes and drop them into the water as you work. You should have about 3 cups of sunchokes.

2. Coarsely chop about two-thirds of the sunchokes and transfer them to a large saucepan. Add the cream, thyme, and bay leaf and bring to a boil over medium-high heat. As soon as the cream starts to boil, reduce the heat to low and simmer for about 1 hour or until the sun-chokes are soft. Remove from the heat, set aside to cool slightly, and remove and discard the bay leaf.

3. Transfer the chopped sunchokes and cream to a blender and puree until smooth. You will have to do this in batches. Strain through a chinois or fine-mesh sieve into a bowl. Season to taste with salt and white pepper. Cover with plastic wrap and refrigerate.

4. Drain the remaining sunchokes, cut them into thin slices, and transfer to a medium-sized saucepan. Add the vinegar, verjuice, honey, coriander seeds, and mustard seeds. Place over medium-high heat and bring to a boil. As soon as the liquid comes to a boil, remove it from the heat and set aside at room temperature for at least 3 hours.

5. Serve the chilled soup in small chilled bowls (see Note) and garnish each with 3 to 4 slices of the pickled sunchokes, caviar, a drizzle of coriander-orange oil, and a chervil sprig.

NOTE: *To chill glass bowls, run water over them and freeze the wet bowls. Remove from the freezer after 24 hours or when ready to serve. Immediately ladle soup into the iced bowls and serve on a bed of crushed ice.*

ABOUT THE WINE: *The silky richness of the velouté, the mouthwatering vibrance of the pickled sunchokes, and the alluring brininess of sevruga caviar are a high-wire act in perfect balance. Here, the wine choice should function as a safety net. Opt for a citrusy, mineral-rich, lightly oaked white such as a Chablis Grand Cru Valmur William Fevre.*

CHILLED TOMATO WATER WITH BABY HEIRLOOM TOMATOES AND OLIVE OIL

Serves 16

I have been making clear, tomato-flavored water since my days at Trio in the 1990s. It's astounding because it has no trace of the red tomato color but all of its flavor, and so it's something of an illusion. At Tru, I wanted to serve the crystal-clear broth with pretty pieces of tomato and herbs floating in it, but quickly realized that if I did, no one would realize the intense tomato flavor came from the clear broth. What fun is that? To compensate, we pour the clear soup at the table and our customers are amazed by the magic of the authentic tomato flavor. David Copperfield would be proud! You have to start with really delicious, ripe tomatoes. Make this in high summer when the tomatoes are at their best. There is a lot you can do with it!

5 pounds large ripe tomatoes, peeled, cored,
*   seeded, and chopped*
1 cup fresh basil leaves
10 coriander seeds
10 juniper berries
2 sprigs fresh thyme
Kosher salt and freshly ground black pepper
½ cup assorted baby heirloom tomatoes
¼ cup micro basil, for garnish
¼ cup extra-virgin olive oil, for garnish

1. Put the tomatoes, basil, coriander seeds, juniper berries, and thyme in the bowl of a food processor fitted with a metal blade and process until smooth. Transfer to a bowl, cover with plastic wrap, and refrigerate for 24 hours.

2. Line a chinois or fine-mesh sieve with a paper coffee filter and place over a large bowl. Pour some of the tomato mixture into the filter and allow the liquid to drip through into the bowl. Replace the coffee filter with a new one and repeat the process until all the tomato mixture has been strained. This process will take 3 to 4 hours.

3. Strain the tomato soup again through a chinois or fine-mesh sieve lined with a fresh coffee filter into a clean bowl. Season to taste with salt and pepper, cover with plastic wrap, and refrigerate for at least 6 hours or until chilled.

4. Peel the baby heirloom tomatoes and, if necessary, cut them in half so they are all the same size.

5. Scatter a few of the baby tomatoes and some micro basil along the bottom of shallow bowls. Spoon about ½ cup of tomato soup into each bowl and drizzle with a little olive oil.

ABOUT THE WINE: *The golden-hued Greco di Tufo Villa Giulia Giovanni Struzziero from the Campania zone in southern Italy is redolent of citrus, spice, and orange blossoms. The palate is round and fruity with great length and excellent structure. Most important, the wine has ample acidity that won't be overpowered by the acidity of the tomatoes.*

CARROT AND HAWAIIAN GINGER SOUP
WITH CARROT SALAD

Serves 6 to 8

This is a deliciously potent soup, which I suggest serving in a pretty demitasse cup or other diminutive vessel. I created it as a dairy-free soup to complement my vegetarian collection menu at Tru. To heighten the flavor, I infuse it with Hawaiian ginger and serve it with a great little carrot-chive salad. The flavor wallop is tremendous! Hawaiian ginger provides good balance because it's neither too hot nor too strong. I learned about it from chef Sam Choy, who has a restaurant of the same name in Honolulu, Hawaii. He explained how it's imbued with floral flavors and aromatics not found in other ginger and I have been hooked ever since. This young, pink, fresh ginger has an especially pleasing mildness, but you can use any fresh ginger you like. If you don't care about the dairy-free aspect of this, garnish it with steamed milk for a cappuccino-like finish.

2 tablespoons canola oil
4 cups chopped carrots
2 cups carrot juice (see page 281)
2 cups Vegetable Stock (see page 266)
2 tablespoons finely grated Hawaiian pink ginger or
*   other fresh ginger*
Kosher salt and freshly ground white pepper
¼ cup Ginger Syrup (recipe follows)
6 to 8 Carrot-Chive Spoons, optional (recipe follows)

1.   In a medium-sized saucepan, heat the oil over medium heat. Add the carrots and cook, stirring occasionally, for about 8 minutes or until they begin to soften.

2.   Add the carrot juice, stock, and ginger. Raise the heat to medium and bring to a simmer. Reduce the heat to low and simmer gently, partially covered, for about 30 minutes or until the carrots are very soft. Remove from the heat and set aside to cool slightly.

3.   Transfer the soup to a blender and puree until smooth. You will have to do this in batches. Strain through a chinois or fine-mesh sieve into a bowl. Season to taste with salt and white pepper. If necessary, reheat the soup in a small saucepan over medium heat.

4.   To serve, ladle the soup into bowls. Drizzle each with ginger syrup and lay a carrot-chive spoon alongside each bowl.

ABOUT THE WINE: *The bold spiciness of the ginger determines the wine choice with this soup. Again, gewürztraminer provides the complementary flavor profile. Leon Beyer's dry Gewürztraminer Comtes d'Eguisheim possesses structure and flavor to match the sweet-spicy soup.*

GINGER SYRUP

Makes about ½ cup

¼ cup water
¼ cup sugar
2 tablespoons peeled and chopped ginger

1.   In a small, heavy saucepan, bring the water and sugar to a boil over medium-high heat, stirring occasionally, and cook for 2 to 3 minutes until the sugar dissolves and the syrup looks clear.

2.   Add the ginger and bring the syrup back to a boil. Reduce the heat and simmer for about 5 minutes to give the flavors time to develop.

3.   Remove from the heat and allow to cool slightly. Transfer to a glass container, cover, and set aside at room temperature to cool. Refrigerate for at least 6 hours until chilled. The syrup will keep tightly covered in the refrigerator for 2 weeks.

4.   Before using, strain the ginger from the syrup through a fine-mesh sieve.

CARROT-CHIVE SPOONS

Makes about ½ cup

1 large or 2 small carrots, finely sliced into a brunoise
    (small dice)
2 tablespoons sliced fresh chives
2 tablespoons Citrus Vinaigrette (recipe follows)
Kosher salt and freshly ground black pepper

1. In a small bowl, combine the carrots and chives. Toss with the vinaigrette and season with salt and pepper to taste.

2. Cover with plastic wrap and refrigerate until needed.

3. Serve the carrot-chive mixture on decorative spoons, such as long-handled iced-tea spoons.

CITRUS VINAIGRETTE

Makes about 1 cup

1 lemon
1 lime
1 orange
1 tablespoon honey
½ cup olive oil
Salt and freshly ground black pepper

1. Squeeze the juice from the lemon, lime, and orange into the container of a blender. Add the honey.

2. With the motor running, slowly add the oil and blend until emulsified.

3. Strain the vinaigrette through a chinois or fine-mesh sieve into a small glass or ceramic bowl and season to taste with salt and pepper. Use immediately or refrigerate the vinaigrette in a tightly lidded nonreactive container for up to 2 weeks. Whisk well before using.

TRAMONTO'S TOTALLY INSANE BLACK AND WHITE TRUFFLE SOUP

Serves 6 to 8

Until I ate at Jamin, chef Joël Robuchon's Michelin three-star Paris restaurant, in 1980, I had used truffles extremely sparingly, if lovingly. My life changed that day! Robuchon's black truffle soup gave me the courage to use truffles in outrageous ways, and with near wanton abandon. Even today, most chefs use truffles only for garnish, as I had been doing, but I am proud to say I have the courage now to serve them more as a main ingredient.

This soup is one of my favorite representations of my liberated attitude about truffles, those precious, incredibly earthy, musky fungi prized by chefs and food lovers the world around. Yes, they are rare and expensive, and are mainly found in the wild, cultivation being difficult and small-scale. The most prized black truffles are from the Périgord area of France, while the best white truffles are from the Piedmont region of Italy. To make this soup, you need to be committed to the truffle. You may have to save your money all year, or decide to make it only once in your life, but you should still try it! Otherwise, don't bother. There are six other wonderful soups in this chapter to choose from. This is for the fearless cook—and truly glorious.

6 tablespoons olive oil
2 chopped white onions
½ stalk celery (4 to 5 ribs), trimmed and chopped
6 to 10 portabello mushrooms, depending on the size,
    stemmed and chopped
7 ounces fresh or tinned black truffles, chopped
1½ cups dry white wine
8 cups Mushroom Stock (see page 267)
12 sprigs fresh thyme
Leaves from 3 sprigs fresh rosemary
½ cup white truffle oil
3 cups heavy cream, whipped
8 tablespoons unsalted butter, softened and
    cut into pieces

Kosher salt and freshly ground black pepper
12 to 16 tablespoons foamed milk (see Note),
    or unsweetened whipped cream, for garnish
Shaved fresh black truffles, for garnish, optional
Shaved fresh white truffles, for garnish, optional
8 Parmesan Tuiles, for garnish (recipe follows)

1. Heat the oil in a large saucepan over low heat. When hot, add the onions, celery, and portabello mushrooms and cook for 7 to 8 minutes or until softened. Add the truffles and wine, raise the heat to medium-high, and cook for 10 minutes or until the liquid is absorbed. Stir the bottom of the pan with a wooden spoon to deglaze.

2. Add the mushroom stock, thyme, and rosemary and bring to a simmer. Reduce the heat and simmer gently, partially covered, for 40 to 50 minutes. Remove from the heat and set aside to cool slightly.

3. Transfer the soup to a blender and puree until smooth. You will have to do this in batches. Strain through a chinois or fine-mesh sieve back into the saucepan. Return to medium heat and bring to a gentle boil. Whisk in the truffle oil, whipped cream, and butter until incorporated. Season with salt and pepper.

4. Ladle the soup into demitasse cups and garnish with foamed milk and shaved truffles, if using. Place a Parmesan *tuile* beside each cup.

NOTE: *To steam milk, use a home cappuccino maker. One cup of milk yields about 8 tablespoons of steamed milk.*

ABOUT THE WINE: *Don't stop the insanity! Push it over the edge by pairing this soup with a truffle-, cherry-, and rose-scented Barbaresco from Angelo Gaja. It's worth the time, effort, and money to search for a structured, powerful vintage such as 1978 or 1989.*

PARMESAN TUILES

Makes 8 tuiles

*1 pound Parmesan cheese, grated, such as Grana Padano
    or Parmigiano-Reggiano*

1. Preheat the oven to 325 degrees. Line a half-sheet pan with a Silpat sheet or grease and flour the pan and then line it with parchment paper.

2. Using a piece of sturdy cardboard, make a stencil by cutting out a 2-by-4-inch oval. Lay the stencil on the pan. Sprinkle the cheese over the stencil so that it fills the oval. Lift it carefully and repeat, to make 8 ovals.

3. Transfer the baking sheet to the oven and bake for 6 minutes or until golden brown. Using a small offset spatula, remove each *tuile* from the baking sheet and carefully roll it around a rolling pin. You may need more than one rolling pin. Work quickly but carefully. Let the *tuiles* harden on the rolling pin until they turn crisp and then carefully slide them off onto a rack or plate.

Fish and Seafood

MY ENORMOUS APPRECIATION FOR SEAFOOD is fueled by my love of all God has put in the world's oceans, lakes, and rivers. Everything about fish and shellfish satisfies and challenges me, from their rich textures to their fresh aromas and light, subtle flavors. What is better than a perfectly cooked piece of fish, served simply with a wedge of lemon and a drizzle of olive oil?

At Tru, I generally prefer to work with whole fish, which is shipped to us daily from around the world. I marvel at the fact that here in the middle of the country, thanks to air-shipping we have access to fish that is as fresh as it would be if we were on the coast. Most people don't have the luxury of fresh fish arriving at their back door and so should choose the store where they buy fresh fish carefully.

The store should be spotless and smell fresh and clean when you walk in the door—never fishy. If you buy whole fish, look for clear eyes and bright red flesh beneath the gills and along the belly. The skin should be smooth and sleek and the fish should smell sweetly of the ocean—never, ever strong. The recipes here are meant to inspire you to try as many different fish and shellfish as you can. Enjoy them all!

131   *Roasted Sturgeon with Braised Oxtail and Spiced Carrot Puree*

134   *Black Trumpet Mushroom–crusted Ahi Tuna with Scallion and Fava Bean Stew*

137   *Roasted Spiny Lobster with Vanilla-Saffron Beurre Blanc*

140   *Arctic Char Poached in Duck Fat with Spinach-Almond Puree*

143   *24-karat Gold Leaf Rouget with Shellfish and Saffron Broth*

147   *Asian Bouillabaisse with Coconut Broth and Sea Beans*

149   *Steamed Halibut with Cucumber Broth and Asian Pear Salad*

ROASTED STURGEON WITH BRAISED OXTAIL AND SPICED CARROT PUREE

Serves 6

You might be surprised to find oxtail in a chapter on fish and seafood, but I find that full-flavored, meaty, fatty fish such as sturgeon taste fantastic with braised meats. I credit the idea for this dish to chef Jacques Le Divellec of Le Divellec, the famed Paris restaurant that concentrates on seafood, where I first tasted braised meat with fish. You won't be surprised to hear that I loved it! The layers of protein, flavors, and textures were endlessly fascinating to me.

You can use salmon or any other meaty fish, but I strongly recommend you try delicious-tasting sturgeon, which is not as commonplace as salmon, monkfish, or tuna. If you would rather braise lamb or veal shanks instead of oxtail, go right ahead. Matched with the sturgeon and spiced carrot puree, this is an aromatic and luscious dish.

4 cups Vegetable Stock (see page 266)
8 tablespoons unsalted butter
1 teaspoon Pernod
6 whole baby white turnips, peeled
Kosher salt and freshly ground white pepper
6 Thumbelina or baby carrots, with stems
1 cup Beurre Monté (see page 278)
6 Olive Oil Confit Potatoes (recipe follows)
2 tablespoons Clarified Butter (see page 279)
2 pounds sturgeon fillets
Braised Oxtail (recipe follows)
Spiced Carrot Puree (recipe follows), for garnish

1. In a medium-sized saucepan, bring 2 cups of the stock, 4 tablespoons of the butter, and the Pernod to a boil over medium-high heat. Add the turnips, season with salt and white pepper, and reduce the heat. Simmer for 7 to 10 minutes or until fork-tender. Drain and set aside to cool to room temperature. Halve the larger turnips, if necessary.

2. Peel the carrots and clean around the stem ends with a paring knife. Remove all but ½ inch of the stems.

3. In a medium-sized saucepan, bring the remaining 2 cups of stock and 4 tablespoons of butter to a boil over medium-high heat. Add the carrots, season with salt and pepper, reduce the heat, and simmer for 4 to 8 minutes or until fork-tender. Drain and set aside to cool to room temperature.

4. In a small saucepan set over low heat, heat the *beurre monté* until a cooking thermometer registers 180 degrees. Add the carrots and cooked turnips, remove from the heat, and let stand for 5 minutes. Remove with a slotted spoon and drain on paper towels.

5. Lift the olive oil confit potatoes from the oil. Cut the ends off the potatoes and then cut them into ¼-inch-thick slices. Season with salt and pepper. Discard the oil.

6. Heat the clarified butter in a small sauté pan over medium heat. When hot, add the potato slices and sauté for 8 to 10 minutes or until golden brown.

7. Preheat the oven to 400 degrees.

8. Season the sturgeon with salt and pepper. In a large oven-safe skillet, sear the sturgeon, bone side down, until golden brown. Turn the sturgeon over and transfer to the oven. Roast for 4 to 6 minutes or until the sturgeon is cooked through.

9. Meanwhile, in separate saucepans, gently heat the braised oxtail and the carrot puree until hot.

10. Spoon a small mound of the puree in the center of a plate. Top with a spoonful of braised oxtail, drained of excess juices. Garnish the plate with turnips, carrots, and potatoes. Slice each piece of sturgeon into 4 to 6 pieces and lay a portion on top of the vegetables and braised oxtail. Garnish the plate with a drizzle of the oxtail-braising liquid and some carrot puree around the fish. Repeat to make 5 more servings.

ABOUT THE WINE: *The oxtail ragout and spiced carrot puree are the dominant flavors of this dish. A soft-textured, fruit-driven red is best. Here, Merry Edwards Pinot Noir Klopp Ranch Russian River Valley, with its black cherry, blueberry, sweet spice, and velvety tannins, bridges the gap between surf and turf.*

OLIVE OIL CONFIT POTATOES

Makes 6 potatoes

2 cups olive oil
6 fingerling potatoes
4 cloves garlic
2 sprigs fresh rosemary
2 sprigs fresh thyme
1 tablespoon kosher salt
½ teaspoon white peppercorns

1. In a medium-sized saucepan, combine the olive oil, potatoes, garlic, rosemary, thyme, salt, and white peppercorns and place over very low heat. Cook for 15 to 20 minutes or until the oil just starts to bubble.

2. Remove the pan from the heat and set aside for about 30 minutes or until the potatoes are tender. Using a slotted spoon, remove the potatoes from the oil and set aside to cool.

3. Let the oil cool completely and then strain through a chinois or fine-mesh sieve into a bowl. Submerge the potatoes in the oil, cover, and refrigerate until needed.

BRAISED OXTAIL

Makes 3 cups

1 oxtail, about 2 pounds
Kosher salt and freshly ground black pepper
2 tablespoons vegetable oil
2 cups chopped onions
1 cup chopped carrots
1 cup chopped celery
1 bulb garlic, halved, unpeeled
1 750-ml bottle dry red wine
2 gallons Veal Stock (see page 261)
1 bunch fresh thyme
2 bay leaves

1. Trim the oxtail of any visible fat. Using a sharp paring knife, score the tail lengthwise and cut into 6-inch-long pieces. Season with salt and pepper.

2. In a large, heavy-bottomed, ovenproof casserole or Dutch oven, heat the oil over medium-high heat until very hot. Add the oxtail and cook for 12 to 15 minutes or until browned on all sides. Remove and set aside.

3. Reduce the heat to medium and add the onions, carrots, celery, and garlic to the pan. Cook, stirring, for 10 to 15 minutes or until the vegetables are golden brown.

4. Preheat the oven to 300 degrees.

5. Return the oxtail to the pan with the vegetables. Add the wine and bring to a boil over medium-high heat. Stir the pan with a wooden spoon to scrape up any browned solids and dissolve them into the liquid. Reduce the heat slightly and simmer for about 20 minutes or until the liquid is reduced by two-thirds.

6. Add the veal stock, thyme, and bay leaves to the pan. Remove from the heat and cover with a sheet of parchment paper. Place in the center of the oven and cook for 4 to 5 hours or until the meat is tender and falling off the bone.

7. Remove the oxtail pieces and set aside to cool slightly. When cool enough to handle, pick the meat off the bones and set aside to cool. Discard the bones.

8. Meanwhile, skim the fat from the braising liquid. Strain the stock through a fine-mesh sieve into a bowl and then return to the pan. Bring to a boil, reduce the heat, and simmer over medium heat for about 1 hour or until reduced by two-thirds to three-quarters. Return the meat to the liquid and season with salt and pepper. Set aside to cool to room temperature. Use immediately or cover and refrigerate until needed.

SPICED CARROT PUREE

Makes 1½ cups

1 cinnamon stick
2 whole cloves
½ teaspoon cumin seeds
¼ teaspoon cardamom seeds
1½ pounds carrots, peeled and chopped
2 cups carrot juice (see page 281)
Kosher salt and freshly ground black pepper
2 tablespoons unsalted butter
1 tablespoon Cardamom Oil (see page 278)
Vegetable Stock (see page 266), or water

1. Cut a 4-inch square of cheesecloth and put the cinnamon stick, cloves, cumin seeds, and cardamom seeds in the center of the square. Bring the corners of the cloth together and tie the sachet with kitchen string.

2. In a large saucepan, combine the carrots, carrot juice, and spice sachet and bring to a boil over medium heat. Immediately reduce the heat and simmer for 10 to 15 minutes or until the carrots are fork-tender. Remove from the heat and set aside to cool slightly. Remove the spice sachet.

3. Transfer the carrots and enough of the liquid to make pureeing possible to a blender and puree until smooth. Strain through a chinois or fine-mesh sieve into a bowl. Season with salt and pepper. Set aside to cool to room temperature. Cover and refrigerate until needed.

4. To serve, heat the carrot puree in a small saucepan over low heat for about 5 minutes or until heated through. Incorporate the butter, cardamom oil, and a little vegetable stock if the mixture is dry. Using a handheld immersion blender or wire whisk, emulsify the mixture. Season with salt and pepper.

BLACK TRUMPET MUSHROOM—CRUSTED
AHI TUNA WITH SCALLION
AND FAVA BEAN STEW

Serves 6

When I decided to put seared tuna on the menu,
I tried coating the fish with dried mushrooms, with
less than overwhelming success. I next experimented
with powdered mushrooms and the flavor immediately
popped! It was strong and toasty and changed the
whole tenor of the dish. Plus, the tuna looks great
with the near-black crust and red, moist center. The
creaminess of the scallion stew brings the dish together,
and while I love the fava beans with it, if they are not in
season, leave them out. This still will taste great and
look dramatic.

There are many types of tuna swimming in the
world's oceans, which can be confusing for the chef
and the ordinary shopper. When do you use albacore,
bluefin, yellowfin, blackfin, or ahi? When it comes right
down to it, it's vital to know that tuna is sold in different
grades: sashimi-quality number 1 and sashimi-quality
number 2, and then there is grilling-quality tuna.
Because I only sear this tuna, I use sashimi-quality
number 1 or number 2 ahi or yellowfin, but I prefer
ahi for its firm beeflike texture and deep red color.

¼ cup Clarified Butter (see page 283)
18 3-inch pieces Braised Salsify (recipe follows)
Kosher salt and freshly ground white pepper
24 fresh shelled fava beans
6 purple or green scallions, trimmed and cut into
    3-inch lengths
2 cups cleaned and pulled-apart black trumpet
    mushrooms
3 pounds ahi tuna, sashimi-quality number 1 or 2
½ cup black trumpet mushroom powder (see Note)
2 cups Scallion Stew (recipe follows)
½ cup Red Wine Sauce (see page 271)
½ cup Red Wine Essence (see page 142)

1. In a sauté pan, heat 2 tablespoons of the clarified
butter over medium heat and sauté the braised salsify for
about 5 minutes or until golden brown. Season to taste
with salt and pepper.

2. In a large pot of boiling salted water, blanch the fava
beans and scallions for 3 to 4 minutes or until tender. Remove with a slotted spoon. Drain.

3. In another sauté pan, heat the remaining 2 tablespoons of clarified butter over medium-high heat and
sauté the mushrooms for 3 to 4 minutes or until softened.

4. Cut the tuna into 6 logs, each about 2 inches by
2 inches by 4 inches. Season lightly with salt and pepper
and roll in the mushroom powder.

5. In a sauté pan, sear each tuna log over medium-high
heat for about 1 minute on each side or until medium-
rare. Remove each log from the pan as soon as it is
seared and set aside to rest for 2 to 3 minutes.

6. To serve, spoon a little scallion stew on each plate.
Scatter the salsify, fava beans, and scallions around the
stew. Place the black trumpet mushrooms on top. Slice
each tuna log on the bias into 3 1-inch-wide chunks and
place 2 chunks on top of the stew. Drizzle the red wine
sauce and then red wine essence around the plate.

NOTE: *Black trumpet mushroom powder is available in*
    some gourmet stores and shops specializing in fancy
    foods.

ABOUT THE WINE: *The subtle earthiness of the*
    black trumpets, the meaty texture of tuna, and the
    accompanying red wine essence call for a vibrant,
    lightly oaked, and fruit-driven red wine. The black
    cherry and truffle—scented Barbara from Aldo
    Conterno is the perfect partner for this dish.

BRAISED SALSIFY

Makes 18 3-inch pieces

3 stalks salsify
1½ cups half-and-half
2 cloves garlic
2 sprigs fresh thyme
2 sprigs fresh rosemary
Kosher salt and freshly ground white pepper

1. Trim, peel, and cut the salsify into 3-inch-long lengths. As you cut each one, drop it into a bowl of acidulated water to prevent discoloration. (Or submerge them immediately in the half-and-half.)

2. Drain the salsify and transfer to a saucepan. Add the half-and-half, garlic, thyme, rosemary, and salt and white pepper to taste, and cook on low heat for 25 to 30 minutes or until the salsify is tender. Remove from the heat and drain through a chinois or fine-mesh sieve into a bowl. Set aside to cool. When cool, cut the salsify lengths in half lengthwise.

SCALLION STEW

Makes about 2 cups

1 bunch scallions (5 to 6 scallions)
1 tablespoon unsalted butter
1 tablespoon sherry vinegar
Kosher salt and freshly ground white pepper
2 tablespoons Onion Soubise (recipe follows)
2 tablespoons Homemade Crème Fraîche (see page 280)
¼ cup Scallion Puree (recipe follows)

1. Thinly slice the scallions on the diagonal.

2. In a small sauté pan, melt the butter over low heat. When hot, add the scallions and sauté for 5 minutes or until softened.

3. Add the vinegar and cook over medium heat for 2 to 3 minutes or until the liquid evaporates. Season with salt

and white pepper. Stir in the onion soubise and crème fraîche and bring to a simmer. Stir the ingredients gently.

4. Remove from the heat and set aside to cool to room temperature. Use immediately or cover and refrigerate until needed.

5. Reheat over low heat until simmering. Stir in the scallion puree.

ONION SOUBISE

Makes about 2 cups

2 large white onions, thinly sliced
3 tablespoons unsalted butter
Kosher salt and freshly ground white pepper

1. In a large sauté pan, combine the onions and butter and bring to a simmer over medium heat. Cover, reduce the heat, and simmer gently, stirring occasionally, for about 30 minutes or until the onions are soft. Remove from the heat and let cool slightly.

2. Transfer to a blender and puree until smooth. Strain through a chinois or fine-mesh sieve into a bowl. Season to taste with salt and white pepper. Use immediately or cover and refrigerate until needed.

SCALLION PUREE

Makes about ½ cup

2 bunches scallions (15 to 18 scallions), trimmed

1. Cut about 2 inches of the dark green ends from the scallions and discard.

2. In a large pot of boiling, lightly salted water, blanch the scallions for about 3 minutes or until soft. Drain immediately and submerge in ice-cold water. Drain again.

3. Transfer to a blender and puree, with a little water if necessary, until smooth. Strain through a chinois or fine-mesh sieve into a bowl. Cover and refrigerate until needed.

ROASTED SPINY LOBSTER WITH VANILLA-SAFFRON BEURRE BLANC

Serves 6

I was fortunate to *stage* at Michel Guerard's renowned restaurant in the early 1990s in the village of Eugenie-Les-Bains called Les Pres d'Eugenie, a lovely old place surrounded by herb gardens, trailing rose bushes, and leafy walks. The chef constructed a wood-burning oven in the center of his kitchen that is more of an open fireplace. He cooks wonderful things over the wood fire, but I was most intrigued by the grilled lobsters liberally brushed with vanilla butter. Frankly, this was the inspiration for my fascination with the marriage of these two flavors—lobster and vanilla—and so I invented this dish. It's very simple yet very elegant.

I was so charged up about Guerard's recipe, I couldn't wait to try something similar. When I got home from France, I bought lobsters and invited my neighbors for supper. I blanched the lobsters, split them, and cooked them on a grate I had rigged over the open fire in my living room fireplace. I basted the lobsters with vanilla-infused butter as they cooked. They were awesome—and so is this more upscale version of the dish!

4 cups heavy cream
1 cup Vegetable Stock (see page 266)
1 tablespoon saffron threads
3 vanilla beans, split lengthwise
5 tablespoons unsalted butter
2 tablespoons Homemade Crème Fraîche (see page 280)
Kosher salt and freshly ground black pepper
3 spiny lobsters
4 tablespoons Clarified Butter (see page 279)
*1 cup peeled and blanched edamame beans, tossed with a
    little butter, for garnish*
1 cup Diced Purple Potatoes (recipe follows), for garnish

1. Preheat the oven to 350 degrees.
2. To make the vanilla-saffron butter, combine the cream, stock, and saffron in a medium saucepan. With the tip of a small, sharp knife, scrape the seeds from the 3 vanilla beans into the cream and bring to a boil over medium heat. Reserve 2 of the pods for drying (see Note).
3. Whisk in 2 tablespoons of the butter and the crème fraîche. When the butter emulsifies and the sauce is smooth, taste and season with salt and pepper. Remove from the heat. Using a slotted spoon, remove the vanilla seeds. Whisk before using.
4. Cut the lobsters in half lengthwise and thoroughly clean out the cavity above the tail.
5. In a large sauté pan, heat the clarified butter over medium heat. Put the lobsters, meat side down, in the pan and cook for 3 to 4 minutes. Turn and cook for an additional 3 to 4 minutes on the other side, or until the shells turn red.
6. Transfer the lobsters to a baking sheet and dot each lobster with about 1 tablespoon of the remaining butter. Bake for 3 to 4 minutes or until heated through.
7. Remove from the oven and set aside for 5 minutes.
8. Place half a lobster on each plate and garnish each with edamame, potatoes, and vanilla-saffron butter.

ABOUT THE WINE: *The rich, opulent honeysuckle, apricot, and tropical-fruit character of Condrieu Les Chaillées de l'Enfer from masterful Georges Vernay elevates this dish. The surprising lively acidity helps cut the buttery sauce while the perfumed Viognier enhances the sweet lobster.*

DICED PURPLE POTATOES

Makes 1½ cups

6 purple potatoes, peeled and cut into ¼-inch cubes
Kosher salt
2 tablespoons unsalted butter
Freshly ground black pepper

1. In a saucepan, cover the potatoes with cold water and season lightly with salt. Bring to a boil over medium-high heat, reduce the heat, and simmer for 15 to 20 minutes or until tender. Drain in a colander and spread the potatoes on a baking sheet to cool.

2. To serve, melt the butter in a sauté pan over low heat until foaming. When the foam subsides, add the potatoes and sauté for about 5 minutes or until heated through. Season to taste with salt and pepper.

ARCTIC CHAR POACHED IN DUCK FAT WITH SPINACH-ALMOND PUREE

Serves 6

If I had not known how to make classic sole amandine, I would never have created this recipe. As in the original, I pair almonds and fish, but use a subtle, almond-flavored spinach puree to introduce the flavor. Yet, without question, it's the duck fat that sets this apart from other recipes. Again, had I not understood how integral duck fat is to classic French cuisine, I might not have integrated it here. In France, high-end chefs cook with duck fat more frequently than we do— they even cut butter with duck fat!—and so I looked for ways to use it at Tru. I found it works especially well with char, a fatty, firm-fleshed fresh-water fish related to the trout. The play on sole amandine is obvious, but the overall flavors are more intense yet still perfectly balanced.

It's critical for young cooks to understand what has gone before them. They should know about Auguste Escoffier, perhaps the greatest French chef of all time and certainly of his time, and Fernand Point, who revolutionized French classic cuisine in the first half of the twentieth century. Equally important is to read reference books such as *Larousse Gastronomique,* written by Prosper Montagné and published in 1938. Escoffier himself wrote the preface for the book, although he died before it was published. (The master wrote the preface based on the manuscript's first draft.) This kind of knowledge is vital for holding on to old techniques, such as making confits and curing meats, but it's also crucial to understanding modern methods. You can't modernize a dish if you don't know what you're updating! As Point is credited with saying, "In all professions without doubt, but certainly in cooking one is a student all his life."

3 cups duck fat (see Note)
6 4-ounce pieces arctic char
4 tablespoons unsalted butter
½ cup finely diced potatoes
Kosher salt and freshly ground white pepper

½ cup Spinach-Almond Puree (recipe follows)
1 cup Mousseron Mushroom Confit (recipe follows)
1 cup julienned leeks, blanched
½ cup warm Red Wine Essence (recipe follows)
Chopped chives, for garnish
18 purple Johnny-jump-ups, for garnish, optional

1. In a large saucepan, heat the duck fat over low heat until a cooking thermometer reads 160 degrees.

2. Carefully submerge the char in the duck fat and poach for 5 to 6 minutes or until the fish begins to firm up slightly. With a wide, slotted spatula, lift the char from the duck fat. Set it aside, covered with foil, to keep warm.

3. In a small sauté pan, heat the butter over medium-high heat and cook the potatoes, stirring, for 8 to 10 minutes or until cooked through and crispy. Remove from the heat and spread the potatoes on a double thickness of paper towels to drain. Season to taste with salt and white pepper. Set aside in a warm place.

4. Gently heat the spinach-almond puree over low heat, stirring constantly, for about 5 minutes or until heated through.

5. In a small sauté pan, warm the mushroom confit over medium heat for about 5 minutes or until heated through. Add the leeks and sauté for 2 to 3 more minutes, until heated through. Season to taste with salt and pepper.

6. Spoon a small amount of spinach-almond puree in the center of a plate. Place some of the mushroom confit and leeks in the center of the puree. Drizzle a little of the warm wine essence around the plate. Place a piece of arctic char on top of the vegetables. Garnish the fish with some of the crispy potatoes, chopped chives, and 3 Johnny-jump-ups, if using. Repeat to make 5 more servings.

NOTE: *Duck fat is sold in specialty stores and by some high-end butchers.*

ABOUT THE WINE: *Arctic char, with its salmonlike flavor, pairs very well with lean, elegant red wines. A mature premier cru red Burgundy, such as Volnay Les Champans 1990 from Hubert de Montille, offers pure fruit flavors and ample acidity to deal with the natural fish oils and duck fat.*

SPINACH-ALMOND PUREE

Makes about ½ cup

3 tablespoons unsalted butter
2 shallots, thinly sliced
1 clove garlic, thinly sliced
4 cups fresh spinach, stems removed
Kosher salt and freshly ground white pepper
3 tablespoons almond oil (see Note)

1.   In a large sauté pan, melt the butter over low heat and cook the shallots and garlic for 4 to 6 minutes or until softened but not brown.

2.   Add the spinach and cook, stirring, for 4 to 5 minutes or until wilted. Season to taste with salt and white pepper.

3.   Transfer to a blender and puree until smooth. With the motor running, slowly add the almond oil and puree until thick and smooth.

4.   Strain through a chinois or fine-mesh sieve into bowl. Cover and refrigerate until needed.

NOTE: *You can buy almond oil in specialty stores and some grocery stores.*

MOUSSERON MUSHROOM CONFIT

Makes about 1 cup

1 cup duck fat
2 cloves garlic
3 sprigs fresh thyme
Kosher salt and freshly ground white pepper
1½ cups stemmed mousseron, yellowfoot, or chanterelle
    mushrooms

1.   Preheat the oven to 250 degrees.

2.   Combine the duck fat, garlic, and thyme in a medium-sized ovenproof saucepan and heat over low heat until the fat melts. Season with salt and white pepper. Stir the mushrooms into the fat.

3.   Cover the pan with aluminum foil and transfer to the oven. Bake for 15 to 20 minutes, stirring every 5 minutes. Remove from the oven and set aside to cool slightly.

4.   Strain through a chinois or fine-mesh sieve into a bowl. Set aside at room temperature to cool.

RED WINE ESSENCE

Makes about ½ cup

2 750-ml bottles dry red wine
1 750-ml bottle port wine
1 large tart apple, peeled, cored, and quartered
¾ cup sugar
2 whole cloves
1 cinnamon stick

1.   In a large saucepan, combine the red wine, port, apple, sugar, cloves, and cinnamon stick and bring to a simmer over medium heat. Reduce the heat and simmer gently for 1 hour.

2.   With a slotted spoon, remove the apple quarters. Continue to simmer the wine mixture for 1 hour longer or until the sauce thickens and coats the back of a spoon without running.

3.   Remove from the heat and set aside to cool slightly. Strain through a chinois or fine-mesh sieve into a bowl. Set aside to cool completely.

24-KARAT GOLD LEAF ROUGET WITH SHELLFISH AND SAFFRON BROTH

Serves 6

Without doubt, the 24-karat gold leaf accent provides high drama, but it's not necessary in order to enjoy the full flavor of the fish mixed with calamari, mussels, and scallops. The sweet shellfish complement the rouget, which is a European fish and not often available in the United States. Try it if you see it; otherwise, substitute snapper or black bass. The harmless gold leaf is lovely, and it's a great conversation starter, too!

I saw gold leaf on rouget at Outhier, a marvelous restaurant in the south of France owned by chef Louis Outhier. I knew that Jean-Georges Vongerichten, one of my culinary heroes, had studied with Outhier while coming up through the ranks in his native France, and since I admire Jean-Georges, I wanted to try his teacher's food, too. I was not in the least disappointed! The meal, which included the rouget with gold leaf, was as incredible as the south of France is beautiful.

6 2- to 3-ounce rouget or small red snapper fillets,
*   scaled, skin on*
Kosher salt and freshly ground black pepper
2 tablespoons olive oil
3 cups Saffron Broth (recipe follows)
1 ounce calamari rings (about 8 rings)
6 mussels, rinsed and scrubbed
6 bay scallops
2 tablespoons finely diced tomato
1 tablespoon finely diced zucchini
1 tablespoon finely diced yellow squash
1 tablespoon unsalted butter
6 small capers
3 pitted black olives, such as Kalamata, sliced
6 3-by-3-inch pieces 24-karat gold leaf (see Note)
6 long chives

1.   Season the fillets with salt and pepper.

2.   In a large sauté pan, heat the oil over medium heat and sear the fillets, skin side down, for 2 to 4 minutes until lightly browned or until the edges are opaque.

3.   In a medium saucepan, bring the saffron broth to a simmer over medium-high heat. Add the calamari, mussels, scallops, tomato, zucchini, and squash. Reduce the heat and simmer for 5 to 7 minutes or until the mussels open, the scallops are opaque and cooked through, and the vegetables are tender.

4.   Add the butter, capers, and olives to the pan, stir until the butter is incorporated, and season to taste with salt and pepper.

5.   Using a slotted spoon, remove the seafood and vegetables from the broth and divide among 6 small bowls. Ladle the broth over the seafood and vegetables. Place a rouget or red snapper fillet on top of the ragout and garnish the fish with a sheet of gold leaf and a single long chive.

NOTE: *Sheets of 24-karat gold leaf are available in markets that sell Indian food products and in cake-decorating stores. The gold leaf is completely edible and comes in very thin, fragile sheets packaged between two sheets of paper. Remove only one sheet of paper, invert the gold leaf onto the food, and peel off the remaining paper. In Indian markets, the gold leaf is called* varak *or* vark.

ABOUT THE WINE: *In keeping with the Mediterranean nature of this dish, serve a rustic, dry white wine. Clos Ste. Magdelaine from the tiny coastal appellation of Cassis in southern France is an aromatic, refreshing, moderately acidic wine perfect for this bouillabaisse-inspired presentation.*

SAFFRON BROTH

Makes about 3 cups

2 tablespoons saffron threads
1 tablespoon olive oil
2 shallots, finely chopped
1 sprig fresh thyme
1 bay leaf
1 750-ml bottle dry white wine
4 cups Fish Stock (see page 266)
Kosher salt and freshly ground black pepper

1. In a dry frying pan, cook the saffron over medium heat, shaking the pan gently to prevent burning, for about 1 minute or until fragrant. Remove the saffron from the pan and set aside.

2. In a large saucepan, heat the oil over low heat, add the shallots, thyme, bay leaf, and saffron and cook, stirring, for about 5 minutes or until the shallot softens but does not color.

3. Add the white wine, raise the heat to medium-high, and bring to a boil, stirring the bottom of the pan with a wooden spoon to deglaze. Reduce the heat slightly and cook for 3 to 5 minutes to concentrate the flavors. Add the fish stock, bring to a simmer, reduce the heat, and simmer for 30 to 40 minutes or until reduced by half. Season to taste with salt and pepper.

4. Remove from the heat and set aside to cool slightly. Strain through a chinois or fine-mesh sieve into a bowl. Set aside to cool to room temperature, cover, and refrigerate until needed.

ASIAN BOUILLABAISSE WITH COCONUT BROTH AND SEA BEANS

Serves 6

After traveling through the south of France—my favorite place in the world because it combines great food, great weather, and beautiful surroundings—I fell in love with bouillabaisse, the traditional seafood stew of the region, which has as many variations as there are fish in the Mediterranean Sea. I returned from Europe and put bouillabaisse on the menu at Bella Luna, where I was cooking at the time in 1988, and it has been in my repertoire ever since.

Since those days, I have learned to appreciate Thai and other Asian food, much of which involves seafood. I have also been inspired by chef Eric Ripert of Le Bernardin in New York, who prepares amazing contemporary seafood dishes. With these two influences in my mind, I came up with the idea of marrying East with West in a bouillabaisse. I introduce Asian ingredients for a fresh interpretation of this grand old Mediterranean dish. It's cooking out of the box—the way I like it—and I encourage you to interpret my recipe any way you like, using whatever seafood is freshest.

1 pound soba noodles
6 cups Curried Coconut Broth (recipe follows)
1 cup thinly sliced scallions
½ cup sea beans (see Note)
1 cup peeled and finely diced tomatoes
18 Prince Edward Island mussels, rinsed and scrubbed
6 fresh lobster claws
6 sea scallops
6 2-ounce pieces halibut
6 Manila clams
6 langoustines
6 large shrimp, peeled and cut in half lengthwise
1 6-inch-long baguette
4 to 6 heaping tablespoons Red Pepper Rouille
    (recipe follows), for garnish
¼ cup chopped fresh cilantro, for garnish
Toasted black and white sesame seeds, for garnish
1 tablespoon lobster roe, for garnish, optional

1. In a large saucepan of boiling water, cook the soba noodles for about 10 minutes or until al dente. Drain.
2. In a large saucepan, heat 1 cup of the coconut broth over medium-high heat until boiling. Reduce the heat to a simmer and add the soba noodles, scallions, sea beans, and tomatoes. Warm for 1 to 2 minutes.
3. Meanwhile, in a large stockpot bring the remaining 5 cups of coconut broth to a boil over medium heat, and add the mussels, lobster, scallops, halibut, clams, langoustines, and shrimp. Simmer for 5 to 7 minutes or until the lobster shells are red, the mussels and clams open, the fish is cooked through, and the shrimp are pink.
4. Slice the baguette lengthwise into 6 very thin, long slices, about the thickness of melba toast. Toast under the broiler for about 1 minute on each side or just until crisp.
5. Mound some of the noodles, sea beans, scallions, and tomatoes in the center of 6 bowls. Using a slotted spoon, remove the shellfish and fish from the broth and arrange them around the noodles. Ladle some of the broth around the noodles. Spread red pepper rouille on one side of each of the toasts. Garnish each bowl with the toast, cilantro, and a sprinkling of sesame seeds. Decorate the bouillabaisse and a small portion of the rims of the bowls with lobster roe.

NOTE: *Sea beans are also called samphire, and the variety that is most available in the United States is known as salicornia, glasswort, or sea pickle. Fresh sea beans are available in the spring and summer, and are sold most often in Asian markets and specialty stores. Look for bright green, spiky leaves and refrigerate for no more than a few days before using. Sea beans can be eaten raw in salads or, as in this recipe, lightly cooked.*

ABOUT THE WINE: *The supreme versatility of German Riesling is never more evident than when it is juxtaposed with Asian-influenced cuisine. The sweet, hot, briny, and herbal components become tightly knit together when a Spätlese-level Riesling is introduced to the mix. Consider the sublime Kiedricher Gräfenberg Riesling Spätlese Robert Weil Rheingau.*

CURRIED COCONUT BROTH

Makes 6 cups

2 tablespoons unsalted butter

4 Kaffir lime leaves

1 leek, white and some light-green parts, cleaned,
    trimmed, and chopped

¾ of 1 stalk lemongrass, tough outer leaves removed and
    roughly chopped

½ cup thinly sliced fresh ginger

2 cloves garlic, minced

2 star anise

¼ cup Lobster Glace (see page 268)

2 tablespoons red curry paste

4 cups coconut milk

4 cups Vegetable Stock (see page 266), or Fish Stock
    (see page 266)

2 cups vermouth

Kosher salt and freshly ground black pepper

1. In a large saucepan, melt the butter over medium
heat. Add the Kaffir leaves, leek, lemongrass, ginger, garlic, and star anise and cook gently for 2 to 3 minutes or
until fragrant. Add the lobster glace and curry paste and
stir until all ingredients are combined.

2. Add the coconut milk, stock, and vermouth. Bring to
a simmer over medium heat and cook gently for 45 to 60
minutes or until reduced by a third. Season to taste with
salt and pepper.

3. Strain through a chinois or fine-mesh sieve and set
aside to cool. Use immediately or cover and refrigerate
for 2 to 3 days.

RED PEPPER ROUILLE

Makes about 1 cup

2 red bell peppers, seeded and coarsely chopped

4 cloves garlic, coarsely chopped

2 teaspoons paprika

¼ teaspoon cayenne pepper

3 large egg yolks or pasteurized egg yolks

1 tablespoon fresh lemon juice

Kosher salt and freshly ground black pepper

2 cups olive oil

1. In the bowl of a food processor fitted with a metal
blade, combine the peppers, garlic, paprika, cayenne, egg
yolks, and lemon juice and process until finely chopped
but not smooth. Season with salt and pepper. With the
motor running, slowly pour in the olive oil and process
until smooth. Taste and adjust the seasoning.

2. Strain through a chinois or fine-mesh sieve into a
bowl. Use immediately or cover with plastic wrap and
keep refrigerated until needed.

STEAMED HALIBUT WITH CUCUMBER BROTH AND ASIAN PEAR SALAD

Serves 6

Living in a town with a world-acclaimed chef as your neighbor is constantly inspiring. Charlie Trotter always reinvents his cooking, and in so doing raises the bar for the rest of us. A few years after I worked at Charlie's restaurant, I ate there and was blown away by a luscious oyster and cucumber soup. I recall thinking that the cucumber soup base would make a great sauce and work well with other dishes. I was so right!

This is a wonderful dish with great depth of flavor and marvelous textures, as found in the soft tenderness of the fish, the crunch of the pears, and the crispiness of the leeks. With its clean, light, refreshing taste, the cucumber broth pulls everything together in a magical way.

2 pounds halibut fillets, cut into 6 pieces
Kosher salt and freshly ground white pepper
1 cup dry white wine
¼ cup fresh lemon juice
1 cup chopped onions
⅓ cup chopped celery
1 tablespoon fresh thyme
4 cups water
1½ cups Shiitake Mushrooms, Zucchini,
*   and Scallion Sauté (recipe follows)*
1½ to 2 cups warm Cucumber Broth (recipe follows)
1 cup Asian Pear Salad (recipe follows)
½ cup Fried Leeks (recipe follows)

1. Season the halibut fillets with salt and white pepper and set aside.
2. In a medium-size saucepan, bring the wine, lemon juice, onions, celery, and thyme to a simmer over medium heat. Simmer for about 15 minutes, or until the liquid is reduced to about ¼ cup. Strain through a chinois or fine-mesh sieve into a 4-inch-deep casserole with a tight-fitting lid. Add the water to the casserole and position a steaming rack in the casserole.

3. Put the lid on the casserole and set over medium-low heat. When the liquid starts steaming, put the halibut on the rack. Cover and steam for 8 to 10 minutes or until cooked through, moist, and tender.
4. To serve, divide the sautéed shiitake mushrooms, zucchini, and scallion sauté among 6 bowls. Ladle about ¼ cup of the warm cucumber broth into each bowl. Lay a halibut piece on top of the mushroom, zucchini, and scallion sauté. Top each with some of the Asian pear salad and fried leeks.

SHIITAKE MUSHROOMS, ZUCCHINI, AND SCALLION SAUTÉ

Makes about 1½ cups

8 ounces shiitake mushrooms
2 bunches scallions, white and light green parts
2 tablespoons unsalted butter
3 baby zucchini, trimmed and cut on the bias into
*   ½-inch-thick slices*
Kosher salt and freshly ground black pepper

1. Remove the stems from the mushrooms, and then cut the tops into quarters. Set aside.
2. Cut the scallions into 1-inch-long pieces.
3. In a large pot of lightly salted boiling water, blanch the scallions for 3 to 4 minutes or until tender. Drain and immediately submerge the scallions in ice-cold water. Drain again. Pat dry with paper towels.
4. Melt the butter in a sauté pan over medium heat. When the butter has stopped foaming, add the mushrooms and zucchini and sauté for 7 to 8 minutes or until golden brown. Add the scallions to the pan. Season to taste with salt and pepper. Reduce the heat and sauté the mushroom mixture for an additional 4 minutes or until the scallions are heated through. Set aside until needed.

CUCUMBER BROTH

Makes 1½ to 2 cups

4 English cucumbers
2 tablespoons fresh lemon juice
Kosher salt

1. Juice the cucumbers. Strain through a chinois or fine-mesh sieve into a small saucepan.
2. Add the lemon juice and salt to the pan.
3. Put the pan over low heat. Slowly heat the juice for 5 to 7 minutes or until just warm. Make sure not to boil the juice or it will turn brown.

ASIAN PEAR SALAD

Makes 1 cup

2 Asian pears
¼ cup daikon sprouts
2 tablespoons olive oil
1 tablespoon fresh lemon juice
Kosher salt and freshly ground black pepper

1. Cut the Asian pears into 2-inch-long julienned slices. You should have about ¾ cup.
2. In a small bowl, combine the pears and daikon sprouts. Drizzle with the olive oil and lemon juice. Season to taste with salt and pepper. Gently toss to combine.
3. Cover and refrigerate until needed.

FRIED LEEKS

Makes ½ cup

2 cups vegetable oil
½ cup julienned leeks, white and
*   light-green parts*
Kosher salt

1. Pour the oil into a deep, heavy saucepan and heat over low heat until a deep-frying thermometer registers 150°F. Blanch the leeks in the oil for 3 to 5 minutes or until tender. Remove the leeks from the oil with a slotted spoon and set aside.
2. Raise the heat to high and heat the oil until it registers 250 to 275 degrees on the deep-frying thermometer. Return the leeks to the oil and deep-fry for 3 to 4 minutes or until golden brown and crisp. Remove the leeks from the oil and transfer to paper towels to drain. Season to taste with salt.

CHAPTER EIGHT

Meat and Poultry

WITH FEW EXCEPTIONS, MEAT IS the centerpiece of most meals, particularly celebratory ones. Who doesn't look forward to the roast at Christmas, turkey at Thanksgiving, and lamb or ham at Easter? I grew up in an Italian household, and while we traditionally served pasta for big family meals, I always eagerly anticipated the meat course that followed. At most parties, the host plans the meal around meat or poultry. Even a summer backyard picnic commands hot dogs and hamburgers!

I love the techniques of cooking meat. Slow braising, grilling, and roasting produce lusty aromas that fill the house and luscious juices that seep into the pan. No matter how many times I cook meat or poultry, I always look forward to plucking browned, crunchy bits or crispy skin from the roasting pan. Who doesn't?

Good-quality meat demands respect for the farmers who raise it and keep the traditions of responsible farming alive and well, for the butchers who dress it, and for the cooks who prepare it. At Tru, I buy large cuts of meat and we butcher them ourselves. These may be whole lambs and pigs, or sides of beef, which we age in our cooler. Finally, when all is said and done, I am gratified at how well a glass of Burgundy or Cabernet Sauvignon enhances the flavor of meat. So, where's the beef?

154   *Roasted Beef Tenderloin, Truffled Potato Puree, and Bone Marrow Foam with Red Wine Sauce*

157   *Braised Beef Short Ribs with Parsnip Puree*

161   *Assiette of Milk-fed Veal: Roasted Loin, Butter-poached Breast, Crispy Sweetbreads*

167   *Tramonto's Backyard BBQ: Smoked Pork Belly, Pork Tenderloin, and Pig-tail Roulade*

172   *Malaysian-crusted Rack of Lamb with Truffled Bread-and-Butter Pudding and Mint Paint*

177   *Roasted Poussin and French Lentils with Bacon Lardons and Truffled Green Brussels Sprouts*

ROASTED BEEF TENDERLOIN, TRUFFLED POTATO PUREE, AND BONE MARROW FOAM WITH RED WINE SAUCE

Serves 6

I am crazy in love with bone marrow. When I am in New York, I like to go to the Blue Ribbon in SoHo, the casual late-night French restaurant where, among other things, I can order bone marrow off the menu. I developed a fondness for bone marrow when I first ate at Georges Blanc's restaurant, George Blanc, in Vonnas, France. Since, I have encouraged my customers and friends to try it but often they are resistant. It's too weird, too oily, too fatty, they say.

When I started making savory foams, it seemed logical to make one with marrow. This way, I could serve the marrow in a creamy, light, and more acceptable form to American diners. It caught on like wildfire at Tru! Those who are used to eating horseradish cream with beef not only feel comfortable with this, they absolutely love it. It's another example of how I like to layer flavors and textures throughout my food, as I do here with the bone marrow foam and the beef. A home run!

2½ to 3 pounds beef tenderloin
Kosher salt and freshly ground black pepper
2 tablespoons olive oil
2 bunches asparagus (10 to 12 stalks)
¾ cup Asparagus Puree (recipe follows)
1 cup Red Wine Sauce (see page 271)
3 cups Truffled Potato Puree (recipe follows)
6 beef bone marrow bones
Beef Bone Marrow Foam (recipe follows)
6 sprigs fresh rosemary, for garnish
Cracked black pepper, for garnish

1. Preheat the oven to 450 degrees.
2. Season the tenderloin with salt and pepper. In a large skillet, heat the oil over medium-high heat and sear the tenderloin until browned and a crust begins to form.
3. Lay the beef tenderloin in a shallow roasting pan. Roast for 15 to 20 minutes or until cooked to desired de-gree of doneness. For medium-rare meat, an instant-read thermometer will register 140 degrees. Let the beef rest for about 10 minutes before slicing. The temperature will rise about 10 degrees as the meat rests.
4. Meanwhile, cut the tips from the asparagus stalks. Peel the stalks below the tips. Reserve the stems for another use. Blanch the tips in boiling water for 2 to 3 minutes or until tender and bright green. Drain, season with salt and pepper, and set aside.
5. To serve, using a squeeze bottle, garnish 6 plates with some asparagus puree and spoon on the red wine sauce. Center a dollop of potato puree on each plate and top with the beef and the asparagus tips. Put a bone marrow bone on each plate. Shake the foamer vigorously and fill each bone marrow bone with beef bone marrow foam. Garnish the foam with a sprig of rosemary. Sprinkle each plate with cracked black pepper.

ABOUT THE WINE: *A softly textured, fruit-driven New World blend of Cabernet Sauvignon and Cabernet Franc, Crocker and Starr Stone Place Cuvée Napa Valley is tailor-made to pair with this elegant interpretation of the meat-and-potatoes theme.*

ASPARAGUS PUREE

Makes about ¾ cup

½ pound green asparagus, trimmed and cut into
2-inch lengths
6 tablespoons Chlorophyll (recipe follows)
Kosher salt and freshly ground black pepper

1. In a large pot of lightly salted boiling water, blanch the asparagus for 5 to 10 minutes or until fork-tender.
2. Drain immediately and submerge in ice-cold water. Drain again.
3. Transfer the asparagus to a blender and puree until almost smooth. Add the chlorophyll and puree until smooth. Season to taste with salt and pepper.
4. Strain through a chinois or fine-mesh sieve into a bowl. Cover and chill.

CHLOROPHYLL

Makes about ½ cup

¼ cup fresh spinach leaves
¼ cup fresh flat-leaf parsley
2 tablespoons ice water

1.   In a pot of lightly salted boiling water, blanch the spinach for 2 to 3 minutes or until wilted. Remove with a slotted spoon and immediately submerge in ice-cold water. Drain. Transfer the spinach to a blender.

2.   In the same pot of boiling water, blanch the parsley for 30 seconds to 1 minute or until wilted. Drain and immediately submerge in ice-cold water. Drain again. Transfer to the blender.

3.   Add the ice water to the blender and blend until smooth.

4.   Strain through a chinois or fine-mesh sieve into a bowl. Cover and chill.

TRUFFLED POTATO PUREE

Makes 3 cups

6 russet potatoes, peeled and cubed
3 tablespoons kosher salt
8 tablespoons unsalted butter
½ cup heavy cream
2 tablespoons chopped black truffles
Kosher salt and freshly ground black pepper

1.   Put the potatoes in a large saucepan, add enough water to cover the potatoes by 1 inch, and add the salt. Bring to a boil over medium-high heat, reduce the heat to medium, and simmer gently for about 20 minutes or until the potatoes are tender.

2.   Drain the potatoes and then pass them through a ricer into a large bowl.

3.   In a small saucepan, heat the butter and cream over medium-low heat. When the butter melts and the cream

is hot, gently stir into the potatoes. Fold in the truffles and season to taste with salt and pepper. Set aside, covered, to keep warm.

BEEF BONE MARROW FOAM

Makes about 2 cups

8 ounces bone marrow
2 cups heavy cream
1 sprig fresh thyme
½ cup riced, cooked potato (1 medium potato)
Kosher salt and freshly ground white pepper
2 N_2O cream chargers

1.   In a small saucepan, cook the bone marrow over low heat for about 10 minutes or until the marrow liquefies. Strain through a chinois or fine-mesh sieve into a small bowl.

2.   In the same or another small saucepan, bring the cream to a boil over medium-high heat. As soon as the cream boils, remove it from the heat and add the thyme.

3.   Add the potato and stir with a wooden spoon until incorporated. Add the marrow and stir vigorously with a wooden spoon until smooth.

4.   Strain through a chinois or fine-mesh sieve into a bowl and season to taste with salt and white pepper. Set aside to cool to room temperature.

5.   Pour the marrow mixture into a chilled iSi Gourmet Whip canister. Refrigerate for at least 1 hour. Charge the foam canister with 1 or 2 N_2O cream chargers.

BRAISED BEEF SHORT RIBS
WITH PARSNIP PUREE

Serves 6

This simple, straightforward dish—one of my favorites—is dedicated to chef Daniel Boulud, chef-owner of Daniel in New York City. He is a great friend, supporter, and mentor who always inspires my staff and me. Without doubt, he is one of the most influential French-American chefs in the world. Among other techniques, Daniel is a master of braising, and I hope this dish does him proud.

To be done correctly, braised meats require hours in a low oven. You need time, patience, and love for this technique to really shine. Once you taste the short ribs, cooked to an incredibly tender turn in a very slow oven, you, too, will be sold on braising. I like this with parsnip puree, but you can substitute celery root or potato puree instead. Or try the shredded meat on a great hard roll as a sandwich—that works, too!

6 pieces Braised Beef Short Ribs (recipe follows)
2 cups Parsnip Puree (recipe follows)
12 baby carrots
4 tablespoons unsalted butter
Kosher salt and freshly ground black pepper
6 large Brussels sprout leaves
1 cup Short Rib Sauce (recipe follows)
Parsnip Curls, for garnish (recipe follows)

1. Preheat the oven to 350 degrees.
2. Put the braised short ribs and braising liquid in a roasting pan. Cover with foil and roast for about 30 minutes or until hot.
3. Meanwhile, in a small saucepan, heat the parsnip puree over low heat for 7 to 10 minutes or until hot.
4. In a large pot of lightly salted boiling water, blanch the carrots for 4 to 6 minutes or until tender. Remove with a slotted spoon.
5. In a small sauté pan, melt 2 tablespoons of butter over medium heat. Add the carrots and cook for 3 to 4 minutes or until the carrots are glazed. Season to taste with salt and pepper.

6. Remove the cores from the Brussels sprouts with a paring knife and separate the leaves. In the same pot of boiling water, blanch the Brussels sprout leaves for 2 to 3 minutes or until wilted. Drain and immediately transfer to a small sauté pan with the remaining 2 tablespoons butter. Cook over medium heat for 3 to 4 minutes or until coated with butter. Season to taste with salt and pepper.
7. To serve, put about 1/3 cup of parsnip puree in the center of a plate. Arrange carrots and Brussels sprout leaves around the puree and center a short rib on top of the puree. Drizzle some short rib sauce around the plate and garnish the short rib with parsnip curls. Repeat to make 5 more servings.

ABOUT THE WINE: *The pinnacle in comfort food, these ultratender short ribs deserve a generous, plush red wine. The powerful wines of Priorat in Spain's Catalan region offer myriad options. My choice is the Garnacha-based* Doix *from Mas Doix Winery. Its core of deep, fleshy pepper-spiked blackberry fruit is the perfect match for the luxurious reduced short rib sauce.*

BRAISED BEEF SHORT RIBS

Serves 4 to 6

1 head garlic, root end trimmed
1 sprig fresh thyme
1 bay leaf
1 tablespoon black peppercorns
10 pounds short ribs
Kosher salt and freshly ground black pepper
2 tablespoons Clarified Butter (see page 279)
1 cup chopped onion
½ cup chopped carrots
½ cup chopped celery
1½ cups dry red wine
16 cups Beef and Veal Stock (see page 262), heated

1. Preheat the oven to 250 degrees.

2. Cut an 8-inch square of cheesecloth and mound the garlic, thyme, bay leaf, and peppercorns in the center of the square. Bring the corners of the cloth together and tie the bouquet garni with kitchen string. Set aside until needed.

3. Season the short ribs with salt and pepper.

4. Put a large sauté pan over high heat. When hot, add the clarified butter, let it get hot, and then sear the ribs on all sides until dark golden brown. Transfer the ribs to a plate. Add the onion, carrots, and celery to the pan. Lower the heat to medium and cook the vegetables for 8 to 10 minutes or until softened and golden brown.

5. Add the wine to the pan and raise the heat to high, scraping up any browned bits from the bottom of the pan with a wooden spoon. Cook until the wine is reduced by at least half.

6. Transfer the vegetables and liquid to a large roasting pan. Place the short ribs on the vegetables. Add enough of the hot stock to cover the ribs. Cover the pan with aluminum foil and braise in the oven for 8 to 10 hours or until the ribs are very tender.

7. Remove the ribs and set aside to cool to room temperature. Strain the braising liquid through a chinois or fine-mesh sieve into a saucepan. Discard the vegetables and bouquet garni. Remove and set aside half of the braising liquid to make the Short Rib Sauce (recipe follows).

8. Bring the braising liquid left in the pan to a boil over medium-high heat. Reduce the heat and simmer the liquid until reduced by half.

9. When the meat is cool enough to handle, trim it from the bones. Cut the meat into 2- to 4-inch pieces and transfer to a large bowl. Pour in the braising liquid, allow to cool to room temperature, cover, and chill.

PARSNIP PUREE

Makes 2 cups

3 to 5 parsnips (about 1 pound), peeled and quartered
3 cups heavy cream
1 Bouquet Garni (see page 271)
Kosher salt and freshly ground black pepper

1. Put the parsnips, cream, and bouquet garni in a medium-sized saucepan over medium heat. Bring the liquid to a simmer and continue to simmer for 15 to 20 minutes or until the parsnips are tender.

2. Strain through a chinois or fine-mesh sieve. Reserve the liquid and discard the bouquet garni.

3. Transfer the parsnips to a blender and puree until smooth, adding some of the reserved cooking liquid if necessary. Season to taste with salt and pepper.

SHORT RIB SAUCE

Makes 1 cup

1 tablespoon olive oil
½ cup chopped onion
¼ cup chopped carrots
¼ cup chopped celery
2 tablespoons fresh thyme
2 bay leaves
8 cups short ribs braising liquid
Kosher salt and freshly ground black pepper

1. Heat a large saucepan over medium-high heat until hot. Add the olive oil and, when hot, add the onion, carrots, and celery and cook for 5 to 7 minutes or until the vegetables have softened and are golden brown. Stir in the thyme and bay leaves.

2. Pour in the braising liquid, reduce the heat to low, and simmer for 1 hour, skimming off any fat and froth that float to the surface of the liquid.

3. Strain through a chinois or fine-mesh sieve into a saucepan. Discard the vegetables.

4. Simmer the liquid over low heat for 1 hour or until reduced to 1 cup. Season with salt and pepper. Cover and keep warm until needed.

PARSNIP CURLS

Makes 40 to 60 curls

1 parsnip, peeled
4 cups corn or canola oil
Kosher salt

1. Using a vegetable peeler, peel down the length of the parsnip to create long, thin ribbons.

2. Pour the oil into a deep, heavy saucepan and heat over medium heat until a deep-frying thermometer registers 340 degrees.

3. Fry the parsnip ribbons for 3 to 4 minutes or until golden brown. Drain on paper towels. Season to taste with salt. Set aside until needed for garnishing. The curls will keep for 2 to 3 days in a tightly lidded container.

ASSIETTE OF MILK-FED VEAL: ROASTED LOIN, BUTTER-POACHED BREAST, CRISPY SWEETBREADS

Serves 6

How proteins react with one another fascinates me. This recipe is a veritable study in proteins and progressions of flavors, textures, and cooking techniques. I begin with three different cuts of veal—tenderloin, veal breast, and sweetbreads, going from the lightest to the heaviest—and cook them in three very different ways but so that they are harmonious on the plate. Despite the obvious differences, this works. The light flavors and textures of the tenderloin give way to the heavier ones of the breast and sweetbreads. This is a complicated, challenging dish but it's an exciting one.

I encourage you to try this technique. Young and curious cooks, especially, should explore this philosophy of using different cuts from the same animal. This kind of "vertical cooking" teaches you so much about the animal and how flavors interact.

Buy the youngest veal you can. If it's not pure white, which indicates milk-fed veal, it should be light, pale pink with no visible graining. This assures you of tenderness.

¾ to 1¼ pounds milk-fed veal tenderloin
Kosher salt and freshly ground black pepper
2 tablespoons olive oil
1 cup Roasted Vegetables and Fried Celery Leaves
    (recipe follows)
1 cup Braised Red Cabbage (recipe follows)
6 circles from 6 slices Brioche (see page 280)
6 Torchons of Sweetbreads (recipe follows)
2 tablespoons Clarified Butter (see page 279)
½ pound grade A foie gras, cut into 6 slices
½ cup braising liquid from Butter-poached Veal Breast
    (recipe follows)
½ cup Port Wine Reduction (recipe follows)
½ cup Madeira Sauce (recipe follows)
6 rounds Butter-poached Veal Breast (recipe follows)

1. Preheat the oven to 400 degrees.
2. Cut the tenderloin into 6 medallions, tie each with kitchen string, and season with salt and pepper.
3. In a large cast-iron skillet, heat the olive oil over medium-high heat and sear the veal medallions for 1 to 2 minutes on each side, until golden brown. Transfer to a plate to rest for 5 minutes. Return the veal to the skillet and transfer the skillet to the oven. Roast for 3 to 5 minutes.
4. In separate saucepans, heat the roasted vegetables (not the fried celery leaves) and the braised red cabbage over medium heat for 5 to 8 minutes or until heated through.
5. Toast the brioche circles until golden brown on both sides.
6. To cook the torchons of sweetbreads, heat the clarified butter in a large skillet over medium heat until hot. Add the sweetbread medallions and cook for 3 to 4 minutes on each side, until crispy and golden brown. Season with salt and pepper. Drain on paper towels.
7. To prepare the foie gras, heat a dry cast-iron skillet over medium-high heat. When hot, sauté the foie gras for about 1 to 2 minutes on each side, until lightly browned.
8. In separate saucepans, heat the braising liquid, port wine reduction, and Madeira sauce over medium heat for 5 to 7 minutes or until the sauces are heated through.
9. To serve, arrange a portion of the roasted vegetables at the top of a plate and place some braised cabbage and a brioche circle on opposite sides of the plate to form a triangle. Put a veal tenderloin on top of the brioche, sweetbreads on top of the cabbage, and a veal breast on top of the roasted vegetables. Drizzle braising liquid over the tenderloin, port wine reduction over the sweetbreads, and Madeira sauce over the veal breast. Top the veal breast with the fried celery leaves. Repeat to make five more servings.

ABOUT THE WINE: *There are various flavor and textural contrasts at work in this dish: tender veal, creamy sweetbreads, rich foie gras, and piquant citrus-spice braised cabbage. An oaked wine is not welcome here. Instead, try the fruity* Forster

Ungeheuer *Riesling Spätlese von Bühl from Germany's Pfalz region. The persistent acidity of the wine will temper the richness of the organ meats and match the vivid tang of the cabbage while the striking white peach fruitiness refreshes the palate.*

ROASTED VEGETABLES AND FRIED CELERY LEAVES

Makes about 1 cup

2 ounces bacon, finely diced
1 celery root, trimmed, peeled, and finely diced
1 carrot, finely diced
3 shallots, minced
Kosher salt and freshly ground white pepper
Vegetable oil
½ cup celery leaves

1. To prepare the roasted vegetables, in a skillet, cook the bacon over medium heat until the fat renders and the bacon begins to crisp.

2. Add the celery root, lower the heat slightly, and cook, stirring occasionally, for about 10 minutes or until the celery root is tender. Add the carrot and shallots and cook for 5 to 7 minutes longer or until the carrots are tender. Season to taste with salt and white pepper and set aside, covered, to keep warm.

3. To prepare the fried celery leaves, pour vegetable oil into a deep, heavy saucepan to a depth of about 2 inches and heat over medium-high heat until a deep-frying thermometer registers between 250 and 275 degrees. Using a slotted spoon, carefully put the celery leaves in the hot oil and fry for 2 to 3 minutes or until crispy. Remove with the slotted spoon and drain on paper towels. Season with salt and pepper and set aside until ready to use.

BRAISED RED CABBAGE

Makes 2 cups

1 head red cabbage, cored and trimmed
2¼ cups dry red wine
¾ cup port wine
Kosher salt
2 pieces star anise
1 teaspoon juniper berries
1 teaspoon black peppercorns
2 bay leaves
¼ cup sugar
¼ cup duck fat
½ onion, finely chopped
3 strips orange rind, each the length of the fruit
3 strips lemon rind, each the length of the fruit
6 tablespoons red wine vinegar
¼ cup frozen and defrosted lingonberries or
    red currants with juice
Freshly squeezed lemon juice
Freshly ground black pepper

1. Cut the cabbage into julienne strips. Transfer to a large bowl and add the red wine, port, and a little salt. Cover with plastic wrap and refrigerate for at least 8 hours or overnight.

2. Strain the cabbage and reserve the marinade.

3. Cut an 8-inch square of cheesecloth and mound the star anise, juniper berries, black peppercorns, and bay leaves in the center of the square. Bring the corners of the cloth together and tie the sachet with kitchen string.

4. In a large sauté pan, bring the sugar and ¼ cup of water to a boil over medium heat and cook for about 5 minutes or until the sugar dissolves and the syrup turns a light caramel color. Slowly add the reserved marinade, stirring to blend.

5. In another pan, heat the duck fat and add the cabbage, onion, spice sachet, and orange and lemon rinds to the pan and cook, stirring, until the cabbage begins to wilt. Add the vinegar and sugar mixture. Bring to a simmer over medium heat, cover with parchment paper, and simmer for about 45 minutes or until the cabbage is tender and most of the liquid evaporates.

6. Add the lingonberries and their juice. Season to taste with lemon juice, salt, and pepper. Stir and cook just until heated through. Use immediately or set aside to cool. When cool, cover and refrigerate until needed.

TORCHONS OF SWEETBREADS

Makes 6 medallions

2 lobes veal sweetbreads
Milk
10 large egg whites
8 cups Sweetbread Poaching Liquid (recipe follows)

1. Soak the sweetbreads in milk in the refrigerator for 3 to 4 hours.

2. Remove the sweetbreads from the milk and pat them dry. Trim off any visible fat, membranes, and sinews. Discard the milk.

3. Put the egg whites in a medium bowl and add the sweetbreads. Let the sweetbreads soak for 10 to 20 minutes.

4. Roll the sweetbreads in plastic wrap and tie the ends with kitchen string. Break any air pockets with a thumbtack or the tip of a small, sharp knife.

5. In a wide, deep skillet, heat the sweetbread poaching liquid over low heat until it reaches 160 degrees. Lower the sweetbreads into the liquid and poach for 12 to 14 minutes. Remove from the poaching liquid and set aside to cool.

6. Remove the plastic wrap and slice the sweetbreads into 6 medallions. Cover and refrigerate until needed.

SWEETBREAD POACHING LIQUID

Makes 16 cups

2 tablespoons olive oil
½ cup chopped leeks, white part only
¼ cup chopped celery
4 ounces white button mushrooms, chopped
3 sprigs fresh thyme
2 bay leaves
1 tablespoon black peppercorns
1 cup dry white wine
16 cups Vegetable Stock (see page 266)

1. In a large stockpot, heat the olive oil over low heat and cook the leeks, celery, and mushrooms for about 5 minutes or until softened without coloring. Add the thyme, bay leaves, and peppercorns and cook for 2 to 3 minutes longer.

2. Add the white wine, raise the heat to medium-high, and simmer for 8 to 10 minutes or until most of the wine has evaporated and the bottom of the pot is almost dry.

3. Add the vegetable stock, bring to a boil, and immediately remove the pot from the heat. Strain through a chinois or fine-mesh sieve into a large bowl and chill in an ice bath. Discard the vegetables. Cover the chilled liquid and refrigerate for up to 2 days.

BUTTER-POACHED VEAL BREAST

Makes 6 rounds

1 4- to 5-pound veal breast
Kosher salt and freshly ground black pepper
2 tablespoons olive oil
2 carrots, chopped
2 leeks, white and light-green parts only, chopped
2 ribs celery, chopped
1 onion, chopped
2 heads garlic, root ends trimmed
8 medium tomatoes, peeled, seeded, and chopped
½ bunch fresh thyme
2 tablespoons black peppercorns
4 bay leaves
10 cups Veal Demi-glace (see page 268)
2 cups Beurre Monté (see page 278)

1. Preheat the oven to 300 degrees.

2. Remove the excess fat and silver skin from the veal. Season generously with salt and pepper.

3. In a roasting pan, heat the olive oil over high heat, using 2 burners if necessary, and sear all sides of the veal until it's a deep golden brown. Transfer to a plate and drain off all but 2 tablespoons of the fat from the roasting pan.

4. Place the pan over medium heat and add the carrots, leeks, celery, onion, garlic, tomatoes, thyme, peppercorns, and bay leaves and season with salt and pepper. Cook for 2 to 3 minutes, stirring the bottom of the pan with a wooden spoon to deglaze.

5. Return the veal to the roasting pan, rib side down. Pour in enough veal demi-glace to come three-quarters up the side of the veal breast and then add enough cold water to cover the breast. Raise the heat to medium-high and bring to a boil. Lower the heat and simmer for about 10 minutes, skimming any fat or foam that rises to the surface.

6. Cover the roasting pan with parchment paper and transfer to the oven. Poach for 4 to 5 hours or until tender.

7. Remove the breast from the pan and set aside for 20 to 30 minutes to cool. Strain the braising liquid through a chinois or fine-mesh sieve into a saucepan. Discard the vegetables.

8. Put the saucepan over medium heat and simmer the liquid, skimming off any fat or foam that rises to the surface, for 30 to 60 minutes or until the liquid reaches a saucelike consistency. Strain twice through a chinois or fine-mesh sieve into a bowl. Cover and refrigerate until needed.

9. Clean the veal breast of bones, cartilage, and all fat. Wear rubber gloves if the veal is still hot. Season all over with salt and pepper.

10. Line a 2-inch-deep pan with parchment paper. Fold the veal breast in half, as you would a book, and place it in the pan. Cover with another sheet of parchment paper and put another pan on top to weight down the veal. Refrigerate for 12 hours or overnight.

11. Using a 2-inch-wide ring cutter, stamp out 6 rounds from the veal breast. Cover and refrigerate until needed.

12. To heat, put the *beurre monté* in a deep skillet large enough to hold the veal rounds. When warm, gently lay the veal in the butter sauce and cook until the veal is heated through. Be sure to test the center, which takes the longest to heat up.

13. Remove the veal rounds with a slotted spoon, blot the excess butter with a paper towel, and serve.

PORT WINE REDUCTION

Makes ½ cup

1 750-ml bottle port wine
2 tablespoons honey

In a small saucepan, bring the port and honey to a slow simmer over low heat and cook for 30 to 40 minutes or until reduced to ½ cup. Set aside at room temperature until needed.

MADEIRA SAUCE

Makes about 1 cup

½ 750-ml bottle Madeira wine
2 cups Veal Demi-glace (see page 268)
1 cup Vegetable Stock (see page 266), or Chicken Stock
(see page 265)
¼ pound unsalted butter
¼ cup heavy cream
10 ounces French truffle juice (see Note)
Kosher salt

1. In a medium saucepan, bring the Madeira to a simmer over medium heat. Reduce the heat to low and simmer for about 30 minutes or until reduced to a syrup.

2. Add the veal demi-glace and stock, raise the heat to medium, and bring to a simmer. Reduce the heat to low and slowly simmer, skimming off any fat and froth that float to the surface, for 45 minutes to 1 hour or until reduced by a third.

3. Using a handheld immersion blender, blend in the butter and cream until fully incorporated.

4. Add the truffle juice and salt to taste. Set aside to cool. Cover and refrigerate until needed.

NOTE: *Truffle juice is sold at specialty stores.*

TRAMONTO'S BACKYARD BBQ:
SMOKED PORK BELLY, PORK TENDERLOIN,
AND PIG-TAIL ROULADE

Serves 6

I named this dish in a lighthearted moment. Not because everything is cooked in the backyard on the grill (far from it; most of this recipe is done in the kitchen), but because the flavors are reminiscent of the best southern barbecue. There's irony here, too, because, let's face it, this recipe is pretty over-the-top and removed from the laid-back style of most traditional southern barbecue cooks.

As I have mentioned before, we are spoiled at Tru because we get whole pigs that we can butcher as we see fit. I've seen my sous-chefs walking down North St. Clair Street, in the heart of metropolitan Chicago, carrying a slaughtered pig on each shoulder from the Green City Market! Now, that's not something urban sophisticates see every day! We were using as much of the pig as we could, making head cheese and using the trotters, but I thought we could dig deeper and use even more. I remembered a pig-tail roulade I had in London at Marco Pierre White's original restaurant, Marco Pierre White's, and decided to follow suit because it was such a great idea. It's easy to think of ways to use the primary cuts of the pig, but not so easy to come up with ways to use the pig tails!

PIG-TAIL ROULADE:
10 pounds pig tails
¼ cup olive oil
1 cup chopped onion
½ cup chopped carrots
½ cup chopped celery
2 tablespoons fresh thyme leaves
3 bay leaves
2 tablespoons black peppercorns
16 cups Chicken Stock (see page 265)
2 tablespoons Dijon mustard
1 cup fresh bread crumbs
3 tablespoons Clarified Butter (see page 279)

CURED PORK BELLY:
1½ cups kosher salt
1 cup brown sugar
10 cups water
1 cup chopped Granny Smith or other tart apple
½ cup chopped onion
¼ cup chopped carrots
¼ cup chopped celery
2 tablespoons fresh thyme leaves
2 tablespoons fresh sage
2 tablespoons black peppercorns
1 pound pork belly or slab bacon
¼ pound unsalted butter

PORK TENDERLOIN:
2 pounds pork tenderloin
Kosher salt and freshly ground black pepper
¼ cup canola oil
3 cups Boniato Mash (recipe follows)
¾ cup Sautéed Baby Spinach (recipe follows)
1 cup Smoked Pork Jus (recipe follows)
2 cups J-Rob's Barbecue Sauce (recipe follows)
About 6 teaspoons purple bachelor's button flowers,
*   for garnish*

1. To prepare the pig tails, put them in a large bowl and add enough lightly salted water to cover. Cover with plastic wrap and refrigerate overnight.

2. Preheat the oven to 300 degrees.

3. Thoroughly rinse the pig tails in cold water.

4. In a large, deep roasting pan, heat the olive oil over medium-high heat, add the onion, carrots, and celery, and cook, stirring occasionally, for 7 to 8 minutes or until the vegetables are evenly browned. Stir in the thyme, bay leaves, and peppercorns.

5. Add the pig tails and chicken stock. Cover with aluminum foil, transfer to the oven, and roast for 2 to 3 hours or until the meat is very tender.

6. Remove the pig tails with a slotted spoon and transfer them to baking sheets, spreading them into a single layer. Let them cool slightly. Reserve the braising liquid. When the pig tails are cool enough to handle, remove the

meat and transfer it to a large, shallow pan. Cover and refrigerate until ready to use.

7. Strain the braising liquid through a chinois or fine-mesh sieve into a saucepan. Place over low heat and simmer for 45 minutes to 1 hour or until reduced by three-quarters. Let cool to room temperature. Strain again through a chinois or fine-mesh sieve and pour over the pig-tail meat.

8. Place an 18-inch-long sheet of plastic wrap on a work surface, with the long side facing you. Spread out the meat along the bottom edge, leaving a 2-inch border at each end, and roll the plastic wrap over the meat to make a log. Hold both ends of the plastic wrap and roll it along the work surface to tighten the roll, which should be about 2 inches in diameter. Prick a few holes in the log with a small pin to release any trapped air. Refrigerate overnight.

9. Unwrap the log and slice it into 6 ½-inch-thick slices. Brush the cut sides of the roulade with Dijon mustard.

10. Spread the bread crumbs on a plate. Dip the coated pig-tail slices in the crumbs and transfer to a plate. Cover with plastic wrap and refrigerate for at least 30 minutes and for up to 1 hour.

11. Just before serving, heat the clarified butter in a sauté pan over medium heat. When hot, add a few slices of the roulade and cook on both sides until golden brown and crispy. Repeat with the remaining pieces. Cover to keep warm.

12. To prepare the pork belly, start by mixing the salt and brown sugar with the water in a large bowl until the sugar dissolves. Add the apple, onion, carrots, celery, thyme, sage, and peppercorns. Submerge the pork belly in the liquid. Cover with plastic wrap and refrigerate for 12 hours.

13. Remove the pork belly from the brining liquid and set the pork aside at room temperature for 30 minutes to dry. Discard the brining liquid.

14. Prepare a smoker according to the manufacturer's instructions. Smoke the pork belly at a low setting for 1 to 2 hours. Remove from the smoker and allow to cool at room temperature.

15. In a large sauté pan, heat the butter over medium heat, and when melted, add the smoked pork and sauté for 3 to 4 minutes or until tender but not colored. Drain on paper towels and cut into six equal portions. Set aside, covered, to keep warm.

16. To prepare the pork tenderloin, preheat the oven to 350 degrees.

17. Season the pork with salt and pepper.

18. Heat a dry cast-iron skillet or ovenproof sauté pan over medium-high heat until very hot. When hot, add enough canola oil to lightly cover the bottom of the pan. Sear the pork on all sides until well browned.

19. Transfer to the oven and roast for 8 to 10 minutes or until an instant-read thermometer registers 140 to 145 degrees. Transfer the pork to a cutting board and allow to rest for 5 minutes. Slice into 6 pieces.

20. To serve, spoon boniato mash into the center of a plate. Place a slice of tenderloin on one side of the mash, at about "one o'clock." Put a slice of pig-tail roulade on one side of the tenderloin, at "three o'clock." Slice the belly into 4 to 5 slices and fan near the bottom of the plate at "six o'clock." Put spinach at "ten o'clock." Drip the pork jus around the plate. Using a paintbrush, brush some barbecue sauce on the side of the plate.

21. Fill 1-ounce ramekins with some of the remaining barbecue sauce. Sprinkle the dish with purple bachelor's buttons. Repeat to make 5 more servings.

ABOUT THE WINE: *The pervasive hickory-smoke flavor and rich texture of the three pork components call for a wine with crisp acidity, firm tannic backbone, and earthy fruit flavor. I prefer to serve a traditionally styled Rioja with this dish. Prado Enea Gran Reserva from Bodegas Muga is a fine example with its cherry, strawberry, sweet vanilla, and smoky nature.*

BONIATO MASH

Makes about 3 cups

3 boniatos or other sweet potatoes (about 1 pound),
*   peeled and cut into equal-sized pieces (see Note)*
3 tablespoons kosher salt
1 cup heavy cream
¼ pound unsalted butter
Kosher salt and freshly ground black pepper

1.   Put the potatoes and enough cold water to cover in a large saucepan. Add the salt, bring to a boil over medium heat, reduce the heat, and simmer gently for about 20 minutes or until tender. Drain in a colander. Press through a potato ricer into a bowl.

2.   In a small saucepan, heat the cream and butter until the butter is melted. Gently fold the cream mixture into the boniato. Season to taste with salt and pepper. Keep warm until needed.

NOTE: *Boniatos, which are also called Cuban sweet*
*   potatoes, have drier, whiter flesh than the common*
*   sweet potato and are not as sweet. They are*
*   irregularly shaped and their jackets range in color*
*   from red to beige. Look for them in Cuban and other*
*   markets that sell the produce of the Caribbean.*

SAUTÉED BABY SPINACH

Makes about ¾ cup

2 tablespoons olive oil
1 large clove garlic, minced
1 large shallot, minced
2 cups baby spinach, cleaned, washed, and drained
Kosher salt and freshly ground black pepper

1.   In a large skillet, heat the olive oil over medium heat. Add the garlic and shallot and cook for 1 to 2 minutes or until softened but not colored.

2.   Add the spinach and cook for about 1 minute or just until wilted. Season to taste with salt and pepper. Spread the spinach on a double thickness of paper towels to drain. Use immediately.

SMOKED PORK JUS

Makes 1 cup

½ cup chopped onion
¼ cup chopped carrots
¼ cup chopped celery
1 cup Calvados
¼ cup apple cider vinegar
4 cups Veal Demi-glace (see page 268)

1.   Wrap the onion, carrots, and celery in aluminum foil. Add the vegetables to the smoker along with the pork belly (see page 169, step 14) and smoke for 1 hour.

2.   Remove the vegetables from the aluminum foil, and then transfer them to a medium-sized saucepan along with the Calvados and apple cider vinegar.

3.   Put the pan over low heat and simmer for 30 to 40 minutes or until most of the liquid has evaporated and the bottom of the skillet is almost dry.

4.   Add the veal demi-glace, and then raise the heat to medium-high. When the liquid starts to simmer, reduce the heat to low and simmer for 1 hour.

5.   Strain through a chinois or fine-mesh sieve into a saucepan. Discard the vegetables. Put the pan over low heat and simmer, skimming off any fat and froth that float to the surface, for about 1 hour or until reduced to 1 cup. Allow to cool in an ice bath. Cover and refrigerate until chilled, and then remove the layer of congealed fat from the surface.

6.   Transfer to a covered storage container and refrigerate for up to 3 days.

J-ROB'S BARBECUE SAUCE

Makes 2 cups

2 tablespoons vegetable oil
½ cup chopped onion
½ cup chopped carrots
2 jalapeño peppers, seeded and chopped
2 ripe mangoes, peeled and chopped
1 cup fresh orange juice
½ cup brewed coffee
¼ cup honey
1 cup ketchup

1. Heat the oil in a medium-sized saucepan over low heat. When the oil is hot, add the onion, carrots, and jalapeño peppers. Stirring occasionally, cook for 5 to 7 minutes or until the vegetables have softened without coloring.

2. Add the mangoes, orange juice, coffee, and honey. Stirring occasionally, cook over low heat for 10 to 15 minutes or until the liquid is reduced by three-quarters.

3. Add the ketchup, and then stir the ingredients. Raise the heat to medium and simmer for 10 to 15 minutes or until slightly thickened. Transfer to a blender and puree until smooth.

4. Strain through a chinois or fine-mesh sieve into a metal bowl. Allow to cool in an ice-water bath. Use when cool or cover and refrigerate for up to a week.

MALAYSIAN-CRUSTED RACK OF LAMB WITH TRUFFLED BREAD-AND-BUTTER PUDDING AND MINT PAINT

Serves 6

The flavor of this rack of lamb is just unbelievable. I became interested in Malaysian food when I spent three weeks in New Zealand. I sampled a loin of lamb there, rolled in similar spices and Kaffir lime leaves. When I created rack of lamb with these flavors, I decided it would taste terrific with the truffled bread-and-butter pudding, one of my all-time favorites. I was right! And for even deeper depth of flavor, I pair it with broccoflower puree. Delicious.

A rack of lamb is a connected series of rib chops, usually with cracked bones that make it easy to separate into individual chops. Despite some preconceived notions, it's an easy cut to work with, and if you like lamb chops, you will be in lamb paradise with this recipe.

½ cup olive oil

¼ cup plus 1 tablespoon oyster sauce

3 tablespoons rice wine vinegar

3 tablespoons toasted sesame oil

2 tablespoons soy sauce

1 tablespoon fish sauce

1 tablespoon crushed dried chili

2 racks of lamb (at least 18 ribs)

12 cloves garlic, unpeeled

2 bunches Swiss chard

½ cup Dijon mustard

½ cup sambal or other hot, spicy chili paste

2 cups homemade Brioche cubes (see page 280), or from a good bakery

1 tablespoon finely chopped ginger

4 cloves garlic, finely chopped

1 stalk lemongrass, tough outer stems removed, finely chopped

3 Kaffir lime leaves, finely chopped

8 mint leaves, finely chopped

1 teaspoon finely chopped fresh cilantro

1 tablespoon paprika

1 teaspoon turmeric

¼ cup olive oil

Truffled Bread-and-Butter Pudding (recipe follows)

2 tablespoons unsalted butter

Kosher salt and freshly ground white pepper

1 cup Broccoflower Puree (recipe follows)

½ cup Red Wine Lamb Sauce (recipe follows)

Mint Paint (recipe follows)

1. In a large bowl, whisk together the olive oil, oyster sauce, rice wine vinegar, sesame oil, soy sauce, fish sauce, and chili. Remove ¼ cup of the marinade and set aside for later use. Put the racks of lamb in the marinade, making sure the meat is coated with the marinade. Cover with plastic wrap and refrigerate for at least 3 hours or overnight.

2. In a large pot of lightly salted boiling water, blanch the garlic cloves for 4 to 5 minutes or until just tender. Drain and immediately submerge in ice-cold water. Drain again and set aside.

3. Trim the stems of the chard and separate the leaves. Wash the leaves thoroughly and dry well with paper towels. Wash and cut enough of the stems on a diagonal into ½-inch-long pieces to measure ½ cup. In a large pot of lightly salted boiling water, blanch the stems for 3 to 4 minutes or until tender. Drain, immediately submerge in ice-cold water, and drain again.

4. Remove the lamb from the marinade and pat dry with paper towels. Whisk together the mustard, sambal chili paste, and the reserved ¼ cup of lamb marinade. Brush the mustard mixture on the lamb.

5. Put the brioche pieces into the bowl of a food processor fitted with a metal blade and process until crumbly. Add the ginger, garlic, lemongrass, Kaffir lime leaves, mint, cilantro, paprika, and turmeric. Process until finely chopped. Spread the bread crumbs on a flat plate and then coat the lamb on all sides with the bread crumbs.

6. Preheat the oven to 450 degrees.

7. Heat the olive oil in a cast-iron skillet over medium-high heat until hot. Add the racks of lamb and sear on all sides until they are a deep brown. Remove from the pan and place on a rack in a roasting pan. Transfer the pan to the oven and roast for 10 to 12 minutes for medium-

rare, or longer, if desired. Remove from the oven and transfer to a plate. Set aside to rest for 10 minutes.

8. Meanwhile, reheat the bread-and-butter pudding in a 325-degree oven for about 10 minutes or until heated through.

9. In a large sauté pan, melt the butter over medium-high heat and sauté the Swiss chard stems for 2 to 3 minutes. Add the leaves and sauté for 2 to 3 minutes longer or until the leaves have wilted. Season to taste with salt and white pepper.

10. To serve, slice the racks of lamb into chops. Using 2 spoons, make a quenelle (oval-shape mound) of broccoflower puree and place it on the side near the top of a plate. Put 2 cloves of garlic directly above the puree. Put a scoop of the bread-and-butter pudding on the other side of the plate. Put Swiss chard in the center of the plate and arrange 2 lamb chops against the chard with the bones pointed toward the top of the plate. Spoon some of the lamb sauce around the chops. Using a clean ½-inch-wide paintbrush, paint a line of mint paint along the bottom of the plate, below the bread pudding. Repeat to make 5 more servings.

ABOUT THE WINE: *The perfumed, spicy Asian elements call for a bold red wine with full-on fruit. The power, big fruit, and full body of Australian Shiraz dazzles next to this dish. For a rare, unequaled pleasure, try procuring a bottle of Henschke Hill of Grace from the Barossa Valley. The intense concentration of its licorice, plum, chocolate, and vanilla flavors and great length are an excellent match for the assertively seasoned lamb.*

TRUFFLED BREAD-AND-BUTTER PUDDING

Makes 1 9-inch loaf

2 tablespoons unsalted butter
¼ cup chopped shallots
1 clove garlic, chopped
1 sprig fresh thyme
1 sprig fresh rosemary
2½ cups heavy cream
1½ cups half-and-half
9 large egg yolks
Kosher salt and freshly ground black pepper
1 loaf homemade Brioche (see page 280),
    or from a good bakery
1 tablespoon unsalted butter
2 tablespoons Black Truffles in Oil (recipe follows)
½ cup chopped Vidalia onion
¼ cup Madeira wine

1. In a medium-sized saucepan, melt the butter over medium heat and cook the shallots, garlic, thyme, and rosemary for 3 to 4 minutes or until the shallots soften. Add the cream and half-and-half and bring to a boil.

2. Meanwhile, in a small bowl, whisk the egg yolks. When the cream starts to boil, whisk a little of the cream into the egg yolks to temper them. Whisk this egg yolk mixture into the cream, remove the pan from the heat, and continue whisking until smooth. Season to taste with salt and pepper. Strain through a chinois or fine-mesh sieve into a bowl. Cover with plastic wrap, pressing the plastic directly on the surface of the custard to prevent skin from forming. Refrigerate for at least 4 hours or until chilled.

3. Preheat the oven to 300 degrees.

4. Remove the crust from the brioche and cut the bread into ¼-inch cubes. Spread on a baking sheet, transfer to the oven, and toast for about 10 minutes or until nicely browned. Remove from the oven and set aside to cool.

5. Transfer the brioche cubes to a large bowl and pour the chilled custard over them. Toss gently, cover with plastic wrap, and refrigerate overnight.

6. In a sauté pan, melt the butter over medium heat. Add the black truffles in oil and Vidalia onion and cook, stirring occasionally, for 6 to 7 minutes or until the onion softens and turns deep amber. Add the Madeira and simmer until most of the wine has evaporated and the bottom of the pan is almost dry. Set aside at room temperature to cool.

7. Remove the bowl from the refrigerator and toss the truffles and onion with the bread cubes and custard.

8. Preheat the oven to 300 degrees. Lightly grease a 9-by-5-by-3-inch loaf pan.

9. Spread the brioche and custard mixture in the loaf pan. Put the loaf pan in a larger roasting pan, add enough water to come halfway up the sides of the loaf pan, and carefully transfer the roasting pan to the center rack of the oven. Bake for 40 to 50 minutes. Rotate the pan and bake for another 40 to 50 minutes. Add more water as needed during baking. Remove from the oven and set aside at room temperature to cool, still in the water bath. Use immediately or cover and refrigerate until needed.

BLACK TRUFFLES IN OIL

Makes ¾ cup

1 7-ounce can black truffles
½ cup white truffle oil

1. Strain the canned truffles through a chinois or fine-mesh sieve. Rinse well under cold water. Pat dry with paper towels.

2. Transfer the truffles to the bowl of a food processor fitted with a metal blade. Process until the truffles are finely chopped.

3. Scrape the chopped truffles into a bowl. Add the white truffle oil. Cover with plastic wrap and refrigerate until needed. The oil will keep for up to 3 weeks.

BROCCOFLOWER PUREE

Makes 1 cup

6 tablespoons unsalted butter
¼ cup water
1 head broccoflower or green cauliflower, cut into florets
½ cup heavy cream, scalded
Kosher salt and freshly ground white pepper

1. In a small saucepan, bring the butter and water to a simmer over medium heat and heat until the butter melts. Add the florets, lower the heat, and simmer gently for 8 to 10 minutes or until tender. Drain in a colander.

2. Transfer the broccoflower to a blender. Add the cream a little at a time and puree until smooth. Season to taste with salt and white pepper. Strain through a chinois or fine-mesh sieve into a bowl. Set aside at room temperature to cool. Use immediately or cover and refrigerate until needed.

RED WINE LAMB SAUCE

Makes 2 cups

8 quarts Lamb Stock (see page 263)
2 pounds lamb scraps
1 750-ml bottle dry red wine
1 750-ml bottle port wine
2 cloves
1 teaspoon allspice
1 teaspoon star anise
½ cinnamon stick
1 sprig fresh rosemary

1. In a very large stockpot, bring the lamb stock to a simmer over medium heat. Reduce the heat to low and simmer very gently, skimming off any fat and froth that float to the surface, for 30 to 40 minutes or until reduced by a quarter.

2. Meanwhile, heat another large stockpot over medium-high heat, and when hot, sear the lamb scraps for about 5 minutes or until deeply browned. You might want to do this in batches. Remove the lamb from the pot and set aside.

3. Add the red wine and port to the second stockpot, and then add the cloves, allspice, star anise, and cinnamon stick. Stir the bottom of the pot with a wooden spoon to deglaze. Bring the wine to a simmer.

4. Return the meat to the pot and add the stock. Bring to a simmer over low heat and cook for about 2½ hours, frequently skimming off any fat and froth that float to the surface of the liquid. Strain through a chinois or fine-mesh sieve lined with cheesecloth into another pot.

5. Set the pot on low heat and simmer the mixture for about 1 hour or until reduced to 2 cups. Cool in an ice bath. Transfer to a bowl, cover with plastic wrap, and refrigerate until chilled. Remove the layer of congealed fat from the surface.

6. Before serving, transfer to a saucepan and add the sprig of fresh rosemary. Place over medium heat for 5 minutes or until heated through.

MINT PAINT

Makes about ½ cup

½ cup fresh mint leaves
¼ cup fresh spinach leaves
¼ cup light corn syrup
Kosher salt and freshly ground black pepper

1. In a large saucepan of boiling water, blanch the mint and spinach leaves for 10 seconds and then shock them in ice water. Drain and gently squeeze out excess water.

2. Transfer to a blender with the corn syrup and blend for 2 to 3 minutes or until pureed and bright green. Strain through a chinois or fine-mesh sieve. Season to taste with salt and pepper. Refrigerate for at least 1 hour until thick.

ROASTED POUSSIN AND FRENCH LENTILS WITH BACON LARDONS AND TRUFFLED GREEN BRUSSELS SPROUTS

Serves 6

I love to spring this peasant-style dish on people at the restaurant, because they don't expect such a simple, homey preparation at Tru. We serve it in a copper pot and carve the poussin at tableside, which makes it more elegant and dramatic. This means our waitstaff must know how to carve chicken flawlessly, which is where our dining room manager, Serge Krieger, steps in. From his days working in Europe in some of the world's finest restaurants, like Georges Blanc, to his time working in the States with Daniel Boulud, he has an impressive background in tableside service and has taught our staff to carve birds to perfection—and shown me a few tricks along the way, too! The staff practices on the whole roasted chickens we serve for staff meals before nightly service begins; this is another reason we have received many outstanding service awards. This dish has the classic Old World flavors of a French country dish: lentils, Brussels sprouts, and chicken. You couldn't find a better rendition at a Paris brasserie!

3 1-pound poussin, wing tips removed and reserved
for sauce
9 tablespoons Herb Butter (recipe follows), softened
Kosher salt and freshly ground black pepper
2 tablespoons Clarified Butter (see page 279)
4 to 6 tablespoons unsalted butter, softened
5 slices thick-cut bacon, cut into 1- to 1½-inch pieces
2 cups French Green and Crimson Red Lentils
(recipe follows)
2 cups Truffled Green Brussels Sprouts with Purple Kale
(recipe follows)
1 cup Natural Poussin Jus (recipe follows)
3 tablespoons Black Truffles in Oil (see page 175)
6 sprigs fresh rosemary

1. Preheat the oven to 425 degrees.
2. Gently slide a finger under the skin of the poussin breasts to create pockets. Stuff 1½ tablespoons of the herb butter under the skin of each side of the breasts and, using your fingertips, gently spread the butter beneath the skin to cover the breast meat evenly.
3. Truss the poussin with kitchen string and season with salt and pepper.
4. Heat the clarified butter in a large skillet over medium-high heat until hot. Add the 3 poussin and brown on all sides until golden brown. Remove from the skillet and transfer to a rack positioned in a roasting pan, breast side up.
5. Rub the poussin with softened butter.
6. Transfer to the oven and roast for 10 to 12 minutes or until the juices run clear, basting with the pan juices every 2 to 3 minutes. Remove from the oven and let rest for 8 to 10 minutes. Halve each poussin and carve the meat from the bones.
7. In a small saucepan, cook the bacon over low heat until the fat is rendered and the bacon begins to cook. Increase the heat to medium and cook until the bacon is crisp and golden brown. Remove with a slotted spoon and drain on paper towels.
8. Put the lentils in a small saucepan over low heat for about 5 minutes or until heated through.
9. Mix the bacon and the lentils together and spoon onto the center of a plate. Top with Brussels sprouts and kale and place half a poussin on top of the sprouts and kale. Drizzle jus and about ½ tablespoon of black truffles in oil over and around the poussin. Garnish with a sprig of rosemary. Repeat to make 5 more servings.

ABOUT THE WINE: *The wine choice should pull together the earthy poussin, smoky lentils, and musky flavor of the Brussels sprouts. A bold, deeply hazelnut-scented white Burgundy, Auxey-Duresses Les Clous Domaine d'Auvenay, shows layers of focused ripe fruit, toast, and earth that stand up to the bacon and lentils without overpowering the young chicken.*

HERB BUTTER

Makes about ½ pound

½ pound cold unsalted butter
½ bunch fresh flat-leaf parsley
2 to 3 tablespoons fresh thyme leaves
2 to 3 tablespoons fresh rosemary
2 to 3 tablespoons fresh sage

1. Cut the butter into ½-inch cubes and set aside to come to room temperature.
2. Remove the leaves from the herbs and finely chop.
3. Transfer the herbs to the bowl of a food processor fitted with a metal blade and process until combined. With the motor running, add the cubes of butter, 1 cube at a time, until all the butter is added and the mixture is smooth.
4. Press the butter mixture through a tamis or fine-mesh sieve into a bowl to remove any herb stems missed when the leaves were chopped. Cover tightly with plastic wrap and refrigerate until needed.

FRENCH GREEN AND CRIMSON RED LENTILS

Makes 2 cups

2 tablespoons Clarified Butter (see page 279)
1 small Spanish onion, chopped
1 small carrot, chopped
1 cup French green Puy lentils, rinsed and drained
1 cup Crimson red lentils, rinsed and drained
1 Bouquet Garni (see page 271)
6 cups water or Vegetable Stock (see page 266)

1. Heat the butter in a medium saucepan over low heat until hot. Add the onion and carrot and cook for 10 minutes or until softened without browning.
2. Add the lentils, bouquet garni, and water. Increase the heat and bring to a boil.

3. Reduce the heat and simmer, uncovered, for 25 to 30 minutes or until the lentils are tender. Drain, transfer to a bowl, cover, and set aside to keep warm.

TRUFFLED GREEN BRUSSELS SPROUTS WITH PURPLE KALE

Makes 2 cups

8 ounces green Brussels sprouts
8 ounces purple kale
2 tablespoons unsalted butter
Kosher salt and freshly ground black pepper
2 tablespoons Black Truffles in Oil (see page 175)

1. Remove the cores from the Brussels sprouts with a paring knife and separate the leaves. Cut the veins from the kale leaves.
2. In a large pot of lightly salted boiling water, blanch the Brussels sprouts and kale for 2 to 3 minutes or until just tender. Drain and immediately submerge in ice-cold water. Drain again.
3. Melt the butter in a medium sauté pan over medium-low heat. Add the Brussels sprout leaves and kale and sauté for 3 to 4 minutes or until the leaves are hot and tender. Season with salt and pepper to taste. Add the black truffles in oil. Toss to mix.
4. Transfer to a bowl and cover to keep warm.

Makes about 1 cup

12 poussin wing tips
2 tablespoons vegetable oil
1 cup chopped onion
½ cup chopped carrots
½ cup chopped celery
4 cloves garlic
1 tablespoon fresh thyme
1 tablespoon fresh rosemary
1 cup dry white wine
4 cups Roasted Chicken Demi-glace (see page 269)
Kosher salt and freshly ground white pepper

1. Rinse the poussin wing tips under cold water. Set aside.

2. In a large saucepan, heat the oil over medium-high heat and sear the wing tips on all sides until golden brown.

3. Lower the heat to medium and add the onion, carrots, celery, garlic, thyme, and rosemary. Cook, stirring occasionally, for 10 to 15 minutes or until the vegetables are golden brown.

4. Add the white wine and cook for 8 to 10 minutes or until most of the liquid has been absorbed, stirring the bottom of the pan with a wooden spoon to deglaze.

5. Add the demi-glace and bring to a simmer. Reduce the heat to low and simmer gently for 45 minutes.

6. Strain the stock through a chinois or fine-mesh sieve into a clean saucepan. Discard the vegetables and bones. Simmer the stock over low heat for 1 to 2 hours or until thick and saucelike and reduced to about 1 cup. Season to taste with salt and white pepper.

CHAPTER NINE

Game

I DIDN'T FULLY APPRECIATE GAME until I lived in the countryside of England. I went hunting for the first time in Scotland and met people for whom it's a way of life and rich in tradition. I remember picking shot out of my mouth from game birds I was served in France and realizing how close to the earth I was living and eating. I discovered that grouse, pheasant, squab, and hare were absolutely delicious and lent themselves to mouthwatering and robust preparations.

Since then, I have cooked game whenever I could. If it's seasoned, marinated, and cooked correctly, game can taste better than aged beef. It's leaner, with finer graining, less marbling, and loads of flavor. Even if you rarely cook game, I encourage you to try it every now and then. No doubt, like me, you will come to love it. So, let the game begin!

185   *Duet of Venison with Rutabaga Mash*

188   *Rabbit, Rabbit, Rabbit*

193   *Pomegranate-lacquered Muscovy Duck with Foie Gras Ravioli*

196   *Roasted Squab with Sweet Corn Flan and Gingered Spaghetti Squash*

DUET OF VENISON WITH RUTABAGA MASH

Serves 6

I came up with an earlier version of this recipe for Brasserie T, the restaurant Gale and I owned for about five years during the 1990s. It was an American-style brasserie, and we based our book *American Brasserie* on its food. We served French, Italian, and American food and cooked many of the dishes over an open wood fire. We always had a *plat du jour,* and when we served our French *plat,* we included lamb *navarin.* I serve a similar *navarin* at Tru because of the rich European tradition for this kind of dish. I want to keep the tradition alive and well.

I knew a *navarin* made with venison would taste better than one made the more traditional way, with mutton. A *navarin* is a meat ragout made with potatoes and other root vegetables. It's a rustic, earthy dish that reminds me of the stew my grandmother made in autumn when the weather cooled.

I use root vegetables, but you don't have to rely solely on them. At Tru we serve the *navarin* in its own little pot and pair it with a beautiful venison chop, which reinforces my abiding interest in layering proteins and cooking them quite differently from one another. Serving the venison with a rutabaga mash extends the root-vegetable theme—rutabagas are one of the best root vegetables of all time!

2 pounds rutabaga
2½ cups heavy cream
8 tablespoons unsalted butter
Kosher salt and freshly ground black pepper
3 tablespoons olive oil, plus extra for brushing grill
6 cups thinly sliced red onions
½ cup red wine vinegar
¼ cup grenadine
3 Forelle or other firm, ripe pears
1 vanilla bean
6 venison chops (about 4 to 6 ounces each)
3 cups Venison Navarin (recipe follows)
1 to 1½ cups Venison Sauce (recipe follows)
6 sprigs fresh lavender stems, for garnish

1. Peel the rutabaga and cut them into equal-sized chunks. Transfer to a medium-sized saucepan, add 2 cups of the cream and enough cold water to cover, and simmer over medium heat for 10 to 15 minutes or until tender. Drain the rutabaga in a colander and then run through a food mill fitted with a small-hole disk. Press the rutabaga through a chinois or fine-mesh sieve into a bowl.

2. Meanwhile, in a small saucepan, bring the remaining ½ cup of cream and 4 tablespoons of the butter to a boil over medium heat. Remove from the heat and fold into the rutabaga. Season to taste with salt and pepper. Cover and keep warm until needed.

3. Preheat the oven to 300 degrees.

4. Heat the olive oil in a large sauté pan over low heat. Add the onions and cook, stirring occasionally, for about 10 minutes or until they start to soften. Season to taste with salt and pepper. Continue to cook for 5 to 7 minutes and then add the red wine vinegar and grenadine. Cook for another 10 to 15 minutes or until all the liquid has evaporated and the onions are tender. Season to taste with salt and pepper. Cover and set aside until needed.

5. Cut the pears in half and remove the seeds with a melon baller.

6. In a large ovenproof sauté pan, melt the remaining 4 tablespoons of butter over low heat. Split the vanilla bean in half lengthwise and scrape out the seeds. Add the seeds to the melted butter. Place the pears, cut side down, in the pan and cook for 1 to 2 minutes or until they begin to brown.

7. Transfer the pan to the oven and roast the pears for 10 to 15 minutes or until tender. Lightly season with salt.

8. Prepare a charcoal or gas grill. The coals should be medium-hot.

9. Season the venison chops with salt and pepper. Rub the grill with a little olive oil to prevent the meat from sticking.

10. Grill the chops for 3 to 4 minutes on each side for medium-rare, or longer if desired.

11. To serve, spoon some of the *navarin* into 6 small pots or china cups and put one on the side of each plate. Place a small amount of the sour onions on each plate and place a quenelle (oval-shaped mound) of rutabaga

next to the onions. Place a roasted pear on top of the onions. Lean a venison chop against the pear. Drizzle a little of the venison sauce around the plate and garnish each plate with a sprig of lavender.

ABOUT THE WINE: *Many consider the steeply terraced slopes of the northern Rhône appellation of Côte-Rôtie home to the finest Syrah grapes in the world. The powerful, age-worthy wines, often softened by the addition of Viognier, are redolent of black fruit, game, and smoke flavors. A favorite to serve with this dish is one of the single-vineyard wines of Guigal. Pair the venison with Côte-Rôtie La Turque, a wine that masterfully expresses the personality of its hallowed vineyard site.*

VENISON NAVARIN

Makes 3 cups

2 pounds leg of venison meat
½ cup olive oil
1 head garlic, cloves peeled
1½ cups dry red wine
4 cups Veal or Venison Demi-glace
    (see page 268 or 270)
2 tablespoons black peppercorns
3 sprigs fresh thyme
2 bay leaves
3 ounces haricots verts
12 red pearl onions, peeled
6 baby carrots, peeled
12 shelled fresh fava beans
6 baby turnips, peeled
Kosher salt and freshly ground black pepper

1. Preheat the oven to 400 degrees.
2. Cut the venison into ½-inch cubes.
3. In a large saucepan, heat the olive oil over medium-high heat and cook the venison and garlic for 3 to 4 min-utes or until the meat is brown on all sides. Cook the meat in 2 batches, if necessary.
4. Add the red wine and simmer, stirring the bottom of the pan with a wooden spoon, for 5 to 10 minutes or until most of the wine has evaporated and the bottom of the pan is almost dry.
5. Add the demi-glace, peppercorns, thyme, and bay leaves, bring to a simmer over medium heat, cover, and transfer to the oven. Cook for 1 to 1½ hours or until the meat is tender.
6. Meanwhile, bring a large pot of lightly salted water to a boil. Blanch the haricots verts for 3 to 5 minutes or until tender. Remove with a slotted spoon and immediately submerge in ice-cold water. Drain and set aside on a paper towel. Return the water to a boil and blanch the pearl onions for 2 to 4 minutes or until tender. Remove with a slotted spoon and immediately submerge in ice-cold water. Drain and set aside on a paper towel. Repeating this process, blanch the carrots for 4 to 6 minutes or until tender, blanch the fava beans for 2 to 3 minutes or until tender, and then blanch the baby turnips for 4 to 6 minutes or until tender. Drain. Cut the haricots verts, carrots, and turnips in half.
7. When the venison is ready, remove the thyme sprigs and bay leaves and discard. Add the blanched vegetables to the venison. Season to taste with salt and pepper.

TRU

VENISON SAUCE

Makes about 1½ cups

3 cups Venison Stock (see page 264)
2 tablespoons unsalted butter
1 tablespoon grated orange zest
Kosher salt and freshly ground black pepper

1. In a saucepan, bring the stock to a boil over medium-high heat. Reduce the heat and simmer for about 15 minutes or until reduced by half.

2. Remove the pan from the heat and whisk in the butter. Stir in the orange zest and season to taste with salt and pepper. Strain through a chinois or fine-mesh sieve and serve.

Rabbit is a delicate, light-tasting meat that sadly is underutilized in the United States. When my customers try it, they generally are delighted. Because I am so fascinated with layering the proteins from the same animal, I serve lovely little rabbit chops in the form of a rack, a roasted rabbit loin, and a very rich confit of rabbit legs all on the same plate, which illustrates the progression of light to heavier, deeper flavors. Because of the intrinsic delicacy of rabbit, this is far more subtle than some of my other recipes that involve layering proteins.

I absolutely love the taste of rabbit with spaetzle, too. The first time I tried this combination was when I *staged* with Chef Albert Roux at his famous London restaurant, Le Gavroche, in the early 1990s. I also had the opportunity to *stage* at the Waterside, outside of London, with his brother Michel Roux, who is better known as a pastry chef but is also an extraordinary cook and a master at cooking rabbit as well.

6 legs from Rabbit Leg Confit (recipe follows)
6 racks of rabbit
Kosher salt and freshly ground black pepper
Olive oil, for brushing grill
½ cup Squash Puree (recipe follows)
½ cup Homemade Crème Fraîche (see page 280)
3 cups Squash Spaetzle (recipe follows)
8 ounces black trumpet mushrooms
4 tablespoons unsalted butter
1 tablespoon minced shallots
1 teaspoon fresh thyme
1 pound shelled fresh fava beans
½ cup Clarified Butter (see page 279)
6 Roasted Rabbit Loins (recipe follows)
1 cup Garlic-Chive Emulsion (recipe follows)
¾ cup Rabbit Jus (recipe follows)
1 tablespoon Black Truffles in Oil (see page 175)
6 sprigs fresh chervil, for garnish
6 edible flowers, such as pansies or nasturtiums, for garnish

Micro mizuna or other micro greens, for garnish
Cracked black pepper, for garnish

1. Preheat the oven to 350 degrees.

2. Reheat the rabbit leg confit in the oven for 10 to 15 minutes or until heated through. Remove the rabbit legs but do not turn off the oven.

3. Season the racks of rabbit with salt and pepper. Prepare a charcoal or gas grill. The coals should be medium-hot. Brush the grill with olive oil to prevent the meat from sticking. Grill the racks for 2 to 3 minutes on each side or until medium. Allow the meat to rest for 2 to 3 minutes before slicing.

4. In a small saucepan, stir together the squash puree and the crème fraîche and heat for 5 to 7 minutes over low heat until heated through. Add the squash spaetzle, season to taste with salt and pepper, and cook for 3 to 5 minutes longer or until the spaetzle are warm.

5. Split the mushrooms in half and rinse well under cold water for 10 to 15 minutes. Pat dry with paper towels. In a large sauté pan, melt 2 tablespoons of the butter over medium heat, and when foamy, add the mushrooms and sauté for 2 to 3 minutes. Add the shallots and thyme, reduce the heat to medium-low, and sauté for 2 to 3 more minutes. Season to taste with salt and pepper.

6. In a large pot of lightly salted water, blanch the fava beans for 3 to 6 minutes or until tender. Drain and immediately submerge in ice-cold water. Drain again. Dry on paper towels. In a large sauté pan, melt the remaining 2 tablespoons of butter over medium heat and sauté the fava beans for 3 to 4 minutes or until tender. Season to taste with salt and pepper.

7. In a sauté pan, heat the clarified butter over medium heat and sear the rabbit loins until golden brown on each side. Roast in the preheated oven for 5 to 7 minutes for medium meat. Cut each loin of rabbit into 3 slices.

8. To serve, spoon some of the squash spaetzle in 3 piles on a plate to make the corners of a triangle. Put some of the mushrooms on top of all the spaetzle piles. Place a rabbit leg on the point of the triangle at the top left side of the plate, atop the spaetzle. Fan out a few slices of loin of rabbit on top of the spaetzle on the opposite side of the triangle, to the right of the leg. Place the

racks of lamb on top of the spaetzle on the point of the triangle at the bottom of the plate. Spoon a little of the garlic-chive emulsion around the leg, and then drizzle a little of the rabbit jus around the loin. Drizzle some black truffles in oil around the rack. Garnish the loin with a piece of chervil; garnish the rack with edible flowers; garnish the leg with micro mizuna. Garnish the plate with fava beans and cracked black pepper. Repeat to make 5 more servings.

ABOUT THE WINE: *The delicacy of summer squash and various cuts of rabbit make this dish white-wine friendly. A wine with ample fruit and a slight oak presence is fine here. A Semillon Sauvignon Blanc–based white Bordeaux such as Château de Fieuzal possesses a wonderful creamy texture and muted fig, honey, and melon tones that will not overwhelm the subtle flavors of the dish.*

RABBIT LEG CONFIT

Makes 6 legs of confit

TRU

⅛ *cup juniper berries*

2 tablespoons black peppercorns

½ *teaspoon coriander seeds*

2 bay leaves

1 pound kosher salt

½ *pound granulated sugar*

¼ *pound light brown sugar*

1 tablespoon Sel Rose or other high-quality sea salt

6 rabbit legs (about 4 ounces each)

1 bunch flat-leaf parsley

¼ *bunch fresh sage, coarsely chopped*

¼ *bunch fresh rosemary, leaves coarsely chopped*

¼ *bunch fresh thyme, leaves coarsely chopped*

4 cups duck fat

1. In the bowl of a food processor fitted with a metal blade, combine the juniper berries, peppercorns, coriander seeds, and bay leaves and process until finely chopped.

2. Add the salt, sugars, and Sel Rose and pulse until combined. You will have to do this in 2 or 3 batches. The curing salt may be made in advance and stored in a tightly sealed container for 30 days.

3. Coat the rabbit legs with the curing salt, shaking off any excess.

4. Set a rack on a baking sheet and spread ½ bunch of the parsley over the rack. Lay the legs on the parsley in a single layer and sprinkle the chopped herbs over the legs. Cover with the remaining ½ bunch of parsley.

5. Place another rack on the parsley and top that with another baking sheet.

6. Place weights, such as soup cans, on the baking sheet, and transfer to the refrigerator. Refrigerate for 8 to 12 hours.

7. Preheat the oven to 250 degrees.

8. Remove the legs and rinse off the curing salt under cold water. Pat dry with paper towels. Place the legs in a casserole dish just large enough to hold them.

9. In a small saucepan, melt the duck fat over low heat. Pour over the legs, making sure the duck fat covers the legs. Cover with foil. Bake for 2 to 4 hours or until the meat is tender.

10. Lift the rabbit from the fat and set aside at room temperature to cool slightly. Strain the fat through a chinois or fine-mesh sieve into a bowl and set aside. When the rabbit is cool enough to handle, carefully remove the bones from the legs.

11. Transfer the meat to a casserole dish and cover with the strained duck fat. Set aside at room temperature to cool completely and then cover and refrigerate until needed.

SQUASH PUREE

Makes 2 cups

2 cups roasted butternut squash (see Note)
¼ cup Vegetable Stock (see page 266)
Kosher salt and freshly ground black pepper

1. Put the squash and vegetable stock in a blender or food processor fitted with a metal blade. Process until smooth.
2. Press through a chinois or fine-mesh sieve into a bowl. Season to taste with salt and pepper. Refrigerate until ready to use.

NOTE: *To roast the squash, halve and scoop out the seeds. Put butter in each indentation in the squash, arrange on a baking tray, cover with foil, and roast in a preheated 300-degree oven for about 1 hour or until softened. When cool, scoop the flesh from the shells and mash with a fork.*

SQUASH SPAETZLE

Makes about 3 cups

2 ⅓ cups all-purpose flour
1 tablespoon semolina flour
2 large eggs
4 large egg yolks
1 cup Squash Puree (see above)
Kosher salt and freshly ground black pepper
Olive oil, for drizzling

1. In a large bowl, combine the flours, make a well in the center, and drop the eggs and egg yolks into the well. Add the squash puree and, using your hands, mix with the flour. When the batter is moistened, season with salt and pepper.
2. Bring a large pot of salted water to a boil over high heat. Transfer the batter to a spaetzle-maker or a colan-der with ¼-inch holes. Press on the batter with a rubber spatula to force the spaetzle through the holes into the boiling water. Cook for 1 to 2 minutes or until the spaetzle bobs to the surface. Drain and immediately submerge in ice-cold water. Drain again. Spread the spaetzle out on a baking sheet and allow to cool and dry. Drizzle with olive oil to prevent sticking.

ROASTED RABBIT LOINS

Makes 6 loins

6 loins of rabbit with flap attached (3 to 4 ounces each)
3 rabbit livers
6 sage leaves
½ pound caul fat
¼ cup Clarified Butter (see page 279)
4 sprigs fresh thyme
2 tablespoons unsalted butter

1. Preheat the oven to 350 degrees.
2. Using a meat tenderizer, pound the flaps attached to the loins into even thicknesses.
3. Cut each liver into 2 slices.
4. Slice the sage leaves in half lengthwise.
5. Lay the rabbit loins on a work surface with the flaps facing away from you. Put 2 slices of the liver and 2 sage halves between the loin and the flap. Roll the loin away from you and secure the stuffing in the roll. Wrap each rolled loin in a single layer of caul fat and tie with kitchen string.
6. In a large sauté pan, heat the clarified butter over medium-high heat and sear the loins on all sides until golden brown. Add the thyme and butter and cook for 2 to 3 minutes, basting the loins with the butter.
7. Set the loins on a rack in a roasting pan and roast for 6 to 8 minutes for medium-rare, or longer if desired. Set aside at room temperature for 5 minutes to rest before slicing.

GARLIC-CHIVE EMULSION

Makes about 2 cups

1 bunch garlic chives (see Note)
2 shallots, finely chopped
5 sprigs fresh thyme
2 cups dry white wine
2 cups heavy cream
Kosher salt and freshly ground white pepper

1. In a large pot of lightly salted boiling water, blanch the garlic chives for about 1 minute or until tender. Drain and immediately submerge in ice-cold water. Drain again.

2. Transfer the chives to a blender and puree until smooth.

3. In a medium-sized saucepan, combine the shallots, thyme, and wine and bring to a boil over medium-high heat. Reduce the heat and simmer for 30 to 35 minutes or until most of the wine has evaporated and the bottom of the pan is almost dry.

4. Add the cream and simmer over low heat for 15 minutes. Add the chives to the cream mixture and strain through a chinois or fine-mesh sieve into a bowl. Season to taste with salt and white pepper.

5. Using a handheld immersion blender, whip the mixture until foamy. Use the foamy top emulsion immediately as desired.

NOTE: *Garlic chives look like chives with long, flat stems and have a distinct garlicky aroma and flavor. They can be found in farmers' markets, specialty stores, and Asian markets, where they may be called Chinese chives or* ku chai.

RABBIT JUS

Makes 1 cup

10 pounds rabbit bones
3 onions, chopped
2 carrots, chopped
½ rib celery, chopped
3 cups dry white wine
4 cloves garlic
6 sprigs fresh flat-leaf parsley
3 sprigs fresh thyme
2 fresh sage leaves
10 black peppercorns
8 quarts Chicken Stock (see page 265)

1. Preheat the oven to 450 degrees.

2. Rinse the bones well under cold water and transfer to a large roasting pan. Roast for 45 minutes to 1 hour or until deep golden brown. Stir the bones every 20 minutes during roasting.

3. Remove the bones from the pan and set aside on a plale. Add the onions, carrots, and celery to the pan and roast for about 5 minutes. Add ½ cup of the wine and stir the bottom of the pan with a wooden spoon. Continue to roast the vegetables for another 10 minutes. Add another cup of wine, stirring the bottom of the pan. Roast the vegetables for 10 more minutes or until golden brown and soft.

4. Transfer the pan to the stovetop, heat over medium-high heat, add the remaining wine, and simmer for 10 to 15 minutes or until the wine is reduced to ½ cup.

5. In a large stockpot, combine the rabbit bones, herbs, and peppercorns, and add the wine mixture and chicken stock. Bring to a rapid simmer over medium-high heat, reduce the heat, and simmer for 1 to 2 hours.

6. Strain through a chinois or fine-mesh sieve into another saucepan. Simmer over low heat for 1 to 2 hours or until it is reduced to 1 cup and has a saucelike consistency. Cool in an ice-water bath and, when cold, cover and refrigerate until needed.

POMEGRANATE-LACQUERED MUSCOVY DUCK WITH FOIE GRAS RAVIOLI

Serves 6

Years ago, I tasted a pomegranate-coated duck cooked by the late Jean Louis Paladin, the great chef-owner of Jean Louis at the Watergate in Washington, D.C., who did so much for French-American cuisine in this country and inspired me enormously. He was a generous chef whom I had the honor of cooking with several times. The time I remember most fondly was during a Cuisines of the Sun event in Hawaii during the mid-1990s, where the two of us were teamed in a cook-off and won! The experience cemented our friendship.

The sweetness of the pomegranate lacquer is amazing with the rich duck and the foie gras ravioli. Its mild acidity and subtle sweetness cut right through both, and I pull the entire dish together with the consommé. Don't be afraid to make consommé! It's quite easy and the raft magically clarifies it. Finally, I garnish this dish with lovely, graceful garlic scapes, which are garlic shoots trying to go to seed. If left uncut in the garden, the pods on the ends of the scapes burst and the garlic self-seeds.

1½ teaspoons star anise

1 cinnamon stick

4 cloves

½ cup grated fresh ginger

1 cup rice wine vinegar

2 cups soy sauce

6 cups pomegranate juice

2 cups molasses

1 cup honey

6 4- to 6-ounce duck breasts

½ cup finely diced carrots

½ cup finely diced celery

½ cup finely diced yellow summer squash

½ cup finely diced zucchini

24 Foie Gras Ravioli (recipe follows)

3 cups Duck Consommé (recipe follows)

About 2 tablespoons chopped chives, for garnish

6 long garlic scapes, for garnish

1. In a large saucepan, combine the star anise, cinnamon stick, cloves, and ginger and stir over medium heat. Stir in the rice wine vinegar, soy sauce, pomegranate juice, molasses, and, finally, the honey. Bring to a simmer, reduce the heat to low, and simmer for 45 minutes to 1 hour or until reduced to about 1 cup.

2. Strain through a chinois or fine-mesh sieve into a bowl. Set the lacquer aside until needed.

3. Preheat the oven to 350 degrees.

4. Score the duck breasts in a crosshatch pattern, making sure the marks cut through the fat but do not penetrate the meat.

5. In a large sauté pan set over low heat, sauté the breasts, skin side down, for 8 to 9 minutes or until most of the fat has drained and the skin is crispy. Turn the breasts over and sear for 1 to 2 minutes until a crust forms.

6. Generously brush both sides of the breasts with some of the lacquer.

7. Transfer the breasts, skin side up, to a rack set in a roasting pan and roast for 8 to 10 minutes for medium. Transfer to a plate and let rest for 10 minutes. Brush the breasts with another coat of lacquer, if desired.

8. Just before serving, put the vegetables in a strainer and submerge in boiling water to blanch. (You can use the water from the ravioli.) Remove and use immediately. You may have to do this in batches.

9. To serve, put 4 ravioli in a shallow bowl with a sixth of the blanched vegetables. Ladle hot duck consommé over the ravioli. Sprinkle with chopped chives. Slice each breast into 5 or 6 pieces and lay on top of the ravioli. Garnish each dish with a garlic scape. Repeat to make 5 more servings.

ABOUT THE WINE: *This robust Muscovy duck with its sweet spiced glaze calls for a New World version of Pinot Noir. Oregon's Willamette Valley produces some of the country's most exciting interpretations of this finicky grape. The hillside vineyards of Domaine Serene yield fruit that result in viscous, full-bodied wines with sweet blueberry, cherry, and spice flavors. The Grace Vineyard bottling is a special treat with this dish.*

FOIE GRAS RAVIOLI

Makes 24 ravioli

48 wonton wrappers
1 large egg
2 tablespoons water
6 ounces foie gras terrine (see page 103), or foie gras

1. Lay 24 wonton wrappers on a work surface.

2. Mix the egg with the water and brush the wonton skins with the egg wash.

3. Place about ¼ to ½ teaspoon of the foie gras terrine in the center of each wonton. Top each wrapper with another wrapper and press to seal the edges around the filling. Using a ring cutter, cut out rounds. The ravioli can be frozen at this point.

4. To serve, bring a large pot of lightly salted water to a boil. Add the wontons and cook for 3 to 5 minutes or until cooked through and the wontons bob to the surface of the pot. Remove the wontons with a slotted spoon or spider and serve immediately.

2. In a large stockpot, combine the duck stock with the ground vegetables and meat.

3. Whisking constantly, bring the stock to a simmer over low heat. As soon as a coagulated froth (called a raft) forms on the surface of the liquid, stop whisking. Use the handle of a wooden spoon to poke a hole through the raft so that the stock can bubble through the hole without breaking the raft. Cook at a bare simmer, undisturbed, for 1 hour. At the end of the cooking time, the raft will be a solid crust and the consommé will be clear.

4. Line a chinois or fine-mesh sieve with several layers of moistened cheesecloth or a large coffee filter and set over a large pot. Ladle the consommé up through the hole in the raft into the lined sieve, being careful not to break up the raft more than necessary, and strain. Allow the consommé to cool, then cover and refrigerate until needed. Discard the raft.

DUCK CONSOMMÉ

Makes about 12 cups

½ cup coarsely chopped onion
½ cup coarsely chopped carrots
½ cup coarsely chopped celery
½ pound boned duck or chicken meat, trimmed of fat
1 cup lightly beaten egg whites
1 tablespoon white wine vinegar
16 cups Duck Stock (see page 265)

1. Put the onion, carrots, celery, and duck meat in a meat grinder fitted with the coarse blade, or a food processor fitted with the metal chopping blade, and grind until coarse. Add the egg whites and mix until thoroughly incorporated. Mix in the vinegar.

This is a dish that comes right from my heart. Since my first bite, I have adored squab for its mildness, lightness, and moistness. For a game bird, it's extremely tender and pairs with many different ingredients. I am also a big fan of spaghetti squash, which complements the creaminess of the flan I make with it. I tasted the best spaghetti squash of my life when I was cooking with my good friend chef Michael Chiarello when he was at Tra Vingne in California's Napa Valley. He roasted it in a wood-burning oven with butter, cinnamon, ginger, and vanilla. Outrageous!

The coriander salt kicks up the dish with another element of flavor, accented by the lemon syrup and jus on the plate. What great flavors: citrus, game, corn, and coriander. At Tru, we follow this dish a little later with a small salad garnished with the squab leg, sort of like "part two" of the dish. Squab: the sequel!

*2 breasts of squab (about 8 ounces each),
    or 4 breast halves*

Kosher salt and freshly ground black pepper

6 tablespoons unsalted butter

1 tablespoon minced garlic

4 ounces fresh spinach

1 to 2 cups Roasted Spaghetti Squash (recipe follows)

⅛ teaspoon minced fresh ginger

1 cup Squab Jus (recipe follows)

4 Sweet Corn Flans (recipe follows)

1 cup Frisée and Watercress Salad (recipe follows)

4 Braised Squab Legs (recipe follows)

8 yellow corn shoots, or other micro greens, for garnish

Fresh thyme, for garnish

*2 teaspoons Lemon Verbena Syrup (recipe follows),
    for garnish*

Coriander Salt (recipe follows), for garnish

1. Preheat the oven to 450 degrees.

2. Season the squab breasts with salt and pepper to taste. In a large ovenproof sauté pan, melt 1 tablespoon of the butter over medium-high heat and sear the breasts on both sides until golden brown. Transfer the pan to the oven and roast the squab, skin side up, for about 4 to 5 minutes or until medium-rare. Remove the squab from the pan and set aside on a plate to rest for 5 to 10 minutes.

3. Melt 2 tablespoons of the butter in a large sauté pan over medium-high heat. Add the garlic and sauté for 10 seconds or until fragrant. Add the spinach and toss for 1 to 2 minutes or until wilted. Season to taste with salt and pepper.

4. Melt 1 tablespoon of the butter in a large sauté pan over medium heat. Add the roasted spaghetti squash and ginger and sauté for 3 to 4 minutes or until heated through. Season to taste with salt and pepper.

5. In a small saucepan, bring the squab jus to a boil over medium heat and whisk in the remaining 2 tablespoons of butter. Remove from the heat, cover, and keep warm.

6. Remove the squab breasts from the bone and cut each half into 6 slices.

7. To serve, spoon a small mound of spaghetti squash into the center of a plate and top with sautéed spinach. Arrange 6 slices of squab breast over the spinach. Unmold a corn flan onto the plate. Place approximately ¼ cup of the salad on the plate across from the flan and rest a squab leg against the salad. Lay 2 corn shoots next to it. Drizzle squab jus around the plate. Garnish the plate with the thyme and lemon verbena syrup. Sprinkle the dish with coriander salt. Repeat to make 3 more servings.

ABOUT THE WINE: *The full-flavored meat of the squab is playfully accented by the aromatic gingered spaghetti squash. Perfumed, spicy wines from the southern Rhône work beautifully with this dish. Château Rayas in the historic Châteauneuf-du-Pape appellation produces hedonistically styled wines from 100 percent Grenache. The full-bodied framboise liqueur and herbes de Provence personality of the wine add a further exotic dimension to this dish.*

ROASTED SPAGHETTI SQUASH

Makes 1 to 2 cups

1 1- to 2-pound spaghetti squash, halved
2 tablespoons unsalted butter, at room temperature
1 tablespoon grated fresh nutmeg
Kosher salt and freshly ground black pepper

1. Preheat the oven to 375 degrees.
2. Rub the cut halves of the squash with butter and season with the nutmeg and salt and pepper.
3. Put the squash halves, cut sides up, on a rack on a baking sheet and roast for about 1 hour or until soft. Set aside at room temperature to cool. Scrape out the squash flesh and set aside until needed.

SQUAB JUS

Makes about 1 cup

2 pounds squab wings, necks, and back bones
2 tablespoons Clarified Butter (see page 279)
2 chopped shallots
2 ribs celery, chopped
1 carrot, chopped
½ onion, chopped
3 cups dry red wine
16 cups water
2 sprigs fresh rosemary
2 sprigs thyme

1. Rinse the squab bones under cold water.
2. Heat a cast-iron skillet over medium heat until hot. Add the clarified butter and the squab bones and cook, stirring occasionally, for 15 minutes or until the bones are golden brown. Add the shallots, celery, carrot, and onion and cook for another 15 minutes or until the vegetables have softened and are nicely browned.
3. Add the red wine and bring to a simmer over medium-

high heat. Reduce the heat and simmer for 20 minutes or until reduced by half.

4. Transfer the bones and vegetables to a large stockpot. Add the water and bring to a simmer over low heat. Simmer for 2 to 3 hours or until reduced by half. Using a slotted spoon or spider, remove the bones and vegetables and discard. Add the herbs to the pot and continue to simmer slowly for 2 to 3 hours or until reduced to 1 cup. Strain through a chinois or fine-mesh sieve into a bowl. Allow to cool in an ice-water bath. Cover and refrigerate until chilled, then remove the layer of congealed fat from the surface. Transfer to a covered storage container and refrigerate for up to 3 days.

SWEET CORN FLAN

Makes 4 flans

4 ears fresh sweet corn
1 tablespoon unsalted butter
Kosher salt and freshly ground white pepper
1 ½ cups heavy cream
2 large eggs
4 large egg yolks

1. Slice the corn kernels from the ears of corn.
2. In a sauté pan, melt the butter over medium heat and sauté the corn kernels for 2 to 3 minutes or until soft. Season to taste with salt and white pepper.
3. In a small saucepan, scald ½ cup of the cream over medium-high heat and then pour over the corn. Transfer to a blender and puree until smooth. Strain through a chinois or fine-mesh sieve into a bowl. Set aside to cool to room temperature.
4. Preheat the oven to 300 degrees.
5. Lightly whisk the eggs and eggs yolks together in a small bowl.
6. In the small saucepan, scald the remaining cup of cream over medium heat. Remove from the heat and

whisk in the corn puree. Whisk a little of the cream and puree mixture into the eggs to temper them and then whisk the eggs into the hot mixture. Season to taste with salt and pepper.

7. Spray the inside of each of 4 2-ounce flan molds with vegetable spray. Fill each about three quarters full. Put the flan molds in a roasting pan and pour enough water into the pan to come halfway up the sides of the molds. Carefully transfer the pan to the oven and bake for 1 to 1½ hours or until set.

8. Remove from the oven and lay a mold on its side. Using your finger, gently release the flan from the side of the mold. All in one motion, turn the mold upside down on the plate. Lift the mold from the flan; it should pop out.

FRISÉE AND WATERCRESS SALAD

Makes about 1 cup

¾ cup frisée (about 8 ounces), trimmed and cut into
    ½-inch-long pieces
¼ cup watercress leaves (about 6 ounces)
1 tablespoon extra-virgin olive oil
Kosher salt and freshly ground white pepper

In a mixing bowl, toss the frisée with the watercress. Drizzle with the olive oil, toss, and taste. Adjust the oil and season to taste with salt and white pepper. Serve immediately.

BRAISED SQUAB LEGS

Makes 12 legs

12 squab legs (1 to 2 ounces each)
Kosher salt and freshly ground black pepper
2 tablespoons olive oil
¼ cup chopped onion
¼ cup chopped carrots
¼ cup chopped celery
¼ cup chopped leeks
1 bay leaf
½ cup Madeira wine
4 cups Chicken Stock (see page 265)

1. Preheat the oven to 275 degrees.

2. Season the squab legs with salt and pepper.

3. In a large sauté pan, heat the olive oil over medium-high heat and sear the legs on both sides until golden brown. Remove from the pan and set aside. Add the onion, carrots, celery, leeks, and bay leaf to the pan and sauté for 10 minutes or until the vegetables have softened and are nicely browned.

4. Reduce the heat to medium, add the Madeira wine, stirring the bottom of the pan with a wooden spoon, and cook for 5 to 8 minutes or until the wine has evaporated and the bottom of the pan is almost dry.

5. Return the squab legs to the pan, and then add the chicken stock. Bring to a boil over medium heat. When boiling, cover with parchment paper or aluminum foil. Transfer to the oven and cook for 45 minutes to 1 hour or until the legs are tender.

LEMON VERBENA SYRUP

Makes 1 cup

1 medium lemon, for zest
2 cups granulated sugar
1 ¼ cups fresh lemon juice
¾ cup water

1. Using a vegetable peeler, remove the zest from the lemon, avoiding any white pith.
2. In a small saucepan, combine all the ingredients and bring to a simmer over low heat. Simmer gently for 20 to 30 minutes or until syrupy. Remove the zest with a spider or slotted spoon, chop finely, and return to the syrup.
3. Transfer to a glass jar or bowl and set aside to cool. Cover and refrigerate until needed.

CORIANDER SALT

Makes about ½ cup

3 tablespoons coriander seeds
9 tablespoons kosher salt

1. In a dry sauté pan, toast the coriander seeds over medium heat for 3 to 4 minutes.
2. Transfer the seeds to a spice grinder and grind to a coarse powder. Pour the powder into a small bowl. Add the salt and stir to mix thoroughly.

Tru Desserts

by Gale Gand

ONCE RICK'S PART OF THE MEAL is over, I exuberantly jump into the mix. Who doesn't love dessert? Many of Tru's most popular are on these pages and represent much of what I do as the pastry chef. In some respects, my dessert menu echoes Rick's savory one. I serve dessert collections that include an *amuse-bouche*, followed by two more dessert courses: the main event—the actual dessert   and then the petit four. As I am a pastry chef–owner, we have a very pastrycentric restaurant.

Presenting dessert after a meal as magnificent as the ones Tru serves is an art. Very few of our customers skip dessert, and most eagerly anticipate it. To meet this anticipation, I put enormous energy into flavor and texture combinations designed to clear the palate and then excite the taste buds for the symphony of sensations that are Tru's desserts.

When I design the cheese, *amuse-bouche*, dessert, and petit four repertoire, I not only look forward but I look back. I consider the dishes Rick and our staff have prepared and work off those tastes, sensations, and textures. It's not an easy task, and many of our guests comment on how much they enjoy the dessert courses, even though when they were done with the savory courses they were not sure "if there was any more room at the inn!" The dessert *amuse-bouche*, in particular, is a small bite meant to clear the palate and refresh the diner, to prepare all five senses for the exciting treats and treasures to come.

Customers who order collections, or tasting menus, are treated to a three-course dessert tasting. Designing the dessert tasting to complement the savory menu is one of the most gratifying challenges of being the executive pastry chef at Tru.

We also serve dessert collections, consisting of a dessert *amuse-bouche*, a fruit and custard duo, a chocolate duo, a mini root beer float (I make my own root beer), and selections from the petit four cart. The duos are pairings of two matched demi desserts that offset each other with tastes, textures, temperatures, and appearances. For example, I serve the tiny Apricot Tarte

Tatin with Cinnamon Flan for the fruit and custard duo, and the Concord Cake with Mocha Panna Cotta for the chocolate duo. Each guest gets a different combination of desserts, so everyone can, spoons and forks willing, sample a range of tastes and textures.

Finally, the Tru meal closes with a selection of our estate and hand-picked teas, brewed for the correct amount of time for the particular tea, or freshly brewed coffee. We are as dedicated to our tea and coffee service as we are to the entire meal.

MY DESSERT HERITAGE

I didn't plan to be a pastry chef when I was growing up in Chicago. Instead, I was raised to be an artist. My dad was a musician and my mom was a sculptor. I can still remember the day my father came home from his downtown high-powered sales job and threw away all his suits and ties! I was about ten years old and it made quite an impression on me. He opened a music store in our village, gave guitar lessons, and began his career as a professional folk singer. From that day on, I worked in our music store after school and during the summers. I already knew how to play the guitar, mandolin, banjo, and dulcimer, and soon I joined Dad giving lessons.

I owe a lot of how I view my work and my craft to my family. My brother and I joined our father to form the Gand Family Singers. We performed on holidays and weekends, at Disney World, the World's Fair in Montreal, and similar venues around the country. It has never seemed strange to me to travel, to work on weekends, or to work with my family. This attitude is compatible with the restaurant business, where you are the one "making the party happen," and so expect to work nights and weekends. It's part of the package. And I love it!

Both my parents encouraged my interest in art as well as in music. I went to art school in Cleveland for three years and, to make ends meet, worked as a waitress in a vegetarian restaurant. One day the boss tossed me an apron and asked if I could cook. Although I objected, she insisted I pitch in. I can

still remember the moment I walked into the kitchen. For the first three seconds I was terrified. By the fourth second I was calm and confident. I was home! This was where I was meant to be.

I took some time off after three years of art school and traveled to France. I needed to go to the heart of the culinary universe and see if, as an American girl, I thought I could really do it. After a summer eating and *staging* in France, I was surer than ever—but my parents weren't thrilled. My mother, a dyed-in-the-wool feminist, told me she had struggled to stay *out* of the kitchen; my father was worried I would never get a college degree and would spend my life in greasy short-order kitchens. I moved to Rochester, New York, and finished my BFA degree at the Rochester Institute of Technology's School for American Craftsmen, studying silver- and goldsmithing.

I went to school during the day and, seduced by food, worked nights as the pastry chef for the University Club in Rochester. Greg Bowman was the chef. After graduation, I set up a studio in Rochester and started making a living as a full-time artist and part-time caterer. One afternoon, Greg appeared at my door and asked me to come work for him at the Strathallen Hotel, where he was then the chef. I begged off, but he refused to leave until I agreed. I think I always knew I would end up in a kitchen. My twenty-seventh birthday was coming up and I reasoned this would be the perfect gift: the opportunity to do what I really loved to do and in the medium I liked most—food!

My natural inclination for pastries and desserts happily permitted me to draw on my training and love of design, color, and style, and for a while I was content (it's closer to jewelry-making than you'd think). But after two years I hit a creative wall. I wanted some formal training—and knew I wanted to get it in France. I signed up for a two-week course at La Varenne, a culinary school in Paris (now relocated to Burgundy). I took a month off from the restaurant, scraped my pennies together, and off I went. After taking classes at the school, I *staged* in some of the best pastry shops in Paris and Brittany. The next summer, I repeated the experience. I couldn't afford more education than those two summers at La Varenne, but they provided me with a enormous amount of knowledge and confidence.

I had taught myself to bake from books. The teachers at La Varenne reassured me I had learned correctly. I have always believed in breaking rules, but I also believe you need to know the rules before you can break them. There is a lot to be said for good technique, and as I have worked on mine I have proudly joined a long line of pastry chefs. I have also connected to France, the motherland for pastry chefs.

THE TRU PASTRY KITCHEN

My staff and I have a great responsibility at Tru: What comes out of the pastry kitchen makes the first and the last impression on our guests. First is the bread, last are the sweets. We also make garnitures for many of Rick's savory preparations, including brioche for caviar, foie gras, and bread puddings. If he needs anything that involves flour, I am there.

This makes the Tru pastry kitchen an interesting place to work. We are very much part of the bigger savory kitchen, yet remain our own entity. My staff is a close, smoothly run team.

The lead pastry person has the only day job on our team, and so it's a coveted position. She arrives early to start things that need a lot of time, such as the brioche, which must proof, and the *cannelés,* which take several days to make and then hours to bake. She has to plan so that they bake in our single convection oven and are cooled in time to be wrapped in cellophane for that evening's guests. We make as many as four hundred *cannelés* a day!

By the afternoon, the lead pastry cook is joined by the first and second platers and the petit four person. First plater is in charge of evening service, ably assisted by the second plater. While the first plater prepares the desserts, the second plater is in charge of ice cream and sorbet. She or he also is responsible for tending the ovens for hot desserts and making our nightly duo of soufflés.

The petit four person is in charge of the dessert *amuse-bouche* and the petit four cart. She makes the garnishes and the toasts for the cheese cart and keeps it looking fresh and inviting throughout the evening. This is a fun spot, because petit fours lend themselves to quick creativity and whimsy.

The final person on our staff is the roundsman. Her job is to work a different station every day so the others can have a day off. This is tough, because you really have to know exactly what is going on in the kitchen and be able to fill in at any minute. I encourage everyone on my staff to take different stations whenever they can. We call this cross-training. You learn so much.

When customers, friends, or journalists ask me what my favorite part of the job is, I have to answer, "cooking in the kitchen." Too much of my day is filled with meetings and paperwork, and I cherish the time I have to cook alongside my staff and to teach them new recipes and techniques. I also love coming up with new ideas.

Ideas come from anywhere and everywhere: from a painting I might see in a gallery or a book I might read; from an heirloom recipe from my mom or grandmother; from a childhood memory; from a dessert or pastry I taste when I travel; or from a penny candy I haven't tried in a while. When I think of people I miss or haven't seen in years, I might remember something they like to eat or a meal we shared.

Creating a new dish is a two-way street. It comes from my heart and so is a part of me and my senses, but it's also a part of the person who will eat it. Maintaining the high level of excellence demanded by a restaurant of Tru's caliber is as challenging as it is gratifying and exciting. It also creates an atmosphere in which you are never totally satisfied. I can't rest on my past successes for too long, but always push myself to create even more dramatic, explosive, and seductive desserts. I love them all.

CHAPTER TEN

The Cheese Course

THE CHEESE COURSE IS A pleasing, appealing bridge between savory dishes and dessert. At Tru, we offer at least fifteen different cheeses on our cheese cart every night. I spend hours educating the staff about these various cow's milk, sheep's milk, and goat's milk cheeses through tastings, workshops, and visits from cheesemakers. This means they are able to guide customers to satisfying, tempting, even exhilarating samplings.

A few years back I looked into my culinary crystal ball and predicted the cheese course would come into its own. I think that day is finally here. Selecting our cheeses is one of the best parts of my job as partner and executive pastry chef at Tru. It's how I got my nickname, "the Dairy Queen." I travel extensively throughout the United States, Canada, and Europe, and as I do, I visit large and small cheesemakers, farms, cheese shops, and restaurants. I taste and then taste again—always on the lookout for innovation, interesting flavors, and, quite simply, the best. American artisanal cheesemakers are nothing short of excellent, and these days they can hold their own with their European counterparts. Our country is in the midst of an exciting renaissance when it comes to cheesemaking, and the result is a tasty, sophisticated body of work. I am pleased to serve local Midwest cheeses and other American cheeses side by side with some of the finest from Europe, which broadens our guests' overall culinary experience with a glorious range of tastes and textures.

Pairing cheeses with complementary garnitures is the creative part for me. I combine saltiness with sweet apricots, creaminess with crisp cornmeal shortbread, butteriness with chewy panforte, and mellowness with intense oven-roasted tomatoes. In the recipes that follow, I am specific about the exact cheese to use. I intentionally don't provide a choice, but actually name the cheese that works best on the plate. Once you understand the style of the cheese, you can make your own substitutions with the help of a good cheese shop, but I strongly recommend beginning with the cheese I identify, if possible.

Cheese Notes

CHEESE IS ONE OF THE oldest foods known to man. Cheesemaking is the practice of harnessing bacteria in dairy products for the benefit of flavor and texture. *Affinage/affiner,* or the aging process, which the French perfected, could be called the "finishing school" for cheeses and elevates cheesemaking to an art form. France boasts some 675 varieties of cheeses.

Cheese is made of three ingredients:

- *Milk* that has been soured—from cows, sheep, or goats (or yaks in China)
- *Rennet,* which is an enzyme used to coagulate the milk
- *Salt* for flavor and to encourage the release of moisture

There are three types of cheese production:

- *Fermier or farmstead cheeses* are made from milk that comes from that cheesemaker's herds only and the cheese is produced by hand.
- *Artisanal cheeses* are made from milk from the same controlled region, and the cheese is produced by hand.
- *Industrial cheeses* are made from milk that comes from anywhere and the cheese is produced with the aid of heavy machinery.

There are three types of rinds:

- *Flourished rind,* with or without ash, is usually white and fluffy and looks like velour. It's generally mild-flavored, although it can be strong, and, while edible, it is not always eaten. The application of a mold such as *Penicillium candidum* results in a flourished rind.
- *Washed rind* is usually yellow and almost wet-looking, with a sticky, moist consistency and a pungent flavor. It usually is not eaten. Salt water or a spirit is used to wash the rind. Generally, it is not eaten and is coated with harmless b-linen mold.
- *Natural rind,* with or without ash, herbs, or bandaged with cheesecloth, looks dry and may look gray and thick. It is the skin that develops naturally as the cheese develops. It absorbs dirt and keeps out air. It's inedible. Ash helps the cheese dry.

Cow's milk cheeses are broken into the following categories:

- *Single cream,* which is 45 to 64 percent butterfat
- *Double cream,* which is 65 to 74 percent butterfat
- *Triple cream,* which is at least 75 percent butterfat

Sheep's milk is inherently 50 percent butterfat and rarely increases beyond that percentage. Goat's milk has butterfat percentages lower than sheep's milk.

210   *Pleasant Ridge Reserve with Organic Honey and Panforte*

213   *Oil-marinated Manchego with Oven-roasted Tomatoes*

214   *Roquefort with Pear Chips and Hot Honey Walnuts*

217   *Wabash Cannonball with Cherries and Rosemary*

I tasted a similar panforte in Italy a few years ago in a little restaurant in the walled city of San Gimignano and was so enchanted I brought a few wheels home. Rich Melman took one bite and declared this the best thing I had ever made. Oops! I had not made it, but brought it from Italy. I quickly learned how from my friend, California pastry chef Nancy Silverton, and now my version is on Tru's menu. The recipe makes more than you will need here, but it's tricky to make a smaller batch. Luckily, they keep for months.

The farmstead cheese, made in Dodgeville, Wisconsin, won Best in Show at the 2001 American Cheese Society Conference—and for good reason. It is dense with only a few gas holes, a smooth but not creamy texture, and a buttery flavor with overtones of clover, wildflowers, and herbs. The cheesemaker makes this from raw cow's milk from a single herd. Once the cheese is made in a five-pound wheel with a natural rind, it's aged for up to six months.

Rice paper
1½ cups whole almonds, skins on and toasted (see Note)
½ cup plus 1 tablespoon all-purpose flour
½ tablespoon unsweetened cocoa powder
½ teaspoon ground cinnamon
½ teaspoon finely ground black pepper
Scant ½ teaspoon ground ginger
⅛ teaspoon ground cardamom
⅛ teaspoon freshly grated nutmeg
1 pound 2 ounces dried fruit, such as raisins, figs,
*   cherries, plums, apricots, currants, or a*
*   mixture, cut into ½-inch pieces*
½ cup granulated sugar
⅓ cup plus 2 tablespoons honey, preferably organic
3 tablespoons water
2 ounces Pleasant Ridge Reserve cheese from
*   Uplands Dairy, at room temperature*

1. Preheat the oven to 300 degrees.

2. Lay a sheet of parchment paper on a sheet pan and put a piece of rice paper on top of the parchment paper. Put 4 flan rings measuring 4 inches wide and ½ inch deep on the rice paper.

3. In a large bowl, stir together the nuts with the flour, cocoa, cinnamon, pepper, ginger, cardamom, and nutmeg. Add the fruit and toss to coat it with the dry ingredients.

4. In a small, heavy saucepan, combine the sugar, ⅓ cup of the honey, and water and bring to a boil without stirring. Brush down the sides of the pan occasionally with a wet pastry brush to prevent crystals from forming. Cook until a candy thermometer registers 240 degrees, the soft-ball stage. You may have to tip the pan to submerge the tip of the thermometer. Pour over the fruit mixture and stir quickly to combine. The mixture will be very sticky and thick.

5. Dip your hands in cold water to prevent burns and sticking, and grab handfuls of the mixture. Pack firmly into the rings so that the mixture reaches the top rim. Bake for about 1 hour or until slightly puffed and the surface no longer looks shiny. Cool the panforte on a wire rack, still in the rings and on the sheet pan.

6. While the rings are still warm, cut around the inside of the rings through the rice paper to remove the ring. Wrap the entire panforte in plastic wrap and store at room temperature or serve right away.

7. To serve, put a slice of cheese on a plate. Drizzle with some of the remaining 2 tablespoons of honey. Cut 1 panforte into 6 wedges. Snuggle a wedge of panforte next to the cheese. Repeat to make 3 to 5 more servings. The remaining panfortes keep at room temperature for up to 2 months, wrapped in plastic.

NOTE: *To roast whole almonds, spread them on a baking sheet and roast in a 350-degree oven for 10 to 15 minutes or until the nuts are fragrant and done. Shake the pan 2 or 3 times for even roasting. If all you have are blanched almonds, toast them till they are golden brown.*

ABOUT THE WINE: *Tuscan Vin Santo, a sweet wine made from air-dried grapes, is a ringer for this cheese-and-fruit combination. The panforte ingredients echo the flavors of the wine and complement the buttery nature of the cheese.*

OIL-MARINATED MANCHEGO WITH OVEN-ROASTED TOMATOES

Serves 4 to 6

When I buy Manchego cheese, I buy wheels of Don Enrique, which is artisanal cheese with an herb crust. Happily, this type of raw sheep's milk cheese is getting popular in the United States, and you can find nice ones at good cheese shops. It's aged in caves in Spain from three months to a year and may be pure white or slightly ivory in color. Its mild nuttiness is wonderful with slow-roasted tomatoes flavored with the best extra-virgin olive oil you can find, and then served on chewy ciabatta bread.

I am fond of sheep's milk cheeses in general. The milk is sweeter with a higher lactose content than other milks, and generally has a 50 percent butterfat content. It's higher in calcium than cow's milk and usually easier to digest.

OIL-MARINATED MANCHEGO:

1 6-ounce wedge Manchego cheese
2 cups extra-virgin olive oil
12 black peppercorns
1 ½-inch strip of orange rind from a whole orange
2 sprigs fresh thyme or rosemary

OVEN-ROASTED TOMATOES:

6 plum tomatoes
¼ cup extra-virgin olive oil
2 teaspoons herbes de Provence (see Note)
½ teaspoon coarse salt
¼ teaspoon freshly ground black pepper
8 to 12 thick slices ciabatta or similar crusty bread

1. Up to 1 month and at least 2 days before serving, marinate the cheese. Cut the cheese into ¼-inch-thick triangular slices and put them in a glass jar with a lid. Add the olive oil, peppercorns, orange rind, and thyme, cover with the lid, and refrigerate.

2. To roast the tomatoes, preheat the oven to 325 degrees.

3. Cut the tomatoes in half lengthwise (if they are extra large, cut them into lengthwise quarters). Lay them on a baking sheet, drizzle with olive oil, and sprinkle with herbes de Provence, salt, and pepper.

4. Roast for about 2 hours or until still moist and chewy. Check occasionally to make sure the edges don't get too brown. When done, the edges will look lightly toasted and the tomatoes, dried and wrinkled.

5. Use immediately or store in an airtight container and refrigerate for up to 2 days. Let the tomatoes come to room temperature before serving.

6. To serve, lift a wedge of cheese from the marinade and let the marinade drip back into the jar. Put the cheese on a cheese plate, and tuck a few pieces of roasted tomato next to the cheese. Repeat to make 3 to 5 more servings. Serve each plate with 1 or 2 slices of bread. Put the jar holding the remaining cheese on the table for extra helpings and to show off the marinade.

NOTE: *Herbes de Provence is a mixture of dried herbs commonly used in the south of France and contains dry basil, fennel seed, lavender, marjoram, rosemary, sage, summer savory, and thyme.*

ABOUT THE WINE: *A dry Oloroso picks up the nutty flavor of the Manchego and artfully negotiates the acidity of the tomatoes. A solera-matured Jerez de la Frontera wine is a fine choice.*

ROQUEFORT WITH PEAR CHIPS AND HOT HONEY WALNUTS

Serves 6 to 8

If you've wondered if Roquefort cheese truly is aged in caves, it is. Rick and I visited the limestone caves of Cambalou in the Aquitaine region of France, where you see row upon row of white wheels of cheese on shelves built into the cool, moist underground caverns. This nutty, slightly sharp cheese has been called "the cheese of kings" and "the king of cheeses," and for good reason. In 1411, King Charles VI of France signed a charter to control and protect the cheese's quality, and the French honor it to this day.

The charming legend surrounding Roquefort is that centuries before Charles VI celebrated the cheese, a shepherd put a sandwich of plain bread and sheep's milk cheese in a cave to keep it cool. Distracted by some danger, the shepherd fled with his sheep and didn't return to the region for months, and when he did, he discovered his sandwich had turned into a marvelous, blue-veined cheese. The rest is history.

The cheese is made from sheep's milk, which must come from the region where the cheese is made. The curds are packed by hand into molds and layered with powder made from the naturally occurring *Penicillium roqueforti.* (Some cheeses are injected with *Penicillium.*) The cheese is aged for sixty to ninety days, rubbed with dry salt, and turned several times a day to distribute the moisture evenly. The air wafting through the caves is cool and humid, and nowadays is carefully monitored. The air itself contains tiny particles of the *Penicillium.*

Roquefort is a great favorite with many cheese lovers, and I like to show off its indescribable properties with spicy walnuts and thin, chewy pear chips.

PEAR CHIPS:
1 cup sugar
1 cup water
1 or 2 Bartlett pears

HONEY WALNUTS:
1 tablespoon honey, preferably organic
2 teaspoons olive oil
¼ teaspoon cayenne pepper
1 cup walnut halves

—

2 cups baby frisée
1 teaspoon extra-virgin olive oil
½ teaspoon lemon juice
Kosher salt and freshly ground black pepper

—

1 4-ounce wedge Roquefort cheese
4 tablespoons unsalted butter
6 to 8 slices French-style baguette

1. To make the pear chips, preheat the oven to 200 degrees. Line a baking sheet with a Silpat sheet.

2. Combine the sugar and water in a saucepan and bring to a boil over medium-high heat. Cook for 2 to 3 minutes or until the sugar dissolves. Remove from the heat and let cool for 5 minutes.

3. Slice the pear into very thin slices, using a mandolin or sharp knife. You will need at least 8 slices and may need only 1 pear. Dip each slice in the slightly cooled syrup and lay in a single layer on the baking sheet. Bake for about 2 hours until crisp but not colored. Check the chips several times during baking. To check for doneness, peel a slice off the baking sheet, let it cool on the countertop for 1 minute, and then try to break it. If it does not break crisply, the chips are not done.

4. When done, peel the chips off the baking sheet and let them cool on the countertop. Use immediately or store in an airtight container for up to 3 days.

5. To prepare the walnuts, preheat the oven to 375 degrees. Grease a baking sheet.

6. Combine the honey, olive oil, and cayenne in a mixing bowl. Add the walnuts and toss until well coated. Spread on the baking sheet and bake for 10 to 15 minutes. Check them every 5 minutes to make sure they don't burn. Stir the nuts after 10 minutes, turning them for even cooking.

7. Let the nuts cool on the baking sheet. Use immediately or store in an airtight container for up to 7 days.

8. In a small bowl, toss the frisée with the olive oil and lemon juice. Season to taste with salt and pepper.

9. To serve, put a piece of cheese on a cheese plate and lean a pear chip against it. Arrange a few walnut halves on the plate. Butter a slice of bread and set it on the plate. The bread and butter mellow the flavor of the cheese. Put a little frisée salad next to the cheese. Repeat to make 5 or 7 more servings.

ABOUT THE WINE: *There are several delectable alternatives to enjoy with this cheese dish. A late-harvest Tokay Pinot Gris counters the spicy element and tames the sharpness of the cheese. Sauternes and Monbazillac are viscous, ethereal choices. Banyuls, Maury, and Madeira partner with the nuts and honey and defuse the aggressive nature of the Roquefort.*

WABASH CANNONBALL WITH CHERRIES AND ROSEMARY

Serves 4

One spring, our son Gio and I spent a week at Judy Schad's wonderful Capriole Farm in Greenville, Indiana, not far from Louisville, Kentucky. It was a magical week for us, and I returned to Chicago refreshed and more excited about goat's milk cheeses than ever.

Judy's cheeses are true farmstead cheeses. Not only does she milk her own goat herd and make the cheese exclusively from its milk, but she raises the hay the goats eat! A completely sustainable operation. These little three-ounce balls of curd are hand-rolled and Judy coats them in vegetable ash and lets them age for eight to ten days. The result? A flourishing white rind and a creamy interior. I love the tart citrus flavor of these gems. Ask your favorite cheese shop to order some for you. You won't be disappointed.

½ cup port wine
1 cinnamon stick
½ vanilla bean, split
1 large sprig fresh rosemary, leaves stripped from
    the stem
1 cup fresh Mount Rainier or Bing cherries, pitted
1 3-ounce Wabash Cannonball, at room temperature

1. In an 8-inch sauté pan, combine the port, cinnamon stick, vanilla bean, and rosemary leaves (reserving a few for garnish) and bring to a simmer over medium heat. Remove from the heat and let the mixture steep for about 5 minutes to meld the flavors. Strain through a fine-mesh sieve, reserving the liquid.

2. Return the strained port to the pan, bring to a boil over medium heat, and add the cherries. Gently shake the pan to toss and roll the cherries in the hot port for only 10 seconds, just until barely cooked. Remove from the heat and set aside to cool completely.

3. Cut the Wabash Cannonball into 8 wedges. Put 2 wedges on a cheese plate and spoon some of the cher-ries next to the cheese. Drizzle with a little of the syrupy port and tuck a few rosemary leaves among the cherries. Repeat to make 3 more servings.

ABOUT THE WINE: *A glass of fruity California zinfandel plays up the cherry-and-port theme. For an elegant turn, a glass of mature sparkling rosé provides an interesting textural contrast.*

CHAPTER ELEVEN

Dessert Amuse-Bouche

THE DESSERT FOCUS OF THE TRU MEAL begins with a dessert *amuse-bouche*. As you leaf through the pages of this chapter, you will find fruit-based treats, such as blueberries and tangerines in basil-infused syrup, an icy little clementine granita with a raspberry-mint salad, and a lemonade shooter. All light, refreshing, and playful, devised to restore, soothe, and prepare the palate. The *amuse-bouche* course is the intermission before the all-important final act of the meal.

I start the dessert progression with one of these little bites, meant to inspire and please. These work well at home, too, as a prelude to a larger, more elaborate dessert, or on their own as a finale. Have fun with these; play with the presentation and flavors. They truly are charming.

221 *Szechuan Peppercorn Crème Brûlée Spoonfuls*

222 *Blueberry and Perfection Tangerines with Basil Syrup*

222 *Clementine Granita with Raspberry Micro Mint Salad*

223 *Roasted Lemonade Shooters*

Makes 10 to 15 spoons

This makes a spectacular presentation. I like the elegance of long-handled iced-tea spoons arranged on a large platter, either in rows if the platter is rectangular, or like the spokes of a wheel if it's round. I call for coarse sugar, which is the kind of sugar you find on top of sugar cookies. In the trade it's called "con AA," for confectioners' AA sugar, which refers to the grain size. You might find it in baking-supply stores or specialty markets, or you can order it through baking catalogs such as King Arthur's.

1 cup heavy cream
⅓ cup half-and-half
¼ vanilla bean, split lengthwise
1½ teaspoons Szechuan peppercorns
4 large egg yolks
¼ cup granulated sugar
¼ cup con AA, raw, or demerara sugar
5 to 8 fresh or canned lychees, peeled (if fresh) and
*   halved (if canned, squeeze lime juice over them)*

1. Preheat the oven to 300 degrees.
2. In a medium-sized saucepan set over medium heat, heat the cream, half-and-half, vanilla bean, and Szechuan peppercorns just to a boil. Remove from the heat and set aside for about 10 minutes to infuse the flavors.
3. In a large mixing bowl, whisk the egg yolks and granulated sugar just until mixed. Whisking constantly, gradually pour in the hot cream mixture and whisk until blended.
4. Strain through a fine-mesh sieve into an 8-inch-square nonaluminum baking pan to remove the vanilla bean and peppercorns. Put the baking pan in a larger pan and set on the middle rack of the oven. Pour enough hot water into the larger pan to come halfway up the sides of the baking pan.
5. Bake for 40 to 50 minutes or until set but not too firm. (The crème brûlée will cook a little further as it cools.) Remove the pan from the water bath and let cool

for 15 minutes. Cover tightly with plastic wrap, making sure the plastic wrap does not touch the surface of the custard. Refrigerate for at least 1 hour or up to 3 days.
6. Up to 4 hours before serving, fill decorative, long-handled spoons with the chilled custard by scooping each spoon into the pan of custard. Round the tops with a small spatula or a butter knife. Set on a baking sheet and refrigerate.
7. Right before serving, top each spoonful of custard with an even sprinkling of coarse sugar and return to the baking sheet. Fire up the kitchen torch and move the flame in a circular motion over the spoons to caramelize them evenly for about 1 minute or until the sugar melts and turns brown. Cool for 1 minute before serving.
8. To serve, place a spoon on a plate and nestle a lychee half next to it.

BLUEBERRY AND PERFECTION TANGERINES WITH BASIL SYRUP

Serves 8

When I eat a juicy, sweet tangerine during our long, cold Chicago winters, it's like a tropical vacation in my mouth! Citrus fruit is a great cheer-you-up in the cold months, and tangerines are one of my favorites. Perfection tangerines are perfect little fruits that are especially sweet and available only in the wintertime. If you can't find them, substitute another tangerine or even clementines.

2 cups fresh basil leaves
1 cup fresh spinach leaves
1½ cups light corn syrup
2 Perfection tangerines or other small tangerines
*   or clementines, peeled, strings removed,*
*   sectioned, and chilled*
½ pint blueberries, stemmed, rinsed, and chilled
1 teaspoon basil blossoms, optional

1. Fill a metal bowl with ice and water.

2. Blanch the basil and spinach leaves in a saucepan of boiling water set over medium-high heat for about 10 seconds. Using a spider or slotted spoon, lift the leaves from the boiling water and transfer them to the ice bath. When cold, squeeze as much moisture as possible from the leaves.

3. Put the leaves and corn syrup in a blender and puree for about 2 minutes until very smooth. Strain through a chinois or fine-mesh sieve into a bowl, if desired. Cover and refrigerate until needed.

4. To serve, toss the tangerine sections with the blueberries. Spoon the fruit onto each of 8 individual plates. Drizzle with basil syrup, making sure some of the beautiful green syrup shows on the plate. Sprinkle each plate with a few basil blossoms.

CLEMENTINE GRANITA WITH RASPBERRY MICRO MINT SALAD

Serves 8 to 10

Granita is an icy treat that you can make in the freezer without the aid of an ice-cream machine. Its name derives from the word *granite* because as it freezes it forms sparkling specks—like granite. The sweet clementine juice is lovely here, made just tart enough with lemon juice.

¼ cup water
¼ cup plus 1 to 2 tablespoons granulated sugar
¼ split vanilla bean
2 cups freshly squeezed clementine juice
2 tablespoons fresh lemon juice
1 pint raspberries
1 tablespoon micro mint sprouts
8 to 10 micro mint sprigs, for garnish

1. To prepare the clementine granita, in a saucepan, bring the water, ¼ cup of the sugar, and the vanilla bean to a boil over medium-high heat. Remove from the heat, and set aside to steep for about 10 minutes for the flavors to infuse and the syrup to cool. Remove the vanilla bean.

2. In a shallow metal pan, whisk together the clementine juice, lemon juice, and syrup. Taste and add more lemon juice if necessary. Freeze for 10 to 12 hours or overnight.

3. Using a large spoon, scrape the frozen juice into crystallized shavings and put in a freezer-safe container. Cover and freeze.

4. Put half the raspberries in a fine-mesh sieve and mash with a spoon into a bowl to remove the seeds. Sweeten to taste with 1 to 2 tablespoons of sugar.

5. Toss the remaining berries with the puree. Fold in the mint sprouts.

6. To serve, spoon some granita into a small frozen dish or frozen Asian soup spoon. Lay on a plate and serve with a spoonful of the raspberry salad. Garnish with a mint sprig. Repeat to make 7 to 9 more servings.

ROASTED LEMONADE SHOOTERS

Serves 6 to 8

I learned to make a lemon drink very much like this one from Mark Dissin, one of the producers for *Sweet Dreams,* my Food Network television series. Though he's a producer now, he used to be a line cook, and he told me about roasting lemons to intensify their flavor. What a wonderful tip. I took this back to Tru and tried it as an *amuse-bouche.* Rich Melman just loved it, and so it has stayed on our menu ever since. Sometimes I make more than needed and freeze the extra in mini ice-cube trays, and then use the frozen cubes to chill the drink. (A small raspberry or a perfect mint leaf in each cube dresses them up.) There's something about this shooter that's familiar yet exotic. The roasted lemon keeps it in the comfort zone but boosts it just enough to make it special.

12 lemons
½ cup granulated sugar, plus more for sweetening
½ vanilla bean, scraped
4 to 6 cups water
½ cup freshly squeezed lemon juice
Granulated sugar, to taste
Coarse, raw, or demerara sugar, optional

1. Preheat the oven to 375 degrees.
2. Soften the lemons by rolling them under the palm of your hand or by microwaving them for 30 seconds. Halve the lemons. Transfer to a roasting pan and add ½ cup of the sugar, the vanilla bean, and enough water to cover the lemons. Roast for about 30 minutes, stirring occasionally, until the edges of the lemons begin to caramelize. Remove the pan from the oven and set aside to cool to room temperature.
3. Set a strainer over the bowl of a food processor fitted with the metal blade. Lift the lemons from the roasting liquid and squeeze the lemon juice through the strainer into the food processor.
4. Pour the roasting liquid through a strainer or fine-mesh sieve into the food processor. Seed and roughly chop 2 of the lemon halves, put in the food processor, and process until smooth.
5. Strain into a large pitcher. Add the 4 to 6 cups of water, lemon juice, and sugar to taste. Stir well and refrigerate until cold.
6. Dip the rims of frozen shooter or other glasses in water and then in coarse sugar. Using a kitchen torch, carefully caramelize the sugared rims. Take care that the glasses do not crack. Pour the lemonade into the glasses.

Desserts

NOW IS THE TIME FOR true indulgence. At first, many of my desserts sound familiar, but upon closer inspection you will find something wildly unexpected. The warm chocolate tarts are cuddled next to refreshing almond-flavored sorbet; and a cold chocolate semifreddo is served with chocolate "paint" enhanced with Earl Grey tea (the tea gets its distinctive flavor from citrusy bergamot).

My customers have a passion for chocolate. I pair it with oranges, coconut, strawberries, and coffee—and that's just for starters. Every week in the Tru pastry kitchen, we go through pounds of the finest bitter, semisweet, milk, and white chocolate I can find. I urge you to seek out quality chocolates, too. They are increasingly available and, while more expensive than run-of-the-mill supermarket brands, are well worth it in flavor. Beyond chocolate, we serve desserts made with *fromage blanc*, crème fraîche, and luscious berries, passion fruit, and lychees. Taste them, compare, and enjoy the overall experience.

227 *Tequila Granita with Yuzu Cream and Grapefruit*

229 *Concord Cakes with Coconut Sorbet*

231 *Warm Chocolate Tart with Toasted Almond Milk Sherbet*

235 *Chocolate-Malted Semifreddo with Chocolate-Bergamot Paint*

239 *Roasted Pineapple Carpaccio with Key Lime Sherbet*

243 *Fromage Blanc Mousse*

246 *Apricot Tarte Tatin*

TEQUILA GRANITA WITH YUZU CREAM AND GRAPEFRUIT

Makes 10 servings

When the invitation comes for the Masters of Food and Wine in Carmel, California, I am there! Not only do I enjoy the event, but a trip to warm, sunny California in the middle of a dreary, frigid Chicago February gives me a little taste of summer. This is exactly how I feel about this dessert; it's a little taste of summer.

One of my assistants and I sampled a grapefruit granita in Carmel one year and were so taken with it that when we got back to the Tru pastry kitchen, we decided to make a similar one. That very week, I received a box of fresh lychees from Melissa's/ World Variety Produce, Inc. Now I was really excited! We made a tequila and lime juice ice and garnished with it yuzu cream and lychees. Yuzu, an Asian citrus fruit, is always in our cooler as whole fruit and juiced in bottles. Citrus brightens up any dish and makes it more vibrant, exciting, and fresh-tasting. This is no exception.

1 ½ cups freshly squeezed lime juice
1 ½ cups Simple Syrup (see page 279)
½ cup tequila
2 sheets gelatin
Yuzu Cream (recipe follows)
1 grapefruit, peeled and cut into thin segments,
*   for garnish*
10 fresh lychees, peeled and halved, for garnish
Rose Petal Ribbons (recipe follows), for garnish

1. In a bowl, whisk together the lime juice, simple syrup, and tequila. Set aside.
2. Meanwhile, soak the gelatin sheets in cool water for about 2 minutes. Carefully lift the gelatin sheets from the water and squeeze them gently with your hands.
3. Put ½ cup of the lime juice mixture in a saucepan. Add the gelatin sheets and warm gently over low heat, swirling until the gelatin melts. Remove from the heat and stir in the rest of the liquid.
4. Pour into a shallow metal pan and freeze overnight or

for at least 8 hours. Scrape and place in a freezer container and freeze until ready to serve. The granita will naturally break up as it's scraped.
5. Put a mound of granita in the center of a small bowl. Surround it with a thick ring of yuzu cream and top with grapefruit segments and then lychee halves. Place a rose petal ribbon on top. Repeat to make 9 more servings.

YUZU CREAM

Makes about 3 cups

2 ½ cups heavy cream
3 ½ tablespoons granulated sugar
1 ½ tablespoons yuzu juice or a mixture of freshly
*   squeezed lemon and lime juices*

In the bowl of an electric mixer set on medium-high speed, combine the cream, sugar, and yuzu juice. Beat only until very, very soft peaks form. Set aside. It will thicken further as it sits.

ROSE PETAL RIBBONS

Makes about 10 ribbons

2 cups granulated sugar
¾ cup water
¼ cup glucose (see Note)
½ cup dried rosebuds, with the cores of the
*   buds removed (see Note)*

1. In a saucepan with a candy thermometer clipped to the side, combine the sugar, water, and glucose and heat to 305 degrees over medium heat without stirring.
2. Remove the pan from the heat and carefully and gently stir in the rose petals. Pour onto a Silpat-lined bak-

ing sheet or greased marble or granite countertop and let cool.

3. Preheat the oven to 300 degrees.

4. Warm the rose petal sugar in the oven for 2 to 4 minutes, just until soft.

5. The sugar will be pliable and ready to pull into very thin ribbons and abstract shapes. To do so, pull off a small hunk and stretch it with your fingers and thumbs, as if you were molding and pulling clay. If your hands are sensitive, wear latex gloves. If the sugar is too loose and droops, let it cool a bit. If the sugar is too stiff, return it to the oven until pliable.

6. Lay the ribbons on foam rubber pads and store in an airtight container with limestone pebbles (see Note) lining the bottom. The pebbles absorb moisture so that the ribbons keep their shape.

NOTE: *Glucose is available in some specialty stores and pharmacies.*

Dried rosebuds are sold in bulk at Whole Foods and health food stores.

Gray limestone pebbles are available from candy-making stores and outlets.

CONCORD CAKES WITH COCONUT SORBET

Serves 8

Much of my training comes from books, and I confess that Gaston Lenotre's 1977 classic pastry book, *Lenotre's Desserts and Pastries,* is my dog-eared, page-worn bible. I learned to make this traditional French cake from the book, after tasting it in one of Lenotre's Paris pastry shops and just adoring it. Since then I have changed just about everything to make it my own. It remains a lovely contrast of light, crisp meringue layered with a rich chocolate cake and soft, smooth ganache. Wonderful flavors and sensations! My cake is small with a cocoa-meringue layer, the ganache is spiked with fresh ginger, and I serve it with a smooth coconut sorbet. I love the combination of dark bitter chocolate and sweet, sweet coconut, like a Mounds bar.

COCOA MERINGUE:

¼ cup egg whites (approximately 2 large egg whites)
¼ cup granulated sugar
½ cup powdered sugar
1½ tablespoons unsweetened Dutch-processed
   cocoa powder

GINGER GANACHE:

1 pound semisweet chocolate, coarsely chopped
1 cup heavy cream
¼ cup water
1-inch-long piece fresh ginger, peeled and
   sliced into rounds

CHOCOLATE CAKE:

3 cups granulated sugar
2¾ cups all-purpose flour
1 cup plus 2 tablespoons unsweetened alkalized
   cocoa powder
2¼ teaspoons baking powder
2¼ teaspoons baking soda
1½ teaspoons salt
3 large eggs
1½ cups whole milk

¾ cup flavorless vegetable oil, such as
   canola or safflower
1 tablespoon pure vanilla extract
1½ cups very hot water

—

Cocoa powder, for sprinkling
Powdered sugar, for sprinkling
Coconut Sorbet (recipe follows)

1. To make the meringue, preheat the oven to 250 degrees. Line 2 12-by-17-inch jellyroll or sheet pans with parchment paper.

2. In the bowl of an electric mixer fitted with the wire whisk and set on medium-high speed, whip the egg whites until they almost form soft peaks. Gradually add the granulated sugar and continue whipping until stiff and glossy and the sugar is dissolved.

3. Spoon the powdered sugar and the cocoa powder into a fine-mesh strainer or sifter and sprinkle a third of the mixture over the top of the meringue. Fold into the meringue and repeat 2 more times.

4. Transfer half of the meringue to a pastry bag fitted with a small plain tip and pipe round, spiraled bases onto one of the prepared pans. Each base should measure about 2 inches in diameter. You are making bases for metal collars (see Note), in which you will build the cakes, so be sure the bases are smaller than the collars. You will need only 8 bases, but make extra if you can because meringue breaks easily.

5. Pipe the remaining meringue into long, thin strips that run the entire length of the other pan. If you still have extra meringue after piping it onto the pan, pipe the rest onto another pan.

6. Bake the meringue for about 1½ hours or until dry and stiff. When baked, let cool and then wrap the entire pan with plastic wrap to keep the meringue dry.

7. To make the ganache, put the chocolate in a metal bowl.

8. Put the cream, water, and ginger slices in a saucepan and bring to a boil over medium-high heat. Immediately remove from the heat and set aside to steep for about 10 minutes. Return to the heat and bring to a boil one more time. Pour the mixture over the chocolate to melt it.

Whisk until the chocolate is melted and smooth. Pour the ganache through a chinois or fine-mesh sieve to strain out the ginger. Use immediately or cover and chill for up to 48 hours.

9. To bake the cake, preheat the oven to 350 degrees. Grease a 12-by-17-inch jelly-roll or sheet pan. Line the bottom and up the sides with parchment paper.

10. Sift the sugar, flour, cocoa, baking powder, baking soda, and salt into the bowl of an electric mixer fitted with the wire whisk, and blend for a few seconds. Alternatively, sift the dry ingredients into a bowl and use a handheld electric mixer to blend.

11. In another bowl, whisk together the eggs, milk, oil, and vanilla extract. Add to the dry ingredients and mix at low speed for about 5 minutes, until well blended. Gradually add the hot water, mixing at low speed just until combined. The batter will be quite thin.

12. Pour into the pan and bake for 25 to 30 minutes, until a tester inserted in the center of the cake comes out clean or a few crumbs cling to it and the center feels firm to the touch. Set the pan on wire racks and let the cake cool in the pan. Cover and refrigerate or freeze until you are ready to cut the cake.

13. To cut the cake, use 2-inch-round biscuit or cookie cutters. Cut out 8 rounds and keep them chilled until it's time to assemble the dessert. You may have leftover cake.

14. To assemble the cakes, arrange 8 2-inch-deep, 2¼-inch wide metal collars on a parchment-paper-lined jelly-roll or half-sheet pan.

15. Set a meringue disk inside each one.

16. Warm the ganache until it's barely pourable but not too hot or thin. To do so, put the ganache in a tempered glass pitcher and set it in a saucepan of water that has come to a boil and then been removed from the heat. Watch the ganache carefully until it reaches the right consistency. Alternatively, warm the ganache in a microwave oven.

17. Pour the ganache over the meringue to cover and fill the collars halfway up. Chill for 10 minutes to harden slightly. Set a round of cake on top of the chilled ganache. Pour more ganache over the cake to cover it completely and fill the collar to the rim. The surface may be a little bumpy, which is fine.

18. Arrange 8 dessert plates on the work surface.

19. Gently set a filled collar on each plate. Use a blowtorch or a hot, well-wrung damp cloth to warm the outside of the metal collars, and lift the ring off the dessert. The heat of the blowtorch or cloth will allow the cake to slip out of the collar.

20. Let the cakes sit at room temperature for 1 hour. Just before serving, press the meringue sticks, broken into 1- to 2-inch-long pieces, to the outside wall of the cakes. The sticks should extend above the cakes and point toward the ceiling. Fill in the center of the cakes with meringue sticks.

21. Sprinkle cocoa powder and powdered sugar over the cakes. Put a scoop of coconut sorbet on each plate.

NOTE: *You can buy metal collars in candy-making supply outlets and specialty cookware sites online.*

COCONUT SORBET

Serves 8 to 10

1¼ cups sweetened coconut puree (see Note)
¾ cup Simple Syrup (see page 279)
½ cup water

1. Whisk together the puree, simple syrup, and water in a metal bowl. Cover and chill for at least 2 hours or until cold.

2. Pour the chilled mixture into an ice-cream machine and process according to the manufacturer's instructions. Scrape into a freezer-safe container and freeze for at least 2 hours until firm.

NOTE: *Sweetened coconut puree can be ordered at www.trurestaurant.com*

WARM CHOCOLATE TART WITH TOASTED ALMOND MILK SHERBET

Makes 6 tarts

When a self-professed chocoholic arrives at Tru, this is the dessert we recommend. It satisfies the most primal need for pure chocolate in a nearly unadulterated form. I fill a crumbly, dark cocoa crust with an oozing dark chocolate filling and then garnish it with all things chocolate: chocolate nibs, cocoa foam, and shards of bittersweet chocolate. These are offset by strawberries and toasted almond sherbet, but it's the chocolate that shines in this creation.

CHOCOLATE SABLE:

3 ¼ cups all-purpose flour
⅞ cup granulated sugar
¾ cup unsweetened cocoa powder
1 cup plus 6 tablespoons chilled unsalted butter
2 large egg yolks
1 tablespoon heavy cream
1 tablespoon pure vanilla extract

MELTED CHOCOLATE FILLING:

5 ounces bittersweet chocolate, coarsely chopped
½ cup plus 3 tablespoons unsalted butter
3 large eggs
3 large egg yolks
1 ½ cups powdered sugar
½ cup all-purpose flour
Powdered sugar, for dusting
Cocoa powder, for dusting
Cocoa nibs (see Note), for garnish
Toasted Almond Milk Sherbet (recipe follows)
Strawberry Balsamic Butter (recipe follows)
Cocoa Foam (recipe follows)
12 to 16 tablespoons halved fresh strawberries, for garnish
Irregular shards of bittersweet chocolate, for garnish

1. To make the sable crust, in the bowl of an electric mixer fitted with the paddle attachment and set on low, mix together the flour, sugar, cocoa powder, and the butter until sandy.

2. In a separate bowl, whisk together the yolks, cream, and vanilla extract. Add to the dry ingredients and mix just until the dough comes together. Turn out onto a work surface, form into a disk, wrap in wax paper or plastic wrap, and refrigerate overnight or for at least 4 hours.

3. Cut the disk in half and return the half you are not working with to the refrigerator. (It softens quickly at room temperature.) On a lightly floured surface, roll the disk half to a thickness of ⅛ inch. Put 3 4-inch tart rings or low individual tart pans on a baking sheet. Line the rings with the dough, pushing it well into the corners. Repeat with the other half of the dough and 3 more tart rings.

4. Using a small, sharp knife, trim the edges. Refrigerate the filled rings for at least 20 minutes.

5. To make the filling, in the top of a double boiler or in a heavy saucepan set over medium-low heat, melt the chocolate and butter together, stirring until smooth. Set aside to cool slightly.

6. In a separate bowl, whisk together the eggs and egg yolks. Add the powdered sugar and whisk to blend. Stir into the melted chocolate mixture and then whisk in the flour. Use right away or cover and refrigerate for up to 3 days.

7. Preheat the oven to 375 degrees.

8. Line the tart rings with plastic wrap and fill each with rice to weight them down. Gather the plastic around the rice to make a bundle. Bake for about 8 minutes or until set. Remove the plastic and rice. Bake for about 4 minutes longer, until crisp.

9. Fill the baked shells all the way to the rim with chocolate filling. At this point they can sit for 4 hours at room temperature or can be refrigerated overnight. Bring them to room temperature for baking. Bake for about 8 minutes or until the filling is set, appears mostly opaque, and is slightly puffy with a single shiny spot in the center. To serve, sprinkle the tarts with powdered sugar and cocoa powder and then put on plates. Put a pile of cocoa nibs on top of each tart and set a quenelle (oval-shaped mound) of toasted almond milk sherbet on top.

10. Draw 2 lines of strawberry balsamic butter and place 2 swatches of cocoa foam on each plate. Cascade chopped strawberries off each tart onto the plate and garnish with shards of chocolate.

NOTE: *These little bits of cocoa-bean pieces are available from the Scharffen Berger Chocolate Company in California.*

TOASTED ALMOND MILK SHERBET

Makes about 2 quarts

4 cups sliced almonds
4 cups whole milk, plus more as needed
4 cups chilled Simple Syrup (see page 279)
2 vanilla beans

1. Preheat the oven to 375 degrees.
2. Spread the almonds on a baking sheet or pan and toast for 10 to 12 minutes, shaking the pan 2 or 3 times during roasting, until the nuts are dark brown and very toasty and fragrant.
3. Add the hot, toasted almonds to the milk, stir, and set aside to steep until the milk cools completely.
4. Transfer to a blender and puree until smooth. Strain through a chinois or fine-mesh sieve into a large liquid-measuring cup. Add enough milk to measure 4 cups. Pour into a bowl.
5. Whisk in the simple syrup and scrape the seeds from the vanilla bean into the milk. Freeze in an ice-cream machine following the manufacturer's instructions.

STRAWBERRY BALSAMIC BUTTER

Makes about 1 cup

1 cup Strawberry Juice (recipe follows)
½ cup balsamic vinegar
2 tablespoons unsalted butter, cut into pieces and slightly softened

1. In a saucepan, combine the strawberry juice and balsamic vinegar and cook over medium-high heat for 10 to 12 minutes or until reduced to ½ cup and a syruplike consistency.
2. Whisk in the butter 1 piece at a time, not adding the next piece until the previous is completely incorporated. Whisk constantly to make a thick sauce. Keep warm in a toasty spot on the stove or in a warm, turned-off oven until ready to use. Do not cover or the sauce could break when the heat builds up.

STRAWBERRY JUICE

Makes 2 to 3 cups

6 pints strawberries, hulled and roughly chopped
1 cup granulated sugar

1. In the top of a double boiler or a metal bowl, combine the strawberries and sugar and cover with plastic wrap. Place over water, making sure the water does not touch the bottom of the bowl.
2. Cook over low heat so that the water barely simmers for 1 hour and 15 minutes or until the berry pieces are floating in liquid.
3. Line a bowl with cheesecloth and pour the mixture into the bowl. Set aside to drain for at least 2 hours at room temperature or overnight in the refrigerator. Some solids will pass through the cheesecloth, which is fine.
4. Carefully pour off the clear red juice and chill. (Save the berry "skulls" for ice cream.)

COCOA FOAM

Makes about 2½ cups

2½ cups skim milk
3 tablespoons Ganache (recipe follows)
4 tablespoons unsalted butter

1. In a saucepan, combine the milk, ganache, and butter and bring to a gentle simmer over medium-low heat.
2. Using a handheld immersion blender, blend the mixture to create foam. Skim off the foam and use it immediately.

GANACHE

Makes about ¾ cup

4 ounces semisweet chocolate, coarsely chopped
¾ cup heavy cream

1. Put the chopped chocolate in a bowl.
2. In a saucepan, heat the cream over medium heat just
to the boiling point. Pour the hot cream over the chopped
chocolate and whisk to melt and combine. Transfer to a
bowl and refrigerate until firm. Store covered in the refrigerator for up to 5 days.

CHOCOLATE-MALTED SEMIFREDDO WITH CHOCOLATE-BERGAMOT PAINT

Serves 15 to 20

This recipe is all about my childhood love affair with Fudgsicles combined with my abiding affection for the flavor of malt. Malt powder was a staple in our house when my brother and I were growing up, and my mom often whipped up chocolate malteds in the blender. They were so good! I decided to combine these favorite flavors in a semifreddo, which is a frozen dessert with a lighter texture than ice cream. My semifreddo is lightened with whipped egg whites, beaten cream, and whipped egg yolks, all folded into the chocolate mixture to insert air.

The "boings" are tricky at first, but once you get the hang of them, they are pretty easy. I remember making them to order for 350 guests at the Aspen *Food & Wine* Classic. That was tough! Because of the altitude, the sugar never caramelized quite right and was hard to keep from crystallizing.

Finally, I serve this dessert with *tuiles* flavored with cayenne. When Sara Moulton was a guest on my Food Network show, *Sweet Dreams,* she made very similar ones. I thought they would taste great with chocolate and they do—after all, historically, chocolate and chili go together.

CHOCOLATE MIXTURE:

8 large yolks
⅔ cup granulated sugar
½ cup plus 1 tablespoon whole milk
¼ cup Vanilla Brandy (recipe follows), or brandy
¼ cup malt powder
1 vanilla bean, split
1 cup semisweet chocolate pistols, or coarsely chopped
    semisweet chocolate

CREAM AND MERINGUE:

3½ cups heavy cream
⅓ cup large egg whites (from 2 to 3 eggs)
¼ cup granulated sugar

TO SERVE:

Chocolate-Bergamot Paint (recipe follows)
24-karat Gold Syrup (recipe follows)
About 1 cup finely chopped semisweet chocolate
Cocoa powder, for sprinkling
Powdered sugar, for sprinkling
Pistachio Chili Tuiles (recipe follows)
Caramel Boings (recipe follows)
Oranges in Star Anise (recipe follows)

1. To make the chocolate mixture, line 15 to 20 2½-inch-wide round collars with strips of 2-inch-wide acetate and put them in the freezer. Alternatively, line cupcake tins with paper liners and set aside.

2. In a large metal bowl, whisk together the yolks, sugar, milk, brandy, and malt powder. Add the vanilla bean. Set the bowl over a saucepan holding simmering water. Do not let the bottom of the bowl touch the water. Whisking constantly, cook over medium heat until the mixture thickens and ribbons back on the surface when the whisk is lifted. Remove from the heat and lift out the vanilla bean. Rinse the bean and set aside to dry. (Use it to flavor sugar or brandy.) Whisk the chocolate into the hot mixture until melted and the mixture is smooth and evenly colored. Set aside to cool almost completely.

3. To prepare the cream and meringue, in the bowl of an electric mixer fitted with the wire whisk, whip the cream until stiff peaks form. Refrigerate to keep chilled.

4. In another clean, dry bowl of an electric mixer fitted with the wire whisk, beat the egg whites until nearly stiff. Gradually add the sugar and continue beating until stiff peaks form.

5. Fold the whites into the chocolate mixture in thirds. Do not worry if specks of whites remain in the mixture. Fold the chilled cream into the mixture just until blended. Pour into the collars or cupcake tins, filling them to within ¼ inch of the rim. Freeze for at least 8 hours or overnight.

6. To serve, paint a large swatch of chocolate-bergamot paint on a white plate. Drizzle a swipe of 24-karat gold syrup next to it.

7. Take a semifreddo from the freezer and remove the collar. Spread the chopped chocolate in a shallow dish

and dip the bottom of the semifreddo in it to coat. Sprinkle the top with cocoa powder and then powdered sugar. Remove the acetate and set the semifreddo half on, half off the chocolate paint. Insert a *tuile* in the center of the semifreddo. Lean a boing against the side of the semifreddo. Arrange 2 orange segments on the plate and serve immediately.

VANILLA BRANDY

Makes about 2 cups

2 cups brandy
6 used vanilla beans or 1 fresh vanilla bean, halved

1. Pour the brandy into a glass jar with a lid. Add the vanilla beans and cover.
2. Before using, set aside for 2 days to give the vanilla time to infuse the brandy. The brandy will keep for up to 6 months. Replenish the brandy as you use it. Start fresh when it begins to lose its vanilla flavor.

CHOCOLATE-BERGAMOT PAINT

Makes about 2½ cups

4 ounces unsweetened chocolate
9 ounces semisweet chocolate
½ cup light corn syrup
1 cup strong brewed Earl Grey tea

1. In the top of a double boiler set over barely simmering water, melt the chocolate until smooth.
2. Add the corn syrup and tea at the same time and whisk until smooth. The mixture will appear to break, but if you keep whisking it will come together. Cover and keep warm until ready to use.

24-KARAT GOLD SYRUP

Makes 1 cup

1 cup light corn syrup
1 teaspoon 24-karat gold dust (see Note)

In a small bowl, whisk together the ingredients and keep chilled until ready to use.

NOTE: *Gold dust is sold in gourmet or baking-supply stores.*

PISTACHIO CHILI TUILES

Makes about 30 tuiles

½ cup granulated sugar
5 tablespoons unsalted butter
3 tablespoons light corn syrup
½ cup chopped pistachios
3 tablespoons all-purpose flour
2 tablespoons cornmeal
1 tablespoon fresh lemon juice
¾ teaspoon cayenne pepper

1. Preheat the oven to 325 degrees. Line a baking sheet with a Silpat. (You may need more than 1 baking sheet.)
2. In a small saucepan, bring the sugar, butter, and corn syrup to a boil over medium heat and cook, stirring, for 1 minute.
3. Remove from the heat and stir in the pistachios, flour, cornmeal, lemon juice, and cayenne pepper until well mixed. Let the batter cool to room temperature.
4. Roll the batter into tiny balls, about the size of large chickpeas, between your palms. Arrange about 3 inches apart on the Silpat and bake for 10 to 15 minutes or until the balls have spread, turned glassy, and are light golden brown. Cool on the pan and then remove carefully with a spatula. Store in an airtight container until needed.

CARAMEL BOINGS

Makes about 40 boings

2 cups sugar
½ cup water

1. Pour the sugar into the center of a deep saucepan. Carefully pour the water around the sides of the pan, trying not to splash any sugar onto the sides. Do not stir but gently draw your finger through the water and then twice through the center of the sugar, making a cross, to moisten it. Bring to a full boil over high heat and cook without stirring for 10 to 15 minutes or until amber-colored. Swirl the mixture occasionally to even out the color. Test the color of the caramel periodically by putting a drop on a white plate. When it's slightly lighter than you want, submerge the bottom of the saucepan in an ice-water bath to stop the cooking. (It will continue to cook and darken.) Swirl the pan for even cooling.

2. Meanwhile, oil a sharpening steel very lightly with flavorless vegetable oil. When the caramel has cooled enough to fall slowly from a spoon, gather up about 1 tablespoon and hold it over the sharpening steel, and hold that over the saucepan. Let a strand of caramel fall from the spoon, and wind the strand of caramel over the steel to form a 3-inch coil, or springlike shape. When the coil reaches the end of the steel, pinch the end to cut it. Let it cool for about 10 seconds on the steel and then slide off onto a sheet of parchment paper folded like an accordion. This keeps the boings from sticking to each other. Repeat to make about 40 coils, or boings. Rest the saucepan on a folded kitchen towel to keep it from cooling too quickly. If the caramel cools too much to work with, return to gentle heat until it reaches the correct consistency.

3. Store in an airtight container, with a sheet of accordion-folded parchment paper between each boing.

ORANGES IN STAR ANISE

Makes about 2 cups

1 cup water
1 cup granulated sugar
1 teaspoon star anise pieces
¼ vanilla bean
1 orange, cut away from the membrane to form natural segments (supremes)

1. In a saucepan, combine the water, sugar, star anise, and vanilla bean and bring to a boil over medium-high heat. Remove from the heat and cool slightly.

2. Add the orange segments and let cool. Cover and let the oranges macerate in the refrigerator for at least 8 hours or up to 3 days.

ROASTED PINEAPPLE CARPACCIO WITH KEY LIME SHERBET

Serves 8

This was the very first dessert I developed for Tru, and it embodies what our desserts should be: simple and refreshing, beautiful and light. There's enough going on to make this complex, and yet it maintains its simplicity. I roast the pineapple, which is a savory technique not often found in the pastry kitchen. As the fruit roasts, its carbohydrates cross over to the sweet side, caramelize, and convert to sugar. Even the normally inedible core becomes tender and edible. I slice it thin, like carpaccio, and serve it with tiny cookies. I love this because it looks like a burst of sunshine on the plate.

1 ¼ cups unsalted butter
1 ¾ cups light brown sugar, organic if possible
1 vanilla bean, split
1 pineapple, peeled but left whole
Coconut-Cilantro Dressing (recipe follows)
Freshly ground black pepper
Macadamia Nut Brittle (recipe follows)
Buttermilk–Key Lime Sherbet (recipe follows)
About 16 thin strips fresh coconut (see Note)
16 Crystallized Cilantro Leaves (recipe follows)
Coconut Butter Cookies (recipe follows)

1. In a large sauté pan, melt the butter over medium heat. Add the brown sugar and vanilla bean and cook for 3 to 4 minutes or until the sugar begins to caramelize.

2. Add the pineapple to the pan and cook, turning, to brown on all sides. Reduce the heat to medium-low and add about 1 cup of water to the pan to prevent burning so the caramel will not get too dark.

3. Cook, turning the pineapple with tongs and basting occasionally with the pan juices, for 1 to 1½ hours or until roasted through to the core. The pineapple will be golden brown and appear a little translucent.

4. Remove the pineapple from the pan and cool slightly. Transfer to a dish and refrigerate for at least 2 hours and up to 2 days until thoroughly chilled.

5. Using a large, sharp knife or an electric slicer set on the number 12 setting, slice the pineapple into paper-thin slices, or as thin as you can slice it.

6. Put 5 to 7 slices of pineapple on a plate. Brush the surfaces of all the slices with the coconut-cilantro dressing. Cover with plastic wrap and warm in the microwave on high power for about 1 minute. Remove the plastic and sprinkle the pineapple with pepper and nut brittle.

7. Center a quenelle (oval-shaped mound) of the sherbet on the pineapple slices. Place coconut strips over the sherbet in an X. Garnish with 2 crystallized cilantro leaves. Repeat to make 7 more servings. Reserve the remaining pineapple for another use. Serve with the coconut butter cookies on the side.

NOTE: *To prepare the coconut, crack a fresh coconut in half and use a vegetable peeler to shave strips of coconut.*

COCONUT-CILANTRO DRESSING

Makes about 1¼ cups

1 cup Simple Syrup (see page 279)
¼ cup coconut milk
1½ teaspoons chopped fresh cilantro leaves
½ teaspoon grated fresh ginger

In a mixing bowl, whisk the simple syrup, coconut milk, cilantro, and ginger. Cover and refrigerate until ready to use.

239

MACADAMIA NUT BRITTLE

Makes about 2 cups

2 cups sugar
½ cup water
2 tablespoons unsalted butter
1 cup chopped, toasted macadamia nuts

1. Pour the sugar into the center of a deep saucepan. Carefully pour the water around the sides of the pan, trying not to splash any sugar onto the sides. Do not stir but gently draw your finger through the water and then twice through the center of the sugar, making a cross, to moisten it. Bring to a full boil over high heat and cook without stirring for 10 to 12 minutes or until topaz-colored. Swirl the mixture occasionally to even out the color. Test the color periodically by putting a drop on a white plate.

2. Remove the pan from the heat, add the butter, and stir with a wooden spoon until melted and incorporated. Stir in the nuts. Pour the mixture onto a pan lined with a Silpat. Spread over the pan and set aside to cool.

3. When cool, chop into pieces. Store in an airtight container until needed.

BUTTERMILK–KEY LIME SHERBET

Makes about 4 cups

1 cup water (spring water, if possible, for the best flavor)
1 cup granulated sugar
1½ cups buttermilk
½ cup freshly squeezed Key lime juice

1. In a saucepan, bring the water and sugar to a boil over medium-high heat until the sugar dissolves. Set aside to cool slightly.

2. Add the buttermilk and lime juice and stir to mix. Refrigerate for at least 2 hours or until cold.

3. Pour the chilled mixture into an ice-cream machine and process according to the manufacturer's instructions. Spoon into a freezer-safe container and freeze for at least 2 hours until firm.

CRYSTALLIZED CILANTRO LEAVES

Makes 16 leaves

1 large egg white
¼ cup granulated sugar
16 large cilantro leaves

1. In a small, shallow bowl, lightly whisk the egg white, just to break it up a little. Spread the sugar in another shallow bowl.

2. Dip a leaf in the egg white, then scrape it along the rim of the bowl to remove excess white. Dip the leaf in the sugar and coat both sides. Set aside to dry on parchment paper. Repeat with the remaining leaves.

COCONUT BUTTER COOKIES

Makes about 60 cookies

1 pound unsalted butter, at room temperature
1 cup granulated sugar
1 teaspoon dark rum
½ teaspoon pure vanilla extract
3½ cups all-purpose flour
1½ cups sweetened coconut, toasted (see Note)
½ teaspoon salt

1. In the bowl of an electric mixer fitted with the paddle attachment and set on medium-high speed, whip the

butter until very light and fluffy. Add the sugar and continue to beat until well blended. Add the rum and vanilla extract and beat just until mixed.

2. In another bowl, toss together the flour, coconut, and salt. Stir into the butter mixture and beat until blended.

3. Butter a small rimmed sheet pan and line it with plastic wrap to cover the sides. Spread the dough evenly over the pan, cover with plastic wrap, and freeze for at least 2 hours or until firm.

4. Preheat the oven to 250 degrees. Line a baking sheet with parchment paper.

5. Spread some flour in a shallow bowl.

6. Cut the frozen dough into 2-inch-wide strips and roll in the flour. You can wrap the strips in wax paper or plastic wrap at this point and freeze to bake at a later time. Cut each strip into very narrow slices, about $\frac{1}{8}$ inch wide. Put on the baking sheet about 1 inch apart and bake for about $1\frac{1}{4}$ to $1\frac{1}{2}$ hours or until crisp but barely colored. To test for doneness, remove a baking sheet from the oven and let it cool for 1 minute. Taste for crispiness. If not crispy enough, return to the oven. You may need 2 baking sheets.

7. Cool on the pan. Lift the cookies off the pan with an icing (thin) spatula.

NOTE: *To toast coconut, spread it in an even layer on a baking sheet and bake in a 350-degree oven for 6 to 10 minutes, stirring several times, until golden.*

FROMAGE BLANC MOUSSE

Serves 12

This is one of my favorites! If there is any category of ingredients I love to work with, it's dairy. Give me cheese, milk, yogurt, and cream any day! Essentially, this is a strawberry cheesecake made with fabulous and naturally fat-free *fromage blanc,* which lightens the dessert as it enriches it. Instead of big, hulking strawberries, I use a crimson, gelled distillation of the berries, which sings with full fruit flavor (although it takes hours to make). We use our strawberry "soup" or "juice" in so many ways in our kitchen. Here we jell it; in other preparations it may be added to a sauce or used to flavor a filling. One of the tricks of keeping up with a menu as elaborate as ours is to use the same ingredients in many forms.

1 pound fromage blanc
1 cup granulated sugar
3 sheets gelatin, softened in cool water
3 large egg yolks
1 ½ cups heavy cream, whipped
Strawberry Gelée (recipe follows)
Lemon Curd Paint (recipe follows)
Blueberry Stew (recipe follows)
Lime Gelée (recipe follows)
Coconut Tuiles (recipe follows)
8 to 10 micro mint sprigs, for garnish

1. In a bowl or the top of a double boiler, combine the *fromage blanc* and ¼ cup of the sugar and cook over simmering water on medium heat, stirring, until the sugar dissolves.

2. Squeeze the water from the gelatin sheets and add them to the warm cheese mixture. Whisk until dissolved.

3. Remove the bowl from on top of the simmering water and submerge the bottom of it in an ice-water bath to cool slightly and thicken.

4. Meanwhile, in the bowl of an electric mixer fitted with the paddle attachment and set on medium-high speed, whip the yolks and the remaining ½ cup of sugar until thick and pale. Fold into the cooled cheese mixture. Fold in the whipped cream until blended, but do not overmix.

5. Spoon into 12 2½-inch-diameter metal rings to fill to within ¼ inch of the rim. Smooth the mousse and set on a baking sheet. Refrigerate for at least 2 hours or until set.

6. When set, pour the hot strawberry gelée over the top to fill the molds to the rim. Return to the refrigerator for 1 to 2 hours longer until the strawberry layer is set.

7. Set 1 ring on a dessert plate. Using a small blowtorch, warm the metal and lift the ring off the mousse. If you don't have a blowtorch, use a hair dryer with a directed nozzle, or try a cloth dipped in very, very hot water and wrung out.

8. Paint a swish of lemon curd on the plate. Spoon a tower of blueberry stew near the mousse. Using a demitasse spoon or other small spoon, dig out "rocks" of lime gelée and pile near the mousse. Lean a *tuile* against the mousse. Sprinkle plate with micro mint leaves. Repeat to make 11 more servings.

STRAWBERRY GELÉE

Makes about 1½ cups

3 sheets gelatin
1 ½ cups Strawberry Juice (see page 233)
¼ vanilla bean, split

1. Soak the gelatin in cool water for about 2 minutes to soften.

2. In a small saucepan, heat the strawberry juice and vanilla bean over medium heat until hot. Remove from the heat.

3. Lift the gelatin from the water and squeeze out the liquid. Add to the hot strawberry juice and stir until dissolved.

LEMON CURD PAINT

Makes about 1½ cups

1 cup granulated sugar
½ cup unsalted butter
½ cup freshly squeezed lemon juice
4 large egg yolks
1 large egg
½ vanilla bean, split

1. In a stainless steel saucepan, combine the sugar, butter, lemon juice, yolks, egg, and vanilla bean. Cook over medium heat, whisking constantly, for 5 to 10 minutes or until thickened. Take care that the curd does not scorch.

2. Strain through a chinois or fine-mesh sieve into a bowl. Cool in an ice-water bath, and when cold, cover and refrigerate until needed or for up to 3 days.

BLUEBERRY STEW

Makes about 1 cup

1 pint fresh blueberries
1 cup granulated sugar
½ cup water

1. In a saucepan, bring ½ pint of the blueberries, sugar, and water to a boil over medium-high heat. Reduce the heat and simmer for 15 minutes.

2. Strain through a chinois or fine-mesh sieve. Add the remaining ½ pint of blueberries to the strained liquid and stir gently to coat. Refrigerate until needed.

LIME GELÉE

Makes about 1 cup

½ cup water
¼ cup freshly squeezed lime juice
¼ cup Simple Syrup (see page 279)
3 sheets gelatin

1. In a saucepan, bring the water, lime juice, and syrup to a boil over medium-high heat. Remove from the heat.

2. Soak the gelatin in cool water for 2 minutes. Lift from the water and squeeze gently. Add to the saucepan and stir to dissolve. Pour into a small nonreactive container, let cool, cover, and refrigerate for at least 4 hours or until set.

COCONUT TUILES

Makes about 15 tuiles

1¼ cups granulated sugar
2½ tablespoons unsalted butter
¾ cup plus 2 tablespoons large egg whites
    (from 6 or 7 eggs)
2 cups unsweetened coconut
¼ cup all-purpose flour

1. In the bowl of an electric mixer fitted with the whisk attachment and set on medium-high speed, mix the sugar and butter for about 2 minutes or until well mixed and sandy. Add the egg whites and mix until combined. Scrape down the sides of the bowl once or twice.

2. In another bowl, stir the coconut with the flour, then add it to the batter. Mix on medium speed until incorporated.

3. Refrigerate for at least 4 hours or up to 12 hours.

4. Preheat the oven to 300 degrees. Line a baking sheet with a Silpat.

5. Spread 15 swatches of the batter, each 6 to 8 inches long, on the Silpat. Bake for 12 minutes, turning halfway through baking, until the *tuiles* are lightly browned.

6. Let them cool on the pan and then carefully lift them off with a spatula. Store in an airtight container until needed.

APRICOT TARTE TATIN

Serves 12

I love a classic French *tarte tatin,* made with
caramelized apples and buttery puff pastry. During
July and August, the apricots from Michigan are better
than any apples I can get, and so I seize the moment
and make this elegant little tart with them. Stone fruits
work very well in this tart, and so if you cannot find
wonderful ripe apricots, try peaches or nectarines
(plums don't work as well). Later in the year, make it
with apples or pears. Frozen puff pastry is a marvelous
product if made with all butter; it just gets better all
the time. I use it and so do most chefs. You can make
your own puff pastry, but I suggest you spend your time
with your family instead of rolling and turning puff
pastry dough!

I like to work with pastry, partly because I inherited
my mother's cold hands. I have a theory that if your
hands are too warm, you'll never be a good pastry chef.
When I interview cooks, I ask them to roll cookie dough
between their palms. If their hands are covered with
sticky dough, I know they won't make it in my kitchen.

½ cup unsalted butter
1 cup granulated sugar
½ vanilla bean, split
1 cinnamon stick
1 tablespoon Vanilla Brandy (see page 237)
1 tablespoon freshly squeezed lemon juice
⅛ teaspoon grated orange zest
18 apricots, halved
12 disks frozen puff pastry, each cut to be ½ inch larger
    in diameter than the ramekin
Sour Cream Ice Cream (recipe follows)

1. Preheat the oven to 375 degrees.
2. In a saucepan, melt the butter over medium heat
until it begins to bubble. Add the sugar and stir with a
wooden spoon until blended. Add the vanilla bean and
cinnamon stick. Stir to bring out the vanilla caviar, or
vanilla seeds.

3. Continue simmering until the sugar caramelizes.
Carefully stir in the brandy, lemon juice, and zest and
deglaze the pan. Continue to cook until smooth.
4. Pour 2 tablespoons of the caramel into each of 12
4-ounce ramekins or tall timbales. Put 3 apricot halves in
each ramekin. Top off with the remaining caramel. Set
the ramekins on a sheet pan.
5. Bake for 20 to 25 minutes or until the caramel bubbles and is almost tender.
6. Raise the oven temperature to 425 degrees.
7. Put rounds of puff pastry on top of each ramekin.
Bake for about 10 to 15 minutes longer or until the pastry is golden brown. Let cool for 30 minutes or longer.
8. Invert the ramekins onto each of 12 plates and lift
the ramekins off the dessert. Serve each one with a
quenelle (oval-shaped mound) of sour cream ice cream.

246

TRU

SOUR CREAM ICE CREAM

Makes about 1 quart

2 cups half-and-half
1 cup heavy cream
½ vanilla bean, split
9 large egg yolks
¾ cup granulated sugar
1 cup sour cream

1. In a saucepan, bring the half-and-half, cream, and vanilla bean to a simmer over medium heat. Remove from the heat and set aside for 5 minutes to infuse.

2. In a mixing bowl, whisk together the egg yolks and sugar. Pour about ⅓ cup of the hot cream mixture into the eggs and whisk to temper. Return the tempered custard to the pan, stir to mix, and return to the heat. Cook, stirring occasionally, until the custard thickens and registers 180 degrees on an instant-read thermometer or candy thermometer.

3. Strain through a chinois or fine-mesh sieve into a metal bowl. Stir in the sour cream. Cool in an ice-water bath. When cold, pour the chilled mixture into an ice-cream machine and process according to the manufacturer's instructions. Scrape into a freezer-safe container and freeze for at least 2 hours until firm. Serve on the same day you make it.

CHAPTER THIRTEEN

Petits Fours

AT THE VERY END OF THE MEAL, Tru guests can select from an ever-changing assortment of petits fours—sometimes with as many as sixteen different selections—displayed on a three-tiered granite cart rolled right up to the table. These are pure, unadulterated fun and pair perfectly with our carefully selected estate and first-growth teas and expertly roasted coffees.

From spicy cayenne-tinged chocolate truffles to nut-flavored shortbread, these small delights are an upbeat way to round out an evening. There are always one or two flavors of our signature lollipops on the cart, too. My staff and I love creating these fantasies because, really, anything goes! The little sketches are tiny good-bye kisses from us, and you can try as many from the cart as you like.

As our guests leave the restaurant, completely sated from a lovely meal, we hand them a pair of our now legendary *cannelés*. We suggest eating these tender, rum-kissed cakes the next morning with coffee or tea as a way to recall the experience from the night before, like basking in the glow of a fabulous love affair. The Tru experience extends into the next day. Our very intention!

251   *Cracker Jack with Dried Cherries*

252   *Hickory Nut Shortbread*

253   *Cinnamon-Cayenne Truffles*

255   *Honey-and-Lemon Tea Lollipops*

256   *Cannelés*

CRACKER JACK WITH DRIED CHERRIES

Serves 8

This is what I call "real Chicago regional food"! The recipe is based on one of Chicago's most lasting contributions to the world of candy, Cracker Jack. The caramel-popcorn-and-peanut treat was first introduced at the wildly successful 1893 World's Columbian Exposition, which was Chicago's first large, international fair. The folks loved it but it was too sticky to package. Three years later, Louis Rueckheim (whose brother, F. W. Rueckheim, had sold it at the fair) invented a process for packaging the sweet popcorn so that it didn't stick together. It quickly caught on, and by 1912 the company introduced the "prize in every box" slogan. One of my favorite prizes is a little blue toaster with a tiny slice of blue toast. I keep it with my permanent collection of charms and play food.

Chicago is known as the candy capital of America, partly because treats such as Cracker Jack were invented here. In the days before air travel, we were easily accessible by train, so ingredients could be shipped in and finished product shipped out. We also are literally surrounded by cornfields, which means that corn syrup, a key ingredient in so many candies, is easy to come by.

2 cups granulated sugar
⅔ cup water
1 tablespoon unsalted butter
4 cups popped popcorn (see Note)
½ cup toasted, salted peanuts
½ cup dried cherries or raisins

1. Pour the sugar into the center of a deep saucepan. Carefully pour the water around the sides of the pan, trying not to splash any sugar onto the sides. Do not stir but gently draw your finger through the water and then twice through the center of the sugar, making a cross, to moisten it. Bring to a full boil over high heat and cook without stirring for 10 to 15 minutes or until golden caramel. Swirl the mixture occasionally to even out the color.

2. Turn off the heat and stir in the butter until incorporated. Add the popcorn, peanuts, and cherries and toss until all ingredients are well mixed. Pour onto a Silpat or well-oiled baking sheet and let cool a few minutes. Start breaking the popcorn mixture into small clusters, each about 2 inches wide, working quickly so the mixture does not harden and taking care you don't burn yourself.

3. Store the clusters in an airtight container for up to 1 week.

NOTE: *To pop corn properly, my dad taught me to put the kernels in a large, heavy-bottomed pot and cover with canola or another flavorless oil. Cover and cook on high heat until you hear the first kernel pop. Immediately remove from the heat and let sit for 1 minute. Return the pot to the heat and finish popping the corn, shaking the pan constantly. I don't know why this is better, but this is how my dad cooked popcorn, and his was the best there was! I use Black Jewel popcorn, with its small, "hull-less" kernels.*

HICKORY NUT SHORTBREAD
Makes about 80 small bars

Years ago, I read about how scarce hickory nuts were, and how difficult to shell, but I was curious about them. I heard that American Spoon Foods sold them but, in the interest of fairness, rationed them to a pound per customer. Still, I was determined, and so I drove to Traverse City, Michigan, to the American Spoon Foods store to buy some. Sure enough—only a pound per person! I stood outside the store begging customers to buy me a pound, feeling like a teenager standing outside a liquor store! That day, I ended up with six pounds, which I froze and used sparingly. I still have trouble getting as many hickory nuts as I would like, but customers and friends bring them to me whenever they can—even nuts picked by their grandmothers.

I really like them in this shortbread. They add a kick to the butteriness. I used to bake huge batches of shortbread at Stapleford Park, the country-house hotel where Rick and I worked in the early 1990s. I made it for tea and for evening turndown in the guest rooms. Shortbread originated in the United Kingdom, and so to give an American accent to afternoon tea, I sometimes baked chocolate chip cookies, too. Both the shortbread and the cookies quickly disappeared!

8 tablespoons cool unsalted butter, cut into pieces
¼ cup plus 2 tablespoons granulated sugar
1 cup all-purpose flour
¼ cup cornstarch
¼ teaspoon salt
¼ cup coarsely chopped, toasted hickory nuts

1. Preheat the oven to 350 degrees. Line an 8-by-10-inch baking pan with parchment paper.

2. In the bowl of an electric mixer fitted with the paddle attachment and set on medium-high speed, cream the butter until smooth and fluffy. Add ¼ cup of the sugar and beat until well incorporated.

3. In a medium bowl, stir together the flour, cornstarch, and salt. Add the dry ingredients to the butter, mixing on medium-low speed until incorporated. Add the nuts and beat until the dough comes together.

4. Turn the dough out onto a lightly floured work surface and knead 5 to 10 times until the dough is smooth and cohesive.

5. Sprinkle more flour on the work surface and roll the dough with a rolling pin to a thickness of about ¼ inch and to the right shape and size to fit in the baking pan. Roll the dough around the rolling pin, lift it up, and then unroll it into the pan. Using light strokes of the rolling pin, roll the dough into the corners and edges of the pan or press the dough into the corners with your fingertips. Smooth out any bumps. Prick the shortbread all over with the tines of a fork or a dough docker (also called a *pique-vite*) to prevent buckling and shrinking. Sprinkle evenly with 1 tablespoon of the remaining sugar.

6. Bake for 15 minutes. Pull out the oven rack and knock the pan once against the rack to knock out any air. Rotate the pan to ensure even cooking and a flat surface.

7. Bake for 10 to 15 minutes longer or until a light golden brown. Remove from the oven and immediately sprinkle evenly with the last tablespoon of sugar. Let the shortbread cool in the pan for about 5 minutes.

8. With a very sharp knife, cut the shortbread into slender bars, each about ½ inch by 2 inches. Let cool completely in the pan. Using a small spatula, remove the bars and store in an airtight container for up to 1 week.

CINNAMON-CAYENNE TRUFFLES

Makes 50 or 60

Just about everyone loves rich, smooth chocolate truffles, and Tru's customers are no exception. I make hundreds every week and try to change the flavor from one week to the next. I have made dried plum truffles, passion fruit truffles, even jasmine-flavored truffles I call Jasmine Pearls. These cinnamon-cayenne truffles are sweet and spicy at the same time and among my customers' favorites. They are quite simple to make because the frozen truffle centers are coated in melted chocolate and then dusted in cocoa powder, rather than being dipped in tempered chocolate, which is a more complicated procedure. But they are just as delicious and seductive. Use the very best chocolate you can find for the truffles. That's what you taste most in any truffle and it pays to use the best!

1 ½ cups Homemade Crème Fraîche (see page 280),
    or sour cream
2 tablespoons ground cinnamon
1 to 2 teaspoons cayenne pepper, according to your taste
12 ounces high-quality bittersweet chocolate, coarsely
    chopped
1 ½ pounds semisweet chocolate
1 ½ cups unsweetened Dutch-processed cocoa powder

1. In a saucepan, combine the crème fraîche, cinnamon, and cayenne and bring to a boil over medium heat. As soon as it boils, turn off the heat.

2. Meanwhile, put the chopped bittersweet chocolate in a medium bowl. Strain the hot crème fraîche mixture through a chinois or fine-mesh sieve into the bowl. Whisk until the chocolate melts and the mixture is smooth. If you have a hand blender, blend this ganache for 2 minutes. Cover and let rest overnight in a cool place, but not the refrigerator. The mixture will become firm but not hard.

3. Spoon the cooled ganache into a pastry bag fitted with a large plain tip. Pipe bite-size "kisses" (similar to Hershey's Kisses) onto parchment-paper-lined baking sheets. Refrigerate for about 30 minutes, just until set.

4. Use your palm to press gently on the point of each truffle. Transfer to the freezer and freeze for 2 to 3 hours or overnight, until hard.

5. In the top of a double boiler set over barely simmering water, melt the semisweet chocolate until it is liquid but not so hot that you can't touch it; if it is too hot for you, wear disposable latex gloves.

6. Spread the cocoa powder on a jelly-roll pan.

7. Working in 2 batches if necessary to avoid crowding the pan of cocoa, dip the frozen truffle centers one at a time into the melted chocolate, shake off any excess, and then set them down in the cocoa. When all the truffle centers are dipped and the chocolate has started to set, gently but thoroughly shake the sheet pan to roll the truffles around in the cocoa until coated. Carefully transfer to another jelly-roll pan and refrigerate, uncovered, for 30 minutes. (You can sift the unused cocoa and use it for another purpose.)

8. Transfer to an airtight container and keep chilled until almost ready to serve. Bring to room temperature before serving.

HONEY-AND-LEMON TEA LOLLIPOPS

Makes 30

We always have a few flavors of handmade suckers on the petit four cart. Our customers like lollipops as much as the next person! These require cooking hot sugar, but they are surprisingly easy to make. Be sure you have a good candy thermometer and use a heavy-bottomed pan.

30 to 35 pansy petals
1 cup sugar
½ cup brewed Darjeeling or black tea
6 tablespoons honey
2 tablespoons glucose or light corn syrup (see Note)
½ teaspoon lemon extract

1. Arrange 30 sucker collars (see Note) on a Silpat or an extremely well greased baking sheet. Put 1 pansy petal in each. Use only the prettiest petals; discard any leftovers.
2. Clip a candy thermometer on the side of a small dry saucepan. Make sure the tip does not touch the bottom of the pan.
3. Combine the sugar, tea, honey, and glucose in the pan and bring to a boil over high heat. Do not stir, but as the syrup cooks, occasionally wash down the sides of the pan with a clean pastry brush dipped in water. This will prevent crystallization. Cook until the thermometer registers 305 degrees, or the hard-crack stage. This should take about 10 minutes.
4. Remove the pan from the heat and dip it into a bowl filled with ice and cold water for 15 seconds to stop the cooking. Set the pan on a heat-proof surface and add the lemon extract. Swirl the hot syrup in the pan to reduce the number of air bubbles.
5. Pour the hot syrup into the sucker collars so that it fills them two-thirds of the way. Cool for at least 20 minutes and for no longer than 30 minutes or the lollipops will absorb moisture from the air.
6. Lift the lollipops from the collars and store in an airtight container for up to 3 days.

NOTE: *Glucose is available in some specialty stores and pharmacies.*

You can buy sucker collars in craft shops, candy-making supply outlets, and specialty cookware sites online.

Serves 6 to 8;
makes 12 to 16 cakes

After a trip to southwest France, my friend Larry arrived in my kitchen with a dusty wooden box that looked as if it had been found in a cave. It was packed with six tiny copper molds and a cake recipe in French. As I followed it (slowly), I kept thinking, "This can't be right!" The *cannelés* seemed to have too much sugar, too little flour, and took far too long to make. But they were perfect.

I find them to be like tiny popovers, with a tender, eggy interior perfumed with vanilla and a dark, chewy crust that is baked and baked until dark brown. They are considered classics in southwest France, where they are served with an afternoon cup of tisane (herb tea) or hot chocolate.

We now hand these out to our guests as they leave Tru, with instructions to eat them the next day with their morning coffee or tea. No one has reported being disappointed!

These take two days to make, but each step is utterly simple. While the batter develops in the refrigerator, it becomes tender and smooth and the vanilla permeates it deliciously. These will be the strangest cakes you have ever baked—and you won't know how much you will love them until you taste one.

3 ¼ cups milk
1 vanilla bean, split lengthwise
4 tablespoons unsalted butter
3 large eggs
2 tablespoons dark rum
2 cups plus 2 tablespoons granulated sugar
1 ½ cups all-purpose flour

1. Two days before you plan to serve the dessert, combine the milk and vanilla bean in a saucepan and bring to a boil over medium-high heat. Remove from the heat and set aside to cool to room temperature. Cover and refrigerate for 8 to 10 hours or overnight to infuse the vanilla flavor into the milk.

2. In a small saucepan, melt the butter over medium heat. Whisk the eggs into the chilled-milk mixture, and then whisk in the rum and warm, melted butter. Add the sugar and flour and whisk to mix. Cover and refrigerate for 8 to 10 hours or overnight.

3. Preheat the oven to 400 degrees. Generously butter 12 to 16 2-ounce *cannelé* molds or 2 12-cup muffin pans. Refrigerate until the butter is firm.

4. Remove the vanilla bean from the batter. Whisk again to mix well. Pour or ladle the batter into the molds. Fill them almost to the top (they expand only a little during baking). Put the molds on a baking sheet or in a shallow pan. Bake for 50 minutes to 1 hour, until very dark brown but not turning black. Check the *cannelés* after 45 or 50 minutes to make sure they are not too dark. They should be dark, caramelized, and chewy on the outside and tender and eggy on the inside. Turn out of the molds while still warm. If they stick to the molds, use a table knife to loosen them gently. Cool on a wire rack.

CHAPTER FOURTEEN

Basic Recipes

261   *Beef Stock*

261   *Veal Stock*

262   *Beef and Veal Stock*

263   *Lamb Stock*

264   *Game Stock*

264   *Venison Stock*

265   *Chicken Stock*

265   *Duck Stock*

266   *Fish Stock*

266   *Vegetable Stock*

267   *Court Bouillon*

267   *Mushroom Stock*

268   *Lobster Glace*

268   *Veal Demi-glace*

269   *Roasted Chicken Demi-glace*

270   *Lamb Demi-glace*

270   *Venison Demi-glace*

271   *Red Wine Sauce*

271   *Bouquet Garni*

272   *Vin Blanc*

272   *Tramonto's Ruby Red Grapefruit Dust*

273   *Coriander-Orange Oil*

273   *Herb Oil*

274   *Yellow Curry Oil*

274   *Vanilla Oil*

275   *Basil Oil*

275   *Lobster Oil*

276   *Garlic and Rosemary Oil*

276   *Chive Oil*

277   *Lemon Oil*

277   *Lime Oil*

278   *Cardamom Oil*

278   *Beurre Monté*

279   *Clarified Butter*

279   *Simple Syrup*

280   *Homemade Crème Fraîche*

280   *Brioche*

281   *Juicing Chart*

BEEF STOCK

Makes about 16 cups

2 pounds meaty beef bones
¼ cup vegetable oil
2 cups chopped onions
1 cup chopped carrots
1 cup chopped celery
¼ cup tomato paste
2 tablespoons fresh thyme leaves
2 tablespoons black peppercorns
4 bay leaves
1 cup dry red or white wine, optional
20 cups water

1. Rinse the beef bones well under cold water to remove any blood. Set aside.

2. Heat the oil in a large saucepan over low heat. Add the onions, carrots, and celery to the pan and cook, stirring occasionally, for about 5 minutes or until the vegetables are softened but not browned. Stir in the tomato paste, thyme, peppercorns, and bay leaves.

3. If using the wine, add it now and stir to incorporate the tomato paste. Add the bones and the water. Bring to a boil over medium heat. Carefully skim off any fat and froth that float to the surface of the liquid. Reduce the heat to low and simmer gently for 2 to 3 hours or until somewhat reduced and flavorful.

4. Strain the stock through a chinois or fine-mesh sieve into a large bowl. Discard the bones and vegetables. Allow to cool in an ice-water bath. Cover and refrigerate until chilled, and then remove the layer of congealed fat from the surface.

5. Transfer to covered storage containers and refrigerate for up to 3 days or freeze for up to 2 months.

VEAL STOCK

Makes about 32 cups

10 pounds veal bones
2 cups chopped onions
1 cup chopped celery
1 cup chopped carrots
1 head garlic, root end trimmed
2 tablespoons black peppercorns
2 tablespoons fresh thyme
4 bay leaves
3 tablespoons tomato paste
2 cups dry red wine
40 cups water

1. Preheat the oven to 350 degrees.

2. Put the veal bones in a large stockpot and add enough cold water to cover. Place over medium heat and bring to a boil. As soon as the water starts to boil, remove from the heat and drain the bones in a colander. Rinse well under cold water. Pat dry with paper towels.

3. Transfer the bones to a large roasting pan and put in the oven. Roast, stirring the bones every 20 minutes, for about 1 hour or until they are golden brown. Remove the bones from the pan and set aside.

4. Place the roasting pan over medium heat. Add the onions, celery, carrots, garlic, peppercorns, thyme, and bay leaves and cook for 10 to 15 minutes or until the vegetables are golden brown. Stir in the tomato paste.

5. Add the wine, and then raise the heat to high. Simmer for 15 to 20 minutes or until the wine has almost evaporated and the bottom of the pan is almost dry.

6. Transfer the bones and the vegetables to a large stockpot. Add the water. Place over low heat and gently simmer the stock for 4 to 6 hours.

7. Strain through a chinois or fine-mesh sieve into a bowl. Allow to cool in an ice-water bath. Cover and refrigerate until chilled, and then remove the layer of congealed fat from the surface.

8. Transfer to covered storage containers and refrigerate for up to 3 days or freeze for up to 2 months.

Makes about 32 cups

5 pounds beef bones
5 pounds veal bones
2 cups chopped onions
1 cup chopped carrots
1 cup chopped celery
1 head garlic, root end trimmed
2 tablespoons fresh thyme
2 tablespoons black peppercorns
4 bay leaves
3 tablespoons tomato paste
2 cups dry red wine

1. Preheat the oven to 350 degrees.

2. Put the beef and veal bones in a large stockpot and add enough cold water to cover the bones. Bring to a boil over medium heat. As soon as the water comes to a boil, remove from the heat and strain the bones. Thoroughly rinse the bones in cold water.

3. Spread the bones in a large roasting pan and roast for 40 to 60 minutes or until golden brown, stirring every 20 minutes. Remove the bones from the pan and return them to the stockpot. Set aside.

4. Add the onions, carrots, celery, garlic, thyme, peppercorns, and bay leaves to the roasting pan and place over medium heat. Cook, stirring occasionally, for 10 to 15 minutes or until the vegetables have softened and are golden brown.

5. Stir in the tomato paste and then the wine, raise the heat, and bring to a boil, stirring the bottom of the pan with a wooden spoon to deglaze. Cook until the wine is almost evaporated.

6. Add the contents from the roasting pan to the stockpot with the bones and add enough cold water to cover the ingredients. Bring to a gentle simmer over low heat, making sure the stock does not boil. Simmer gently for 4 to 6 hours.

7. Strain the stock through a chinois or fine-mesh sieve into a large bowl. Discard the bones and vegetables. Allow to cool in an ice-water bath. Cover and refrigerate until chilled. Scrape off the layer of congealed fat from the surface.

8. Transfer to tightly lidded storage containers and refrigerate for up to 3 days or freeze for up to 2 months.

LAMB STOCK

Makes about 32 cups

5 pounds lamb shank bones
5 pounds lamb neck bones
4 cups chopped onions
1 cup chopped carrots
1 cup chopped celery
¼ cup tomato paste
1 head garlic, root end trimmed
1 tablespoon black peppercorns
4 sprigs fresh thyme
2 bay leaves
1 750-ml bottle dry red wine

1. Preheat the oven to 350 degrees.

2. Put the lamb bones in a large stockpot and add enough cold water to completely cover the bones. Place over medium heat and bring to a boil. As soon as the water comes to a boil, remove from the heat and strain in a colander. Rinse the bones under cold water.

3. Transfer the bones to a large roasting pan and place in the oven. Roast the bones, stirring every 20 minutes, for 1 hour or until they are golden brown. Remove from the oven and transfer the bones to a plate.

4. Add the onions, carrots, and celery to the roasting pan, place over medium heat, and cook, stirring occasionally, for 10 to 15 minutes or until the vegetables are soft and golden brown. Stir in the tomato paste. Add the garlic, black peppercorns, thyme, and bay leaves. Pour in the wine and raise the heat to medium-high. Bring to a simmer while stirring the bottom of the pan with a wooden spoon to deglaze. Simmer until most of the wine has evaporated.

5. Put the bones in a large stockpot and add the caramelized vegetables and liquid. Add enough cold water so that the ingredients are covered by 6 inches of water.

6. Put the stockpot over medium heat and bring to a simmer. Reduce the heat and gently simmer for 8 to 10 hours.

7. Strain through a chinois or fine-mesh sieve into a bowl. Set in an ice-water bath to cool. Cover and refrigerate until chilled, and then remove the layer of congealed fat from the surface.

8. Transfer to covered storage containers and refrigerate for up to 3 days or freeze for up to 2 months.

GAME STOCK

5 pounds rabbit, squab, or pheasant bones
1 cup chopped onions
½ cup chopped carrots
½ cup chopped celery
½ cup chopped leeks
2 heads garlic, root ends removed
¼ cup fresh thyme
¼ cup black peppercorns
¼ cup tomato paste
2 cups dry white wine

1. Preheat the oven to 350 degrees.
2. Rinse the game bones under cold water to remove any blood.
3. Transfer the bones to a roasting pan and roast the bones, stirring every 20 minutes, for about 45 minutes to 1 hour or until they are golden brown.
4. Remove the bones from the pan and set aside. Add the onions, carrots, celery, and leeks to the pan and sauté over medium heat for 10 to 15 minutes or until the vegetables are nicely browned. Stir in the garlic, thyme, peppercorns, and tomato paste.
5. Add the white wine and cook, stirring the bottom of the pan with a wooden spoon, for 10 to 15 minutes or until the wine has almost evaporated and the bottom of the pan is almost dry.
6. Transfer the vegetable mixture to a large stockpot and add the reserved bones. Add enough cold water to cover the bones (20 to 22 cups).
7. Put the stockpot over low heat and simmer for 2 to 3 hours, skimming off any fat and froth that float to the surface of the liquid.
8. Strain through a chinois or fine-mesh sieve into a bowl. Discard the bones and vegetables. Allow to cool in an ice-water bath. Cover and refrigerate until chilled, and then remove the layer of congealed fat from the surface. Transfer to covered containers and refrigerate for up to 3 days or freeze for up to 2 months.

VENISON STOCK

10 pounds venison bones
2 cups chopped onions
1 cup chopped carrots
1 cup chopped celery
4 cloves garlic
4 bay leaves
3 tablespoons fresh thyme
1 tablespoon juniper berries
2 cups dry red wine
1 cup port wine
24 cups water

1. Preheat the oven to 350 degrees.
2. Rinse the venison bones well under cold water, then transfer them to a roasting pan. Roast for 45 minutes to 1 hour or until browned. Remove the bones from the pan and reserve.
3. Put the roasting pan over medium heat, add the onions, carrots, celery, and garlic, and cook, stirring occasionally, for 15 to 20 minutes or until the vegetables are golden and soft. Add the bay leaves, thyme, and juniper berries, and stir into the vegetables.
4. Add the red wine and port and raise the heat to high. Bring to a boil, and then reduce the heat to medium and simmer the liquid for 30 minutes or until most of the wine has evaporated and the pan is almost dry.
5. Transfer the ingredients from the roasting pan to a large stockpot, and then add the reserved bones. Add the cold water; it should cover the bones. Place the stockpot over low heat and simmer the stock, skimming off any fat and froth that float to the surface of the liquid, for 2 to 3 hours or until slightly reduced and flavorful.
6. Strain through a chinois or fine-mesh sieve into a large bowl. Discard the bones and vegetables. Cool in an ice-water bath. Cover and refrigerate until chilled, and then remove the layer of congealed fat from the surface. Transfer to a covered storage container and refrigerate for up to 3 days or freeze for up to 2 months.

CHICKEN STOCK

Makes about 16 cups

2 pounds chicken bones
¼ cup vegetable oil
2 cups chopped onions
1 cup chopped carrots
1 cup chopped celery
2 tablespoons fresh thyme leaves
2 tablespoons black peppercorns
4 bay leaves
1 cup dry white wine, optional
20 cups water

1. Rinse the chicken bones well under cold water to remove any blood. Set aside.

2. Heat the oil in a large saucepan over low heat. Add the onions, carrots, and celery to the pan and cook, stirring occasionally, for about 5 minutes or until the vegetables are softened but not browned. Stir in the thyme, peppercorns, and bay leaves.

3. If using the wine, add it now. Add the bones and the water. Bring to a boil over medium heat. Carefully skim off any fat and froth that float to the surface of the liquid. Reduce the heat to low and simmer gently for 2 to 3 hours or until somewhat reduced and flavorful.

4. Strain the stock through a chinois or fine-mesh sieve into a large bowl. Discard the bones and vegetables. Allow to cool in an ice-water bath. Cover and refrigerate until chilled, and then remove the layer of congealed fat from the surface.

5. Transfer to covered storage containers and refrigerate for up to 3 days or freeze for up to 2 months.

DUCK STOCK

Makes about 16 cups

2 pounds duck bones
¼ cup vegetable oil
2 cups chopped onions
1 cup chopped carrots
1 cup chopped celery
¼ cup tomato paste
2 tablespoons fresh thyme leaves
2 tablespoons black peppercorns
4 bay leaves
1 cup dry white wine, optional
20 cups water

1. Rinse the duck bones well under cold water to remove any blood. Set aside.

2. Heat the oil in a large saucepan over low heat. Add the onions, carrots, and celery to the pan and cook, stirring occasionally, for about 5 minutes or until the vegetables are softened but not colored. Stir in the tomato paste, thyme, peppercorns, and bay leaves.

3. If using the wine, add it now and stir to incorporate the tomato paste. Add the bones and water. Bring to a boil over medium heat. Carefully skim off any fat and froth that float to the surface of the liquid. Reduce the heat to low and simmer gently for 2 to 3 hours or until somewhat reduced and flavorful.

4. Strain the stock through a chinois or fine-mesh sieve into a large bowl. Discard the bones and vegetables. Allow to cool in an ice-water bath. Cover and refrigerate until chilled, and then remove the layer of congealed fat from the surface.

5. Transfer to covered storage containers and refrigerate for up to 3 days or freeze for up to 2 months.

FISH STOCK

5 pounds halibut or cod bones
2 tablespoons vegetable oil
1 cup chopped leeks
1 cup chopped onions
1 cup chopped celery
1 bunch fresh flat-leaf parsley
¼ cup fresh tarragon
2 tablespoons black peppercorns
2 bay leaves
2 cups dry white wine
40 cups water

1. Rinse the fish bones well under cold running water for 20 minutes. Set aside.
2. Heat the oil in a large stockpot over low heat and sweat the leeks, onions, and celery, stirring occasionally, for about 10 to 12 minutes or until the onions are translucent. Add the parsley, tarragon, peppercorns, and bay leaves. Stir to combine. Cook for 2 to 3 minutes.
3. Add the white wine, and then raise the heat to medium-high. Bring the wine to a boil. Reduce the heat, and then simmer the wine for 10 to 12 minutes or until most of the wine has evaporated and the bottom of the pot is almost dry.
4. Add the water and fish bones, and then bring to a simmer over low heat. Simmer for 1 hour.
5. Strain through a chinois or fine-mesh sieve into a large bowl. Discard the fish bones and vegetables. Allow to cool in an ice-water bath. Cover and refrigerate until chilled, and then remove the layer of congealed fat from the surface.
6. Transfer to covered storage containers and refrigerate for up to 3 days or freeze for up to 2 months.

VEGETABLE STOCK

¼ cup vegetable oil
4 cups chopped onions
2 cups chopped carrots
2 cups chopped celery
4 Roma tomatoes, peeled and chopped
3 ears fresh corn
¼ cup black peppercorns
3 tablespoons fresh thyme
2 bay leaves
1 cup dry white wine
32 cups cold water

1. Heat the oil in a large stockpot over low heat. Add the onions, carrots, celery, tomatoes, corn, peppercorns, thyme, and bay leaves to the pot and cook, stirring occasionally, for 8 to 10 minutes or until the vegetables are softened but not browned.
2. Add the wine, and then raise the heat to medium-high. Simmer the wine for 5 to 8 minutes or until most of the wine has evaporated and the bottom of the pot is almost dry.
3. Add the water and bring to a boil. Boil for 10 minutes. Remove from the heat.
4. Strain through a chinois or fine-mesh sieve into a large bowl. Allow to cool in an ice-water bath. Cover and refrigerate until chilled.
5. Transfer to covered storage containers and refrigerate for up to 3 days or freeze for up to 2 months.

COURT BOUILLON

Makes about 24 cups

¼ cup vegetable oil
4 cups chopped onions
2 cups chopped carrots
2 cups chopped celery
1 cup chopped leeks
¼ cup black peppercorns
2 tablespoons fresh thyme
2 bay leaves
1 cup white wine vinegar
32 cups water

1. Heat the oil in large stockpot over low heat and sweat the onions, carrots, celery, and leeks, stirring occasionally, for 15 minutes or until the vegetables are softened without browning. Add the peppercorns, thyme, and bay leaves. Stir to combine with the vegetables and cook for 2 to 3 minutes.

2. Add the vinegar, and then raise the heat to medium-high. Bring the vinegar to a boil. Reduce the heat and simmer the vinegar for about 5 minutes or until most of the vinegar has evaporated and the bottom of the pan is almost dry.

3. Add the water, and then raise the heat to medium-high and bring the liquid to a boil. Reduce the heat and simmer the liquid for 30 minutes.

4. Strain through a chinois or fine-mesh sieve into a large bowl. Discard the vegetables.

5. Allow to cool in an ice-water bath. Cover and refrigerate until chilled.

6. Transfer to covered storage containers and refrigerate for up to 3 days or freeze for up to 2 months.

MUSHROOM STOCK

Makes about 16 cups

2 tablespoons vegetable oil
2 portobello mushrooms, chopped
4 ounces shiitake mushrooms, chopped
4 ounces oyster mushrooms, chopped
4 ounces chanterelle mushrooms, chopped
½ cup chopped leeks
5 shallots, chopped
3 tablespoons fresh thyme
3 tablespoons fresh tarragon
1 cup dry white wine
16 cups water

1. Heat the oil in a stockpot over medium-high heat. When the oil is hot, add the mushrooms. Toss the mushrooms in the oil. Reduce the heat to medium and sauté the mushrooms for 8 to 10 minutes or until they are browned and softened.

2. Add the leeks, shallots, thyme, and tarragon, and cook for an additional 1 minute. Reduce the heat to low and cook for 5 minutes or until the leeks and shallots have softened without browning.

3. Add the wine and raise the heat to medium-high, while stirring the bottom of the pan with a wooden spoon to dissolve any browned solids into the liquid.

4. Simmer the wine for 8 to 10 minutes or until most of the wine has evaporated and the bottom of the pan is almost dry.

5. Add the water and bring to a simmer. Reduce the heat to low and simmer the stock for 30 minutes. Remove from the heat.

6. Strain the stock through a chinois or fine-mesh sieve into a large bowl. Discard the mushrooms and vegetables. Allow the stock to cool in an ice-water bath. Cover and refrigerate until chilled.

7. Transfer to covered storage containers and refrigerate for up to 3 days or freeze for up to 2 months.

LOBSTER GLACE

Makes about 1 cup

2 tablespoons canola oil
1 cup chopped onions
1 cup chopped carrots
¾ cup chopped celery
1 6-ounce can tomato paste
5 pounds lobster bodies or shells
1 cup brandy
¼ bunch flat-leaf parsley, roughly chopped
¼ bunch fresh thyme, roughly chopped
¼ bunch fresh tarragon, roughly chopped
1 tablespoon white peppercorns
8 quarts water

1. In a large stockpot, heat the canola oil over low heat and cook the onions, carrots, and celery, stirring occasionally, for 10 to 12 minutes or until onions are translucent and beginning to caramelize. Add the tomato paste and lobster bodies and stir well.

2. Add the brandy, raise the heat to medium-high, and when the brandy is hot, carefully ignite it. Let the alcohol burn off.

3. When the flames subside, stir in the parsley, thyme, tarragon, and peppercorns and cook for 2 to 3 minutes.

4. Add the water and bring to a boil. Immediately reduce the heat and simmer over low heat for 1½ hours or until reduced to about 6 quarts. Periodically skim any foam that rises to the surface.

5. Strain through a chinois or fine-mesh sieve into a large bowl. Discard the solids. Return the broth to the pot and bring to a boil. Immediately reduce the heat and cook over medium-low heat for about 2 hours or until reduced to about 1 cup. Allow to cool in an ice-water bath. Cover and refrigerate until chilled. Transfer to covered storage containers and refrigerate for up to 3 days or freeze for up to 2 months.

VEAL DEMI-GLACE

Makes about 8 cups

1 tablespoon olive oil
1 cup chopped onions
½ cup chopped carrots
½ cup chopped celery
1 750-ml bottle dry red wine
32 cups Veal Stock (see page 261)

1. In a large stockpot, heat the olive oil over high heat, add the onions, carrots, and celery, and cook, stirring, for 10 to 12 minutes or until the vegetables are tender and golden brown. Add the red wine and scrape the bottom of the pot with a wooden spoon to loosen any browned bits.

2. Bring to a simmer and cook for about 30 minutes or until the wine has almost evaporated and the bottom of the pot is almost dry.

3. Pour in the veal stock. Bring to a simmer over medium heat, reduce the heat to low, and simmer gently for about 3 hours.

4. Strain the stock through a chinois or fine-mesh sieve into a smaller saucepan. Discard the vegetables. Simmer the stock over low heat for about 1 hour or until reduced by half. Occasionally skim any fat and froth from the surface. Strain through a chinois or fine-mesh sieve into a bowl.

5. Plunge the stockpot in an ice-water bath to cool. Cover and refrigerate until chilled. Remove the layer of congealed fat from the surface.

6. Transfer to covered storage containers and refrigerate for up to 3 days or freeze for up to 2 months.

ROASTED CHICKEN DEMI-GLACE

Makes about 16 cups

8 pounds chicken bones
2 cups chopped onions
1 cup chopped carrots
1 cup chopped celery
2 heads garlic, root ends trimmed
4 bay leaves
2 tablespoons black peppercorns
2 tablespoons fresh thyme
1 tablespoon fresh rosemary
¼ cup tomato paste
2 cups dry white wine
1 cup sweet red vermouth

1. Preheat the oven to 375 degrees.
2. Rinse the chicken bones under cold water to remove any blood. Pat dry and transfer to a roasting pan large enough to hold them in a single layer. Roast for 30 to 60 minutes or until the bones are golden brown, stirring every 15 to 20 minutes.
3. Transfer the bones to a large bowl and set aside. Drain off the grease from the roasting pan.
4. Add the onions, carrots, celery, garlic, bay leaves, peppercorns, thyme, and rosemary to the roasting pan and set over medium heat, using 2 burners if necessary. Stirring occasionally, cook for 10 to 15 minutes or until the vegetables are golden brown. Stir in the tomato paste.
5. Add the white wine and vermouth. Raise the heat to high, and cook for 20 to 25 minutes or until most of the liquid has evaporated, stirring the bottom of the pan with a wooden spoon to deglaze.
6. Transfer the ingredients from the roasting pan to a large stockpot, add the chicken bones and enough water to cover by about 1 inch. Bring to a simmer over medium heat, reduce the heat to low, and simmer gently for about 3 hours.
7. Strain the stock through a chinois or fine-mesh sieve into a smaller saucepan. Discard the bones and vegetables. Simmer the stock over low heat for about 1 hour or until reduced by half. Occasionally skim any fat and froth from the surface.
8. Plunge the pot in an ice-water bath. When cool, cover and refrigerate until chilled. Remove the layer of congealed fat from the surface.
9. Use immediately or pour into covered storage containers and refrigerate for up to 3 days or freeze for up to 2 months.

LAMB DEMI-GLACE

Makes about 16 cups

1 tablespoon olive oil
½ cup chopped onions
¼ cup chopped carrots
¼ cup chopped celery
2 tablespoons fresh thyme
2 bay leaves
1 cup port wine
32 cups Lamb Stock (see page 263)

1. In a large stockpot, heat the olive oil over medium heat until hot, add the onions, carrots, and celery, and cook, stirring occasionally, for 6 to 7 minutes or until the vegetables are soft and golden brown. Stir in the thyme and bay leaves.

2. Add the port and bring the liquid to a simmer, scraping the bottom of the pan with a wooden spoon to deglaze. Simmer for about 10 minutes or until most of the liquid has evaporated and the bottom of the pan is almost dry.

3. Add the lamb stock and bring to a simmer over medium heat, reduce the heat to low, and simmer gently for about 3 hours.

4. Strain the stock through a chinois or fine-mesh sieve into a smaller saucepan. Discard the vegetables. Simmer the stock over low heat for about 1 hour or until reduced by half. Occasionally skim any fat and froth from the surface.

5. Strain again through a chinois or fine-mesh sieve. Cool in an ice-water bath. Cover and refrigerate for 4 to 6 days or freeze for up to 2 months.

VENISON DEMI-GLACE

Makes about 8 cups

1 tablespoon olive oil
½ pound venison scraps, optional
1 cup chopped onions
½ cup chopped carrots
½ cup chopped celery
½ cup dry red wine
16 cups Venison Stock (see page 264)

1. In a large stockpot, heat the olive oil over high heat until hot and sear the venison scraps until golden brown, if using. Reduce the heat to medium and add the onions, carrots, and celery and sauté for 10 to 15 minutes or until the vegetables are golden brown and softened. Add the red wine and bring to a simmer, stirring the bottom of the pan with a wooden spoon to deglaze, for 10 minutes or until the wine has almost evaporated and the bottom of the pan is almost dry.

2. Add the venison stock and reduce the heat to low. Simmer for 1 hour. Strain through a chinois or fine-mesh sieve into a saucepan. Discard the vegetables. Set the saucepan over low heat and simmer gently, skimming off any fat and froth that float to the surface of the liquid, for about 3 hours or until reduced by half.

3. Strain the stock through a chinois or fine-mesh sieve into a smaller saucepan. Simmer the stock over low heat for about 1 hour or until reduced by half. Occasionally skim any fat and froth from the surface.

4. Strain again through a chinois or fine-mesh sieve. Cool in an ice-water bath. Cover and refrigerate for 4 to 6 days or freeze for up to 2 months.

RED WINE SAUCE

2 tablespoons olive oil
1 cup chopped carrots
1 cup chopped celery
¼ cup chopped shallots
1 head garlic, root end removed
1 750-ml bottle dry red wine
3 sprigs fresh thyme
4 cups Veal Demi-glace (see page 268)
Kosher salt and freshly ground black pepper

1.   In a medium-sized saucepan, heat the olive oil over medium heat. Add the carrots, celery, shallots, and garlic and cook for 8 to 10 minutes or until nicely browned and softened.

2.   Add the wine and thyme and bring to a boil over high heat. Lower the heat and simmer for 10 to 20 minutes or until most of the wine has evaporated and the bottom of the pan is almost dry.

3.   Add the veal demi-glace and bring to a simmer over medium heat. Lower the heat and simmer for about 30 minutes to 1 hour or until the liquid is reduced to about 2½ cups.

4.   Strain through a chinois or fine-mesh sieve into a small bowl. Season to taste with salt and pepper. Allow to cool. Cover and refrigerate for 4 to 6 days, or freeze for up to 2 months.

BOUQUET GARNI

6 stems flat-leaf parsley
6 sprigs fresh thyme
1 bay leaf

Stack the parsley and thyme on top of the bay leaf. Roll the bay leaf around the herbs. Tie with kitchen string.

VIN BLANC

2 tablespoons olive oil
6 shallots, chopped
3 tablespoons fresh thyme
¼ bunch flat-leaf parsley
3 tablespoons black peppercorns
1 750-ml bottle dry white wine
2 cups heavy cream

1. In a medium saucepan, heat the olive oil over low heat, and cook the shallots, thyme, parsley, and peppercorns, stirring, for about 5 minutes or until the shallots have softened without browning.

2. Add the white wine, raise the heat to medium-high, and simmer for about 30 minutes or until most of the wine has evaporated and the bottom of the pan is almost dry.

3. Add the cream. Bring the cream to a boil. As soon as the cream starts to boil, remove the pan from the heat.

4. Strain through a chinois or fine-mesh sieve into a small bowl. Allow to cool in an ice-water bath. Cover and refrigerate for up to 1 day.

TRAMONTO'S RUBY RED GRAPEFRUIT DUST

6 Ruby Red grapefruits
¼ cup sugar
2 tablespoons water
1 teaspoon sea or kosher salt

1. Using a vegetable peeler, remove only the colored part of the grapefruit peel. Cut off any bitter white pith remaining on the peel.

2. Put the peel, sugar, salt, and water in a large bowl and mix well. Spread on a baking sheet and set in a warm, dry place for 2 days (48 hours) or until completely dried.

3. Transfer to a coffee grinder and blend until finely powdered. You may have to do this in batches.

4. Strain the powder through a chinois or fine-mesh sieve into a small container with a tight-fitting lid. It will keep for 3 to 4 weeks.

VARIATIONS:

Tramonto's Lemon Dust: Substitute 8 lemons for the grapefruit.

Tramonto's Orange Dust: Substitute 7 oranges for the grapefruit.

Tramonto's Lime Dust: Substitute 12 limes for the grapefruit.

CORIANDER-ORANGE OIL

Makes about 2 cups

Zest of 18 oranges
¼ cup coriander seeds
2 cups grapeseed oil

1. Remove the zest from the oranges in strips.
2. Put the orange zest, coriander, and grapeseed oil in a small saucepan over low heat and bring to a simmer. Simmer for 20 minutes. Remove from the heat and let cool slightly.
3. Transfer to a glass container and cover. Let it steep in the refrigerator overnight or up to 24 hours.
4. Strain through a chinois or fine-mesh sieve into a small bowl or glass container. Cover and refrigerate the oil for up to 2 days.

HERB OIL

Makes about 2½ cups

1 bunch fresh flat-leaf parsley
2½ cups grapeseed oil
4 ounces fresh chives
4 ounces fresh tarragon
4 ounces fresh chervil
2 tablespoons kosher salt

1. Remove the parsley leaves from the stems. Discard the stems.
2. In a large sauté pan, heat 4 tablespoons of grapeseed oil over high heat. When hot, add the parsley, chives, tarragon, and chervil. Sauté for about 2 minutes or until the herbs are wilted. Season with the salt. Transfer to a tray and let cool.
3. When cool, transfer the herbs to a blender. With the motor running, slowly add the remaining oil and blend for about 2 to 3 minutes.
4. Transfer to a glass container and cover. Let it steep in the refrigerator overnight or up to 24 hours.
5. Strain through a chinois or fine-mesh sieve into a small bowl or glass container. Cover and refrigerate the oil for up to 2 days.

YELLOW CURRY OIL

Makes about 1 cup

½ cup Madras curry powder
1 cup grapeseed oil

1. In a dry skillet, spread the curry powder in a single layer and toast over low heat, shaking the pan gently, for 40 to 50 seconds or until the curry begins to change color.
2. Add the grapeseed oil to the skillet and bring to a simmer. Immediately reduce the heat to very low and steep for 30 minutes. Remove the skillet from the heat and let the oil cool slightly.
3. Transfer to a glass container and cover. Let it steep in the refrigerator overnight or up to 24 hours.
4. Strain through a chinois or fine-mesh sieve into a small bowl or glass container. Cover and refrigerate the oil for up to 2 days.

VANILLA OIL

Makes about 2 cups

7 whole vanilla beans
2 cups grapeseed oil

1. Split the vanilla beans in half lengthwise and scrape the seeds from the beans.
2. Combine the vanilla seeds, vanilla bean pods, and grapeseed oil in a small saucepan. Bring to a simmer over low heat and cook for 20 minutes.
3. Remove from the heat and let cool slightly.
4. Transfer to a glass container and cover. Let it steep in the refrigerator overnight or up to 24 hours.
5. Strain through a chinois or fine-mesh sieve into a small bowl or glass container. Cover and refrigerate the oil for up to 2 days.

BASIL OIL

Makes about 1 cup

4 ounces fresh basil
¼ bunch fresh flat-leaf parsley
1 cup grapeseed oil
1 tablespoon kosher salt

1. Remove the basil and parsley leaves from the stems. Discard the stems.

2. In a large sauté pan, heat ¼ cup of grapeseed oil over medium-high heat. When the oil is hot, add the basil and parsley leaves. Sauté for 1 to 2 minutes or until the herbs are wilted. Season with the salt. Transfer the herbs to a tray and let cool slightly.

3. When cool, transfer to a blender. With the motor running, slowly add the remaining oil and blend for 4 to 5 minutes.

4. Transfer to a glass container and cover. Let it steep in the refrigerator overnight or up to 24 hours.

5. Strain through a chinois or fine-mesh sieve into a small bowl or glass container. Cover and refrigerate the oil for up to 2 days.

LOBSTER OIL

Makes about 2 cups

4 lobster heads
2 cups grapeseed oil

1. Preheat the oven to 325 degrees.

2. Put the lobster heads on a baking sheet and roast for 20 minutes. Set aside to cool.

3. When the lobsters are cool enough to handle, break them up into small pieces. Transfer to the bowl of a food processor fitted with a metal blade. Add 1 cup of the grapeseed oil and process until the lobster is finely chopped.

4. Transfer the lobster mixture and the remaining cup of oil to a small saucepan. Bring to a simmer over low heat and simmer for 20 minutes. Remove the pot from the heat and set aside to cool slightly.

5. Transfer to a glass container and cover. Let it steep in the refrigerator overnight or up to 24 hours.

6. Strain through a chinois or fine-mesh sieve into a small bowl or glass container. Cover and refrigerate the oil for up to 2 days.

GARLIC AND ROSEMARY OIL

Makes about 2 cups

8 cloves garlic
Leaves of 4 sprigs fresh rosemary
2 cups grapeseed oil

1. In a small saucepan, bring the garlic, rosemary leaves, and grapeseed oil to a simmer over low heat and cook for 20 minutes.
2. Remove from the heat and let cool slightly.
3. Transfer to a glass container and cover. Let it steep in the refrigerator overnight or up to 24 hours.
4. Strain through a chinois or fine-mesh sieve into a small bowl or glass container. Cover and refrigerate the oil for up to 2 days.

CHIVE OIL

Makes about 4 cups

2 ½ cups grapeseed oil
2 cups coarsely snipped fresh chives

1. Heat ¼ cup of the grapeseed oil in a skillet over high heat until almost smoking. Add the chives and cook for 1 minute or until wilted. Remove from the heat and allow to cool.
2. Scrape the chives and any oil into a blender. Add just enough of the remaining oil so that the chives spin when the blender is turned on. Blend for about 5 minutes or until the oil is thick, smooth, and evenly green. Strain the oil through a chinois or fine-mesh sieve into a small bowl.
3. Transfer to a glass container and cover. Let it steep in the refrigerator overnight or up to 24 hours. Use right away, or cover and refrigerate the oil for up to 2 days. The oil will turn brown, but the off color does not mean it is bad.

LEMON OIL

Makes about 1 cup

7 lemons
1 cup grapeseed oil

1. Remove the zest from the lemons in strips. In a small saucepan, combine the zest and the grapeseed oil, bring to a simmer, and cook for 20 minutes.
2. Remove from the heat and let cool slightly.
3. Transfer to a glass container and cover. Let it steep in the refrigerator overnight or up to 24 hours.
4. Strain through a chinois or fine-mesh sieve into a small bowl or glass container. Cover and refrigerate the oil for up to 2 days.

LIME OIL

Makes about 1 cup

9 limes
1 cup grapeseed oil

1. Remove the zest from the limes in strips. In a small saucepan, combine the zest and grapeseed oil, bring to a simmer over low heat, and cook for 20 minutes.
2. Remove from the heat and let cool slightly.
3. Transfer to a glass container and cover. Let it steep in the refrigerator overnight or up to 24 hours.
4. Strain through a chinois or fine-mesh sieve into a small bowl or glass container. Cover and refrigerate the oil for up to 2 days.

CARDAMOM OIL

Makes about 1 cup

¼ cup cardamom seeds
1 cup grapeseed oil
1 tablespoon kosher salt

1. Spread the cardamom out in a dry skillet and toast over low heat, shaking the pan gently, for 40 to 50 seconds or until the cardamom becomes fragrant.
2. In a small saucepan, combine the cardamom, grapeseed oil, and salt, bring to a simmer over low heat, and cook for 20 minutes.
3. Remove from the heat and let cool slightly.
4. Transfer to a glass container and cover. Let it steep in the refrigerator overnight or up to 24 hours.
5. Strain through a chinois or fine-mesh sieve into a small bowl or glass container. Cover and refrigerate the oil for up to 2 days.

BEURRE MONTÉ

Makes about 2 cups

½ cup water
2 cups unsalted butter, cut into small pieces

1. In a small saucepan, bring the water to a boil over medium-high heat. As soon as it starts to boil, remove it from the heat. Slowly whisk in the butter, a few pieces at a time, until all the butter is incorporated.
2. Transfer to a bowl. Cover to keep warm and set aside until needed.

CLARIFIED BUTTER

Makes about 1 cup

1 cup unsalted butter

1. Put the butter in a small saucepan over low heat. Let the butter simmer slowly for 8 to 10 minutes, during which time water will evaporate and the milk solids will collect on the bottom of the pan.

2. Skim any foam that gathers on the top of the butter. Very carefully, pour the clear liquid butter through a fine-mesh sieve into a glass measuring cup or jar. Take care that the white milk solids remain in the pan. Discard the milk solids.

3. Cool the golden-colored butter completely before covering and refrigerating. Clarified butter keeps very well for up to 1 week.

SIMPLE SYRUP

Makes about 1 cup

1 cup granulated sugar
1 cup water

1. In a small saucepan set over medium heat, combine the sugar and water and stir until the sugar dissolves. Raise the heat, bring to a boil, and remove from the heat. Set aside to cool.

2. Transfer to a container with a tight-fitting lid and refrigerate for up to 1 week or until needed.

HOMEMADE CRÈME FRAÎCHE

Makes about 4 cups

2 cups buttermilk
2 cups heavy cream
Juice of ½ lemon
⅛ teaspoon kosher salt

1. In a nonreactive bowl, stir together the buttermilk, cream, lemon juice, and salt. Cover with cheesecloth so the mixture can breathe. Set aside at room temperature for 36 to 48 hours or until thickened.

2. Skim and discard the hardened top layer. Mix the crème fraîche well. Use immediately or cover with plastic wrap and refrigerate for up to 2 weeks.

BRIOCHE

Makes 1 9-inch loaf

1 ¼-ounce package active dry yeast (about 1 tablespoon)
2 tablespoons warm water
1 ½ cups all-purpose flour
1 ¼ cups plus 2 tablespoons bread flour
¼ cup granulated sugar
1 teaspoon salt
4 large eggs
1 cup unsalted butter, cut up

1. Sprinkle the yeast over the water. Set aside for about 5 minutes.

2. Put the flours, sugar, and salt in a large mixing bowl of an electric mixer fitted with a dough hook. Beat for 1 minute on low speed until mixed.

3. Add the eggs and yeast and water. With the mixer on medium speed, beat until smooth. Add the butter and mix until all the butter is incorporated.

4. Cover the bowl with plastic wrap and refrigerate for 24 hours. The dough will rise during this time.

5. Without punching it down, remove the dough from the bowl and roll it into a log. Transfer the log to a standard 9-by-5-inch bread pan and cover with plastic wrap. Set aside in a warm, draft-free place for 2 to 3 hours, until it rises so that the dough touches the plastic wrap.

6. Preheat the oven to 350 degrees.

7. Bake for 45 to 60 minutes, until the crust is lightly browned and cooked through in the center.

8. Remove from the pan immediately and cool completely on a wire rack.

VARIATION: *Pull-apart Brioche Fun Buns: Using the brioche dough, form 24 small balls, each about the size of a walnut (each ball should weigh about ½ ounce). Put 3 balls in a small, ungreased loaf pan. You will need 8 small loaf pans, each about 4 inches long. Cover each pan with plastic wrap and set aside in a warm place to rise for about 1 hour, or until the dough rises slightly over the rim of the loaf pans and pushes against the plastic wrap. Bake in a 375-degree oven for 11 to 15 minutes or until golden brown. Remove the buns from the pans immediately and let them cool completely on wire racks. Freeze the leftover dough or use for a small loaf of brioche.*

JUICING CHART

Makes about ¾ cup of juice

Wash the fruits and vegetables before juicing them. Cut off any soft or obvious brown spots and scrub with a soft pad if it seems needed. Cut them into sizes small enough to go through the juicer's feed tube, but don't worry about peeling or removing stems or small seeds. (The exception to this is citrus fruits, which should be peeled to avoid bitterness.) The juicer extracts the liquid from the fruit or vegetable and separates the pulp (skin, seeds, stems, and all). The juice is exceptionally clear and pure. The pulp is not good for much, although it's great for the compost pile.

Although amounts will vary depending on the ripeness and juiciness of the fruit, the amounts listed below yield about ¾ cup of juice.

Apples	1 pound
Apricots	2 pounds
Asparagus	1 pound
Beets	12 ounces
Blood oranges	3 large fruit
Cantaloupe	1 pound
Carrots	1 pound
Celery	¾ pound
Corn kernels	1 pound
Cucumbers	¾ pound
Fennel	¾ pound
Grapefruit	1 pound
Honeydew melon	1 pound
Leeks	1 pound
Pears	1 pound
Tomatoes	1½ pounds
Watermelon	1 pound
Yukon Gold potatoes	18 ounces

Sources for Hard-to-Find Ingredients and Equipment

Following are sources I use at the restaurant for much of our food and equipment. If there is something you cannot find from local purveyors, one of these merchants may well be able to help you.

SEAFOOD & FISH

Browne Trading
260 Commercial Street, Stop 3
Portland, ME 04101
207-766-2402
Fax: 207-766-2404
All fish

Collins Caviar
925 West Jackson Boulevard
Chicago, IL 60607
312-226-0342
Fax: 312-226-2114
Caviar

Fortune Fish
2442 North 77th Street
Elmwood Park, IL 60707
630-860-7100
All fish

Honolulu Fish
1907 Democrat Street
Honolulu, HI 96819
808-833-1123
Fax: 888-475-6244
All fish

International Marine
1021 South Railroad Avenue
San Mateo, CA 94402
650-341-0390
Fax: 650-341-9798
Shellfish

M.F. Foley Fish Company
24 West Howell Street
Dorchester, MA 02125
1-800-225-9995
Fax: 617-288-1300
All fish

Pierless Fish
Brooklyn Navy Yard
Brooklyn, NY 11205
718-222-4441
All fish

Plitt Seafood
1445 West Willow Street
Chicago, IL 60061
773-276-2200
Fax: 773-276-3350
All fish

Seafood Merchants
900 Forest Edge Drive
Vernon Hills, IL 60061
847-634-0900
Fax: 847-634-1351
All fish

Steve Connolly Seafood Company
34 Newmarket Square
Boston, MA 02118
1-800-225-5595
Lobsters, shellfish

MEATS, GAME, AND POULTRY

Elysian Fields Farms
Keith Martin
844 Craynes Run Road
Waynesburg, PA 15370
724-627-9503
Lamb

Jamison Farms
John Jamison
171 Jamison Lane
Latrobe, PA 15650
1-800-237-5262
Lamb

Joseph Baumgardner
312-829-7762
Fax: 312-829-8791
All meat

Millbrook Farms
1-800-774-3337
Fax: 845-677-8457
Venison

Niman Ranch
940 Judson Avenue
Evanston, IL 60202
847-570-0200
Lamb, pork

Stockyards
340 North Oakley Boulevard
Chicago, IL 60612
312-733-6050
Fax: 312-733-0738
All meat

Swan Creek Farms
10531 Wood Road
North Adam, MI 49262
517-523-3308
Lamb, pork, eggs, cheese

Wild Game
2475 North Elston Avenue
Chicago, IL 60647
773-227-0600
Fax: 773-227-6775
All game, wild mushrooms

PRODUCE

Chef's Garden Farms
9009 Huron-Avery Road
Huron, OH 44839
1-800-289-4644
All vegetables, herbs

Cornille and Sons
Tom Cornille
60 West South Water Market Street
Chicago, IL 60608
312-226-1015
Fax: 312-226-3016
All vegetables, herbs

The Culinary Vegetable Institute
Lee Jones & Family
12304 Mudbrook Road
Milan, OH 44846
419-499-7500
Fax: 419-499-7510
info@culinaryvegetableinstitute.com
Vegetable research center

Earthly Delights
720 East Eldorado Street
Decatur, IL 62523
1-800-367-4709
Wild mushrooms

Fresh and Wild
2917 Northeast 65th Street
Vancouver, WA 98663
360-737-3652
Wild mushrooms

Mid-West Foods
3100 West 36 Street
Chicago, IL 60632
773-927 8870, 1-800-930-4270
Fax: 773-932-4280
All vegetables, herbs

Pacific Farms
88420 Highway 101, Box 223
Florence, OR 97439
541-340-0000; 1-800-927-2248
Fax: 541-345-8050
All vegetables

Sid Wainer and Son
George Rasmussen
2301 Purchase Street
New Bedford, MA 20746
1-800-423-8333
Fax: 508-999-6795
Specialty produce, specialty products

Sunkist Growers Farms
818-14130 Riverside Dr.
Sherman Oaks, CA 91423-2313
Citrus fruits, Tramonto's citrus dust

PASTRY SUPPLIES & CHEESES

Nieman Brothers
3322 West Newport Avenue
Chicago, IL 60618
773-463-3000
Pastry supplies

Albert Uster
1-800-231-8154
Fax: 773-761-5412
Pastry supplies

Laura Chenel
707-996-4477
Cheeses

Coach Farms
1-800-999-4628
Cheeses

Heartland Trading
Giles Schnierle
2320 West 110th Street
Chicago, IL 60643
773-779-5055
Fax: 773-779-5227
www.greatamerica.com
Cheeses

Tekla, Inc.
Sofia Solomon
1456 North Dayton Street
Chicago, IL 60622
312-915-5914
Fax: 312-943-0691
Cheeses

EQUIPMENT

All-Clad
424 Morganza Road
Canonsburg, PA 15317
Smallwares

Boelter
847-675-2963
Fax: 847-675-0505
All equipment, smallwares

Chef's Catalog
1-800-884-2433
5950 Colwell Blvd
Irving, TX 75039
Smallwares

ISI North America
175 Route 46
West Fairfield, NJ 07004
1-800-447-2426
Gourmet whip canisters, cream chargers

Korin
57 Warren Street
New York, NY 10007
212-587-7021
Knives, Asian china, Asian equipment

Paco Jet
212-421-1106
Fax: 212-421-1137
Paco jet machine

Tramonto Cuisine
847-932-3657
www.tramontocuisine.com
*Caviar staircases, specialty china, and
other hard-to-find equipment*

Viking
100 Concourse
1052 Highland Colony Parkway
Ridgeland, MS 30157
404-739-0118
All equipment

Williams-Sonoma
877-812-6235
Smallwares

SPECIALTY PRODUCTS

Anson Mills
1922-C Gervais Street
Columbus, SC 29201
803-225-4032
Fax: 803-256-2463
Stoneground grits

Bragard
215 Park Ave South
New York, NY 10003
212-982-8031
Chef's clothing

SOURCES

Chefwear
3111 N. Knox Ave
Chicago, IL 60641-5200
773-427-6734
Chef's clothing

European Imports
2475 North Elston Avenue
Chicago, IL 60647
773-227-0600
Fax: 773-227-6775
Specialty foods

Gourmand
728 South Dearborn Street
Chicago, IL 60605
1-800-627-7272
Fax: 703-708-9393
Specialty foods

Illy Coffee
275 Madison Ave
New York, NY 10016
1-800-872-4559
Coffee

Limoges China
1-800-448-8282
China

Natural Juice
550 Clayton Court
Wood Dale, IL 60191
630-350-1700
Fresh juices

Rosenthal China
201-804-8000
355 Michele Place
Carlstadt, NJ 07072
China

Spiceland
6604 West Irving Park Road
Chicago, IL 60634
773-736-1000
Fax: 773-736-1271
Spices

Tony Polega
Bukiety Florists
2000 West Carroll Avenue
Chicago, IL 60612
312-733-4580
Flowers

Urbani Truffle
2924 40th Avenue
Long Island City, NY 11101
718-392-5050
Fax: 718-392-1704
Truffle products

Index

a

almond(s):
    in Pleasant Ridge Reserve with organic honey and
        panforte, 210
    in seared foie gras with rhubarb ice cream, pickled
        rhubarb, and pomegranate molasses, 91
    -spinach puree, 142
    -spinach puree, arctic char poached in duck fat with,
        140–42
    toasted, milk sherbet, 233
    toasted, milk sherbet, warm chocolate tart with, 231–34
amuse-bouche, 15–32
    black garbanzo bean and celery salad, 31
    carrot parfait with carrot paint, 23
    chilled purple Peruvian soup with chives, 22
    clam foam on the half shell with crispy pancetta, 21
    deconstructed insalata caprese with olive oil sorbet, 28
    Kumamoto oysters with passion fruit gelée on aromatic
        rock salt, 26–27
    marinated white anchovies with green olives and
        tomatoes, 29
    prosciutto di Parma with tricolor melon and mascarpone,
        32
    rabbit roulade with a salad of frisée, French beans, and
        radish, 19–20
    red and yellow teardrop tomatoes stuffed with goat
        cheese, with 100-year-old balsamic, 27
    red watermelon-lavender juice with yellow watermelon
        salad, 17
    Thai snapper with hijiki seaweed, lemon balm salad, and
        yuzu soy dressing, 24
amuse-bouche, dessert, 221–23
    blueberry and Perfection tangerines with basil syrup, 222
    clementine granita with raspberry micro mint salad, 222
    roasted lemonade shooters, 223
    Szechuan peppercorn crème brûlée spoonfuls, 221
anchovy(ies):
    fillets, white, in beef tartar with quail egg and beef gelée,
        51–54
    marinated white, with green olives and tomatoes, 29
appetizers, cold, 35–54
    beef tartar with quail egg and beef gelée, 51–54
    live Japanese fish and chips, 38–41
    mosaic of seafood with saffron foam, 42–44

octopus carpaccio with niçoise vinaigrette, 49–50
    Peekytoe crab salad with crispy Sawagani crab and micro
        greens, 45–47
    Tramonto's caviar staircase with homemade crème
        fraîche, 37
appetizers, hot, 57–63
    black truffle risotto with lobster, French beans, and
        lobster reduction, 84–85
    braised 31-vegetable ragout with chervil butter, 61–63
    braised veal tongue and artichoke napoleon with Asian
        pear and fennel pollen, 68–72
    butter-poached Maine lobster and truffle mashed potato
        "Martini," 80–81
    frog leg risotto with parsley and lots and lots of garlic,
        77–79
    langoustine ravioli with buttered leeks, foie gras sauce,
        and blood orange reduction, 82–83
    oozy quail egg ravioli with porcini mushrooms, 64–67
    roasted sweetbread salad with walnut vinaigrette and beet
        paint, 73–76
    Swan Creek ricotta gnocchi with Parmigiano-Reggiano
        cream and shaved white truffles, 58–60
apple(s):
    caramel taffy, foie gras with lavender salad and green
        apple chip, 97–99
    in curried cauliflower soup with cumin cracker, 116
    in red wine essence, 142
apple(s), Granny Smith:
    in cured pork belly, 167
    in Peekytoe crab salad with crispy Sawagani crab and
        micro greens, 45–47
apple, green:
    chip, caramel taffy apple foie gras with lavender salad
        and, 97–99
    chips, 99
apricot tarte tatin, 246–47
aromatic rock salt, Kumamoto oysters with passion fruit gelée
    on, 26–27
artichoke(s):
    baby, in braised 31-vegetable ragout with chervil butter,
        61–63
    napoleon, braised veal tongue with Asian pear, fennel
        pollen and, 68–72

Asian:
    bouillabaisse with coconut broth and sea beans, 147–48
    pear salad, 150
    pear salad, steamed halibut with cucumber broth and, 149
asparagus:
    in braised 31-vegetable ragout with chervil butter, 61–63
    in braised veal tongue and artichoke napoleon with Asian pear and pollen, 68–72
    puree, 154–56
    in roasted beef tenderloin, truffled potato puree, and bone marrow foam with red wine sauce, 154–56
    in roasted sweetbread salad with walnut vinaigrette and beet paint, 73–76
aspic, Madeira, 44
avocado puree, 40

b
bacon:
    lardons, roasted poussin and French lentils with truffled green Brussels sprouts and, 177–80
    in roasted vegetables and fried celery leaves, 163
    slab, in roasted sweetbread salad with walnut vinaigrette and beet paint, 73–76
baguette:
    in Asian bouillabaisse with coconut broth and sea beans, 147
    for Roquefort with pear chips and hot honey walnuts, 214–16
banana:
    chutney, 100
    French toast and chocolate sauce, macadamia nut-crusted foie gras with, 100–102
barbecue (BBQ):
    sauce, J-Rob's, 171
    Tramonto's backyard: smoked pork belly, pork tenderloin, and pig-tail roulade, 167–71
basic recipes, 261–81
    basil oil, 275
    beef and veal stock, 262
    beef stock, 261
    beurre monté, 278
    bouquet garni, 271
    brioche, 280–81
    cardamom oil, 278
    chicken stock, 265
    chive oil, 276
    clarified butter, 279
    coriander-orange oil, 273
    court bouillon, 267
    duck stock, 265
    fish stock, 266
    game stock, 264
    garlic and rosemary oil, 276
    herb oil, 273
    homemade crème fraîche, 280
    juicing chart, 281
    lamb demi-glace, 270
    lamb stock, 263
    lemon oil, 277
    lime oil, 277
    lobster glace, 268
    lobster oil, 275
    mushroom stock, 267
    red wine sauce, 271
    roasted chicken demi-glace, 269
    simple syrup, 279
    Tramonto's ruby red grapefruit dust, 272
    vanilla oil, 274
    veal demi-glace, 268
    veal stock, 261
    vegetable stock, 266
    venison demi-glace, 270
    venison stock, 264
    vin blanc, 272
    yellow curry oil, 274
basil:
    in chilled tomato water with baby heirloom tomatoes and olive oil, 121
    oil, 275
    puree, 7
    syrup, blueberry and Perfection tangerines with, 222
beans:
    black garbanzo, and celery salad, 31
    in braised 31-vegetable ragout with chervil butter, 61–63
    sea, Asian bouillabaisse with coconut broth and, 147–48
beans, French:
    black truffle risotto with lobster, lobster emulsion and, 84–85
    rabbit roulade with a salad of frisée, radish and, 19–20
beef:
    bone marrow foam, 156
    braised short ribs, 157–59
    braised short ribs with parsnip puree, 157–60
    consommé, 53
    consommé gelée, 53
    stock, in consommé, 53
    tartar with quail egg and beef gelée, 51–54
beef and veal stock, 262
    in braised beef short ribs, 157–59
beef tenderloin:
    in beef tartar with quail egg and beef gelée, 51–54
    in Rick's steak and eggs, 5
    roasted, truffled potato puree, and bone marrow foam with red wine sauce, 154–56
beet(s):
    in braised 31-vegetable ragout with chervil butter, 61–63
    paint, 76
    in roasted sweetbread salad with walnut vinaigrette and beet paint, 73–76
beignets, orange-kissed, Walla Walla onion soup with, 113–15
bergamot-chocolate paint, 237
beurre:
    blanc, vanilla-saffron, roasted spiny lobster with, 137–39
    monté, 278
bisque, lobster, 110–12
black truffles in oil, 175

blueberry(ies):
    Maine, and caramelized white peaches, seared foie gras
        with, 89–90
    Maine, sauce, 89–90
    and Perfection tangerines with basil syrup, 222
    stew, 245
bluefin tuna, pink peppercorn-crusted, with tomato
    marmalade and buttermilk crackers, 12–13
bone marrow foam, roasted beef tenderloin, and truffled
    potato puree with red wine sauce, 154–56
boniato mash, 170
bouillabaisse, Asian, with coconut broth and sea beans,
    147–48
bouillon, court, 267
bouquet garni, 271
braise(d):
    beef short ribs, 157–59
    beef short ribs with parsnip puree, 157–60
    frog leg, 79
    octopus, 50
    oxtail, 132
    oxtail and spiced carrot puree, roasted sturgeon with, 131–33
    red cabbage, 163–64
    salsify, 136
    squab legs, 199
    31-vegetable ragout with chervil butter, 61–63
    veal tongue and artichoke napoleon with Asian pear and
        fennel pollen, 68–72
brandy:
    in lobster bisque, 110
    in lobster glace, 268
    vanilla, 237
bread crumbs, in pig-tail roulade, 167
brioche, 280–81
    in Malaysian-crusted rack of lamb with truffled bread-
        and-butter pudding and mint paint, 172–76
    in Rick's steak and eggs, 5
    in Tramonto's caviar staircase with homemade crème
        fraîche, 37
broccoflower puree, 175
broth:
    coconut, Asian bouillabaisse with sea beans and, 147–48
    cucumber, 150
    curried coconut, 148
    saffron, 145
    shellfish and saffron, 24-karat gold leaf rouget with, 143–45
Brussels sprouts:
    in braised 31-vegetable ragout with chervil butter, 61–63
    truffled green, roasted poussin and French lentils with
        bacon lardons and, 177–80
    truffled green, with purple kale, 179
butter(ed):
    clarified, 279
    coconut, cookies, 241–42
    garlic-parsley, 79
    herb, 179
    leeks, langoustine ravioli with foie gras sauce, blood
        orange reduction and, 82–83
    strawberry balsamic, 233

    tarragon-chervil, 82–83
    truffle, 106
    see also beurre
buttermilk:
    crackers, 13
    crackers, pink peppercorn-crusted bluefin tuna with
        tomato marmalade and, 12–13
    in cumin crackers, 117
    in homemade crème fraîche, 280
    -key lime sherbet, 241
butter-poached:
    breast, assiette of milk-fed veal: roasted loin, crispy
        sweetbreads, 161–66
    Maine lobster and truffle mashed potato "Martini," 80–81
    veal breast, 165

c
cabbage, braised red, 163–64
cake(s):
    chocolate, 229–30
    Concord, with coconut sorbet, 229–30
calamari, in 24-karat gold leaf rouget with shellfish and
    saffron broth, 143–45
calvados, in smoked pork jus, 170
cannclés, 256
cantaloupe, in sautéed foie gras with honeydew melon soup
    and muscat reduction, 94–96
caramel(ized):
    boings, 238
    taffy apple foie gras with lavender salad and green apple
        chip, 97–99
    white peaches and Maine blueberries, seared foie gras
        with, 89–90
cardamom oil, 278
carpaccio:
    octopus, with niçoise vinaigrette, 49
    roasted pineapple, with key lime sherbet, 239–42
carrot(s):
    in braised beef short ribs with parsnip puree, 157–60
    in braised 31-vegetable ragout with chervil butter, 61–63
    -chive spoons, 124
    in court bouillon, 267
    and Hawaiian ginger soup with carrot salad, 122
    in lobster bisque, 110
    in lobster glace, 268
    paint, carrot parfait with, 23
    puree, roasted sturgeon with braised oxtail and spiced, 131–33
    in red wine sauce, 271
    in roasted chicken demi-glace, 269
    in roasted vegetables and fried celery leaves, 163
    in venison navarin, 186
cassis, crème de, in chocolate sauce, 100
cauliflower:
    curried, soup with cumin cracker, 116–17
    puree, 66
caviar:
    sevruga, chilled sunchoke velouté, pickled sunchokes and,
        118
    Tramonto's staircase, with homemade crème fraîche, 37

celery:
    in braised 31-vegetable ragout with chervil butter, 61–63
    in court bouillon, 267
    in lobster glace, 268
    in red wine sauce, 271
    in roasted chicken demi-glace, 269
    salad, black garbanzo bean and, 31
celery root, in roasted vegetables and fried celery leaves, 163
ceviche, lobster, 110
    lobster bisque with a spoon of, 110–12
champagne, in citrus gelée, 47
chanterelles, in mushroom stock, 267
char, arctic, poached in duck fat with spinach-almond puree, 140–42
cheese(s):
    categories of, 209
    ingredients of, 208
    notes, 208–9
    production, types of, 208
    rinds, types of, 208
    sources of, 285–86
    see also specific cheeses
cheese course, 207–17
    oil-marinated Manchego with oven-roasted tomatoes, 213
    Pleasant Ridge Reserve with organic honey and panforte, 210
    Roquefort with pear chips and hot honey walnuts, 214
    Szechuan peppercorn crème brûlée spoonfuls, 221
    Wabash Cannonball with cherries and rosemary, 217
cherries:
    dried, Cracker Jack with, 251
    Wabash Cannonball with rosemary and, 217
chicken, roasted, demi-glace, 269
chicken stock, 265
    in braised squab legs, 199
    in frog leg braise, 79
    in pig-tail roulade, 167
    in rabbit jus, 192
chili tuiles, pistachio, 237
chilled:
    purple Peruvian potato soup with chives, 22
    sunchoke velouté, pickled sunchokes, and sevruga caviar, 118
    tomato water with baby heirloom tomatoes and olive oil, 121
chip(s):
    fried vegetable, 41
    green apple, 99
    live Japanese fish and, 38–41
    pear, 214
    pear, Roquefort with hot honey walnuts and, 214–16
chive(s):
    -carrot spoons, 124
    chilled purple Peruvian soup with, 22
    -garlic emulsion, 192
    oil, 276
chlorophyll, 156

chocolate:
    -bergamot paint, 237
    cake, 229–30
    in cinnamon-cayenne truffles, 253
    filling, melted, 231–33
    in ginger ganache, 229
    -malted semifreddo with chocolate-bergamot paint, 235–38
    melted, filling, 231–33
    mixture, 235–37
    sable, 231–33
    sauce, macadamia nut-crusted foie gras with banana French toast and, 101–2
    warm tart with toasted almond milk sherbet, 231–34
chutney, banana, 100
ciabatta, in oven-roasted tomatoes, 213
cilantro:
    -coconut syrup, 239
    crystallized leaves, 241
cinnamon:
    -cayenne truffles, 253
    sticks, in Kumamoto oysters with passion fruit gelée on aromatic rock salt, 26–27
citrus:
    gelée, 47
    vinaigrette, 124
clam(s):
    foam on the half shell with crispy pancetta, 21
    Manila, in Asian bouillabaisse with coconut broth and sea beans, 147–48
clarified butter, 279
clementine granita with raspberry micro mint salad, 222
cocoa:
    in cinnamon-cayenne truffles, 253
    foam, 234
    meringue, 229–30
coconut:
    broth, curried, 148
    broth and sea beans, Asian bouillabaisse with, 147–48
    butter cookies, 241–42
    -cilantro syrup, 239
    sorbet, 230
    sorbet, Concord cakes with, 229–30
    tuiles, 245
cod bones in fish stock, 266
cold appetizers, *see* appetizers, cold
Concord cakes with coconut sorbet, 229–30
confit:
    potatoes, duck fat, 70
    potatoes, olive oil, 132
    rabbit leg, 190
consommé, beef, 53
    gelée, 53
cookies, coconut butter, 241–42
coriander:
    -orange oil, 273
    salt, 200

corn:
    ears of baby, in braised 31-vegetable ragout with chervil
        butter, 61–63
    oil, for parsnip curls, 160
    sweet, flan, 198–99
    sweet, flan, roasted squab with gingered spaghetti squash
        and, 196–200
    in vegetable stock, 266
court bouillon, 267
    in mosaic of seafood with saffron foam, 42–44
crab, Peekytoe:
    curried salad, kumquats stuffed with, 11
    salad with crispy Sawagani crab and micro greens, 45
cracker(s):
    buttermilk, 13
    buttermilk, pink peppercorn-crusted bluefin tuna with
        tomato marmalade and, 12–13
    cumin, curried cauliflower soup with, 116–17
Cracker Jack with dried cherries, 251
cream:
    in horseradish foam, 54
    and meringue, 235–37
cream, heavy:
    in beef bone marrow foam, 156
    in black truffle risotto with lobster, French beans, and
        lobster emulsion, 84–85
    in boniato mash, 170
    in cauliflower puree, 66
    in chilled sunchoke velouté, pickled sunchokes, and
        sevruga caviar, 118
    in duet of venison with rutabaga mash, 185–87
    in frog leg risotto with parsley and lots and lots of garlic,
        77–79
    in fromage blanc mousse, 243–45
    in garlic-chive emulsion, 192
    in ginger ganache, 229
    in homemade crème fraîche, 280
    in lobster bisque, 110
    in lobster emulsion, 85
    in parsnip puree, 159
    in porcini emulsion, 67
    in savory anglaise, 93
    in sour cream ice cream, 247
    in sweet corn flan, 198–99
    in Szechuan peppercorn crème brûlée spoonfuls, 221
    in truffled bread-and-butter pudding, 174–75
    in vin blanc, 272
    in Walla Walla onion soup with orange-kissed beignets,
        113–15
    in Yukon gold potato puree, 80
    in yuzu cream, 227–28
cream, Parmigiano-Reggiano, Swan Creek ricotta gnocchi
    with shaved white truffles and, 58–60
cream, sour, ice cream, 247
crème:
    brûlée spoonfuls, Szechuan peppercorn, 221
    fraîche, homemade, 280
    fraîche, homemade, Tramonto's caviar staircase with, 37
crème de cassis, in chocolate sauce, 100

Crenshaw melon, in prosciutto di Parma with tricolor melon
        and mascarpone, 32
crispy pancetta, clam foam on the half shell with, 21
cucumber:
    broth, 150
    broth and Asian pear salad, steamed halibut with, 149–50
    -mango salad, 40
cumin cracker, curried cauliflower soup with, 116–17
cured:
    foie gras au torchon with peppered pineapple relish and
        fun buns, 103–6
    pork belly, 167–69
curry(ied):
    cauliflower soup with cumin cracker, 116–17
    coconut broth, 148
    oil, yellow, 274
    Peekytoe crab salad, kumquats stuffed with, 11

d
deconstructed insalata caprese with olive oil sorbet, 28
demi-glace:
    lamb, 270
    roasted chicken, 269
    veal, 268
    venison, 270
desserts, 227–47
    amuse-bouche, see amuse-bouche, dessert
    apricot tarte tatin, 246–47
    chocolate-malted semifreddo with chocolate-bergamot
        paint, 235–38
    Concord cakes with coconut sorbet, 229–30
    fromage blanc mousse, 243–45
    roasted pineapple carpaccio with key lime sherbet, 239–42
    tequila granita with yuzu cream and grapefruit, 227–28
    warm chocolate tart with toasted almond milk sherbet,
        231–34
dough, pasta, 66
dressing, yuzu soy, Thai snapper with hijiki seaweed, lemon
        balm salad and, 24
duck:
    consommé, 195
    pomegranate-lacquered Muscovy, with foie gras ravioli,
        193–95
duck fat:
    arctic char poached in, with spinach almond puree,
        140–42
    confit potatoes, 70
    in mousseron mushroom confit, 142
    in rabbit leg confit, 190
    in rabbit roulade with a salad of frisée, French beans, and
        radish, 19–20
duck stock, 265
    in duck consommé, 195
duet of venison with rutabaga mash, 185–87

e
egg(s):
    in brioche, 280–81
    deviled quail, assortment of, 7

egg(s) (*cont'd*):
    in French toast, 100
    in melted chocolate filling, 231–34
    quail, and beef gelée, beef tartar with, 51–54
    quail, ravioli, 66
    Rick's steak and, 5
    in sweet corn flan, 198–99
egg whites:
    in coconut tuiles, 245
    in torchons of sweetbreads, 164
egg yolks:
    in chocolate mixture, 235
    in lemon curd paint, 245
    in savory anglaise, 93
    in sour cream ice cream, 247
    in squash spaetzle, 191
    in Szechuan peppercorn crème brûlée spoonfuls, 221
    in truffled bread-and-butter pudding, 174–75
emulsion:
    garlic-chive, 192
    lobster, black truffle risotto with lobster, French beans and, 84–85
    porcini, 67
    white truffle, 72
equipment, sources of, 286
essence, red wine, 142

f

fava bean(s):
    in rabbit, rabbit, rabbit, 188–92
    stew, black trumpet mushroom-crusted ahi tuna with scallion and, 134–36
    in venison navarin, 186
fennel:
    baby, in braised 31-vegetable ragout with chervil butter, 61–63
    pollen and Asian pear, braised veal tongue and artichoke napoleon with, 68–72
filling, melted chocolate, 231–33
fish and seafood, 129–50
    arctic char poached in duck fat with spinach-almond puree, 140–42
    Asian bouillabaisse with coconut broth and sea beans, 147–48
    black trumpet mushroom-crusted ahi tuna with scallion and fava bean stew, 134–36
    braised octopus, 50
    clam foam on the half shell with crispy pancetta, 21
    crispy Sawagani crabs, 47
    grilled octopus, 38
    hamachi-salmon tartar spoons, 6
    hamachi tartar, 6
    Kumamoto oysters with passion fruit gelée on aromatic rock salt, 26–27
    kumquats stuffed with curried Peekytoe crab salad, 11
    live Japanese, and chips, 38–41
    marinated tuna, salmon, and hamachi, 40–41
    marinated white anchovies with green olives and tomatoes, 29
    mosaic of seafood with saffron foam, 42–44
    octopus carpaccio with niçoise vinaigrette, 49–50
    octopus terrine, 49–50
    Peekytoe crab salad with crispy Sawagani crab and micro greens, 45–47
    pink peppercorn-crusted bluefin tuna, 12
    pink peppercorn-crusted bluefin tuna with homemade marmalade and buttermilk crackers, 12–13
    roasted spiny lobster with vanilla-saffron beurre blanc, 137–39
    roasted sturgeon with braised oxtail and spiced carrot puree, 131–33
    salmon tartar, 6
    sources of, 283–84
    steamed halibut with cucumber broth and Asian pear salad, 149–50
    Thai snapper with hijiki seaweed, lemon balm salad, and yuzu soy dressing, 24
    Tramonto's caviar staircase with homemade crème fraîche, 37
    24-karat gold leaf rouget with shellfish and saffron broth, 143–45
fish stock, 266
    in saffron broth, 145
flan, sweet corn, 198–99
foam:
    beef bone marrow, 156
    bone marrow, roasted beef tenderloin and truffled potato puree with red wine sauce, 154–56
    clam, on the half shell with crispy pancetta, 21
    cocoa, 234
    horseradish, 54
    saffron, 44
    saffron, mosaic of seafood with, 42–44
foie gras, 87–106
    in assiette of milk-fed veal: roasted loin, butter-poached breast, crispy sweetbreads, 161–66
    au torchon with peppered pineapple relish and fun buns, 103–6
    caramel taffy apple, with lavender salad and green apple chip, 97–99
    macadamia nut-crusted, with banana French toast and chocolate sauce, 100–102
    ravioli, 195
    ravioli, pomegranate-lacquered Muscovy duck with, 193–95
    sauce, 83
    sauce, langoustine ravioli with buttered leeks, blood orange reduction and, 82–83
    sautéed, with honeydew melon soup and Muscat reduction, 94–96
    seared, with caramelized white peaches and Maine blueberries, 89–90
    seared, with rhubarb ice cream, pickled rhubarb, and pomegranate molasses, 91–93
French toast, banana, and chocolate sauce, macadamia nut-crusted foie gras with, 100–102

294

INDEX

fried:
    leeks, 150
    vegetable chips, 41
frisée (lettuce):
    in beef tartar with quail egg and beef gelée, 51–54
    rabbit roulade with a salad of French beans, radish and, 19–20
    in Roquefort with pear chips and hot honey walnuts, 214–16
    and watercress salad, 199
frog leg:
    braise, 79
    risotto with parsley and lots and lots of garlic, 77–79
fromage blanc mousse, 243–45
fruit, dried, in Pleasant Ridge Reserve with organic honey and panforte, 210
fun buns, cured foie gras au torchon with peppered pineapple relish and, 103–6

g
game, 183–200
    duet of venison with rutabaga mash, 185–87
    pomegranate-lacquered Muscovy duck with foie gras ravioli, 193–95
    rabbit, rabbit, rabbit, 188–92
    roasted squab with sweet corn flan and gingered spaghetti squash, 196–200
    sources of, 284
    stock, 264
ganache, 234
    ginger, 229
garbanzo bean(s), black, 31
    and celery salad, 31
garlic:
    -chive emulsion, 192
    cloves, in braised 31-vegetable ragout with chervil butter, 61–63
    cloves, in roasted sweetbread salad with walnut vinaigrette and beet paint, 73–76
    frog leg risotto with parsley and lots and lots of, 77–79
    in game stock, 264
    in Malaysian-crusted rack of lamb with truffled bread-and-butter pudding and mint paint, 172–76
    -parsley butter, 79
    in red wine sauce, 271
    in roasted chicken demi-glace, 269
    and rosemary oil, 276
gaufrettes pommes de terre in fried vegetable chips, 41
gelatin sheets:
    in fromage blanc mousse, 243–45
    in Kracher gelée, 106
    in lime gelée, 245
    in strawberry gelée, 243
gelée:
    beef tartar with quail egg and beef, 51–54
    citrus, 47
    Kracher, 106
    lime, 245
    passion fruit, 27

passion fruit, with Kumamoto oysters on aromatic rock salt, 26–27
    strawberry, 243
ginger:
    ganache, 229–30
    Hawaiian, and carrot soup with carrot salad, 122
    in pomegranate-lacquered Muscovy duck with foie gras ravioli, 193–95
    syrup, 122
glace:
    lobster, 268
    see also demi-glace
gnocchi, Swan Creek ricotta, with Parmigiano-Reggiano cream and shaved white truffles, 58–60
goat cheese:
    gougères, truffled, 8–9
    red and yellow teardrop tomatoes, stuffed with, 100-year-old balsamic with, 27
gold:
    leaf, 24-karat, rouget with shellfish and saffron broth, 143–45
    24-karat, syrup, 237
gougères, truffled goat cheese, 8–9
granita:
    clementine, with raspberry micro mint salad, 222
    tequila, with yuzu cream and grapefruit, 227
grapefruit:
    dust, Tramonto's ruby red, 272
    tequila granita with yuzu cream and, 227
green apple chips, 99
greens, micro, Peekytoe crab salad with crispy Sawagani crab and, 45
grenadine in pickled rhubarb, 91
grilled:
    octopus, 38
    octopus, in live Japanese fish and chips, 38–41
Gruyère in gougères, 8–9

h
half-and-half:
    in sour cream ice cream, 247
    in truffled bread-and-butter pudding, 174–75
halibut:
    in Asian bouillabaisse with coconut broth and sea beans, 147
    bones, in fish stock, 266
    steamed, with cucumber broth and Asian pear salad, 149–50
hamachi:
    marinated tuna, and salmon, 40
    -salmon tartar spoons, 6
haricots verts:
    in braised 31-vegetable ragout with chervil butter, 61–63
    in frog leg risotto with parsley and lots and lots of garlic, 77–79
    in roasted sweetbread salad with walnut vinaigrette and beet paint, 73–76
    in venison navarin, 186

hazelnuts, in braised veal tongue and artichoke napoleon with Asian pear and fennel pollen, 68–72

herb:
    butter, 179
    oil, 273

hickory nut shortbread, 252

hijiki seaweed in mosaic of seafood with saffron foam, 42–44

homemade crème fraîche, 280

honey:
    -and-lemon tea lollipops, 255
    organic, Pleasant Ridge Reserve with panforte and, 210
    in pomegranate-lacquered Muscovy duck with foie gras ravioli, 193–95
    walnuts, hot, 214

honeydew melon:
    in prosciutto di Parma with tricolor melon and mascarpone, 32
    soup, 94
    soup and muscat reduction, sautéed foie gras with, 94–96

hors d'oeuvres, 5–13
    assortment of deviled quail eggs, 7
    hamachi-salmon tartar spoons, 6
    kumquats stuffed with curried Peekytoe crab salad, 11
    pink peppercorn-crusted bluefin tuna with tomato marmalade and buttermilk crackers, 12–13
    Rick's steak and eggs, 5
    truffled goat cheese gougères, 8–9

horseradish foam, 54

hot appetizers, *see* appetizers, hot

i

ice cream:
    rhubarb, 93
    rhubarb, seared foie gras with pickled rhubarb, pomegranate molasses and, 91–93
    sour cream, 247

ingredients and equipment, sources of, 283–87
    meats, game and poultry, 284
    pastry supplies and cheeses, 285–86
    produce, 284–85
    seafood and fish, 283–84
    specialty products, 286–87

insalata caprese, deconstructed, with olive oil sorbet, 28

j

jalapeño peppers, in J-Rob's barbecue sauce, 171

Japanese fish, live, and chips, 38–41

jus:
    natural poussin, 180
    rabbit, 192
    squab, 198

k

kale, purple, truffled green Brussels sprouts with, 179

ketchup, in J-Rob's barbecue sauce, 171

key lime:
    -buttermilk sherbet, 241
    sherbet, roasted pineapple carpaccio with, 239–42

Kracher gelée, 106

Kumamoto oysters with passion fruit gelée on aromatic rock salt, 26–27

kumquats stuffed with curried Peekytoe crab salad, 11

l

lamb:
    demi-glace, 270
    Malaysian-crusted rack of, with truffled bread-and-butter pudding and mint paint, 172–76
    sauce, red wine, 175–76
    stock, 263

langoustine(s):
    in Asian bouillabaisse with coconut broth and sea beans, 147
    ravioli, 82–83
    ravioli with buttered leeks, foie gras sauce, and blood orange reduction, 82–83

lavender:
    -red watermelon juice, yellow watermelon salad with, 17
    salad and green apple chip, caramel taffy apple foie gras with, 97–99

leeks:
    in braised 31-vegetable ragout with chervil butter, 61–63
    buttered, langoustine ravioli with foie gras sauce, blood orange reduction and, 82–83
    in court bouillon, 267
    in fish stock, 266
    fried, 150

lemon:
    balm salad, hijiki seaweed, and yuzu soy dressing, Thai snapper with, 24
    curd paint, 245
    dust, Tramonto's, 272
    oil, 277
    tea-and-honey lollipops, 255
    verbena syrup, 200
    vinaigrette, 71

lemonade, roasted, shooters, 223

lentil(s):
    French, and roasted poussin with bacon lardons and truffled green Brussels sprouts, 177–80
    French green and crimson red, 179
    salad, 105

lime:
    dust, Tramonto's, 272
    gelée, 245
    juice, in tequila granita with yuzu cream and tequila, 227–28
    oil, 277

live Japanese fish and chips, 38–41

lobster:
    bisque with a spoon of lobster ceviche, 110–12
    black truffle risotto with French beans, lobster emulsion and, 84–85
    claws, in Asian bouillabaisse with coconut broth and sea beans, 147
    glace, 268
    Maine, butter-poached, and truffle mashed potato "Martini," 80–81

in mosaic of seafood with saffron foam, 42–44
oil, 275
poached tails and claws, 81
roe, in langoustine ravioli with buttered leeks, foie gras,
    and blood orange reduction, 82–83
spiny, roasted with vanilla-saffron beurre blanc, 137–39
lollipops, honey-and-lemon tea, 255
lotus root, in fried vegetable chips, 41
lychees, in tequila granita with yuzu cream and grapefruit,
    227–28

m
macadamia nut:
    brittle, 241
    -crusted foie gras with banana French toast and chocolate
        sauce, 100–102
mâche, in cured foie gras au torchon with peppered pineapple
    relish and fun buns, 103
Madeira:
    aspic, 44
    sauce, 166
Malaysian-crusted rack of lamb with truffled bread-and-
    butter pudding and mint paint, 172–76
Manchego, oil-marinated, with oven-roasted tomatoes, 213
mango(es):
    -cucumber salad, 40
    in J-Rob's barbecue sauce, 171
marinated:
    oil-, Manchego with oven-roasted tomatoes, 213
    tuna, salmon, and hamachi, 40
    white anchovies with green olives and tomatoes, 29
marmalade, tomato, pink peppercorn-crusted bluefin tuna
    with buttermilk crackers and, 12–13
marrow, beef bone, foam, 156
mascarpone and tricolor melon, prosciutto di Parma with, 32
mash, boniato, 170
meat and poultry, 154–80
    assiette of milk-fed veal: roasted loin, butter-poached
        breast, crispy sweetbreads, 161–66
    braised beef short ribs with parsnip puree, 157–60
    Malaysian-crusted rack of lamb with truffled bread-and-
        butter pudding and mint paint, 172–76
    roasted beef tenderloin, truffled potato puree, and bone
        marrow foam with red wine sauce, 154–56
    roasted poussin and French lentils with bacon lardons and
        truffled green Brussels sprouts, 177–80
    Tramonto's backyard BBQ: smoked pork belly, pork
        tenderloin, and pigtail roulade, 167–71
meats, sources of, 284
melon:
    honeydew, soup, 94
    honeydew, soup and muscat reduction, sautéed foie gras
        with, 94–96
    tricolor, prosciutto di Parma with mascarpone and, 32
melted chocolate filling, 231–33
meringue:
    cocoa, 229–30
    and cream, 235–37
micro green salad, 45

milk, in cannelés, 256
milk, skim, in cocoa foam, 234
mint:
    micro, raspberry salad, clementine granita with, 222
    paint, 176
    paint, Malaysian-crusted rack of lamb with truffled
        bread-and-butter pudding and, 172–76
molasses, in pomegranate-lacquered Muscovy duck with foie
    gras ravioli, 193–95
monkfish, in mosaic of seafood with saffron foam, 42–44
monté, beurre, 278
mosaic of seafood with saffron foam, 42–44
mousse, fromage blanc, 243–45
muscat:
    reduction, 96
    reduction, sautéed foie gras with honeydew melon soup
        and, 94–96
Muscovy duck, pomegranate-lacquered, with foie gras
    ravioli, 193–95
mushroom(s):
    in braised 31-vegetable ragout with chervil butter, 61–63
    mousseron, confit, 142
    porcini, in roasted sweetbread salad with walnut
        vinaigrette and beet paint, 73–76
    shiitake, zucchini and scallion sauté, 149
    stock, 267
mushroom(s), black trumpet:
    -crusted ahi tuna with scallion and four bean stew,
        134–36
    in rabbit, rabbit, rabbit, 188–192
mussels:
    in Asian bouillabaisse with coconut broth and sea beans,
        147–48
    Prince Edward Island, in mosaic of seafood with saffron
        foam, 42–44
    in 24-karat gold leaf rouget with shellfish and saffron
        broth, 143–45

n
navarin, venison, 186
niçoise, vinaigrette, octopus carpaccio with, 49
noodles, soba, in Asian bouillabaisse with coconut broth and
    sea beans, 147–48
N₂O cream chargers:
    for beef bone marrow foam, 156
    for clam foam on the half shell with crispy pancetta, 21
    for horseradish foam, 54
    for saffron foam, 44
nut, hickory, shortbread, 252

o
octopus:
    braised, 50
    carpaccio with niçoise vinaigrette, 49
    grilled, in live Japanese fish and chips, 38–41
    terrine, 49–50
oil:
    basil, 275
    canola, for crispy Sawagani crabs, 47

oil (*cont'd*):
    chive, 276
    coriander-oil, 273
    garlic and rosemary, 276
    herb, 273
    lemon, 277
    lime, 277
    lobster, 275
    -marinated Manchego with oven-roasted tomatoes, 213
    olive, for crispy Sawagani crabs, 47
    vanilla, 274
    yellow curry, 274
olive(s):
    green, and tomatoes, marinated white anchovies with, 29
    niçoise, in octopus carpaccio with niçoise vinaigrette, 49–50
    Peloponnese, in octopus carpaccio with niçoise vinaigrette, 49–50
olive oil:
    chilled tomato water with baby heirloom tomatoes and, 121
    sorbet, deconstructed insalata caprese with, 28
onion(s):
    in braised 31-vegetable ragout with chervil butter, 61–63
    in court bouillon, 267
    in duet of venison with rutabaga mash, 185–87
    in lobster bisque, 110
    in lobster glace, 268
    in natural poussin jus, 180
    in roasted chicken demi-glace, 269
    soubise, 136
    in steamed halibut with cucumber broth and Asian pear salad, 149–50
    in venison demi-glace, 270
    in venison navarin, 186
    Walla Walla, soup with orange-kissed beignets, 113–15
orange(s):
    -coriander oil, 273
    dust, Tramonto's, 272
    juice, in citrus gelée, 47
    juice in J-Rob's barbecue sauce, 171
    -kissed beignets, 113–15
    -kissed beignets, Walla Walla onion soup with, 113–15
    in star anise, 238
orange, blood:
    reduction, 83
    reduction, langoustine ravioli with buttered leeks, foie gras sauce and, 82–83
oven-dried tomato rings, 70
oven-roasted tomatoes, 213
    oil-marinated Manchego with, 213
oxtail, braised, 132
    roasted sturgeon with spiced carrot puree and, 131–33
oyster mushrooms, in mushroom stock, 267

oysters, Kumamoto, with passion fruit gelée on aromatic rock salt, 26–27

p

paint:
    beet, 76
    carrot, 23
    carrot, with carrot parfait, 23
    chocolate-bergamot, 237
    lemon curd, 245
    mint, 176
pancetta, crispy, clam foam on the half shell with, 21
pansy petals, in honey-and-lemon tea lollipops, 255
parfait, carrot, with carrot paint, 23
Parmesan tuiles, 126
Parmigiano-Reggiano cream and shaved white truffles, Swan Creek ricotta gnocchi with, 58–60
parsley-garlic butter, 79
parsnip:
    curls, 160
    puree, 159
    puree, braised beef short ribs with, 157–60
passion fruit:
    gelée, 27
    gelée, with Kumamoto oysters on aromatic rock salt, 26–27
    vinaigrette, 26
pasta dough, 66
pastry:
    puff, in apricot tarte tatin, 246
    supplies, sources of, 285–86
peaches, caramelized white, and Maine blueberries, seared foie gras with, 89–90
peanuts:
    in caramel taffy apple foie gras with lavender salad and green apple chip, 97–99
    in Cracker Jack with dried cherries, 251
pear(s):
    Asian, and fennel pollen, braised veal tongue and artichoke napoleon with, 68–72
    chips, 214
    chips, Roquefort with hot honey walnuts and, 214–16
    in duet of venison with rutabaga mash, 185–87
peas, in braised 31-vegetable ragout with chervil butter, 61–63
Peekytoe crab:
    salad, kumquats stuffed with, 11
    salad with crispy Sawagani crab and micro greens, 45
peppercorn:
    pink, -crusted bluefin tuna with tomato marmalade and buttermilk crackers, 12–13
    Szechuan, crème brûlée spoonfuls, 221
peppered pineapple relish, 106
    and fun buns, cured foie gras au torchon with, 103–6
peppers:
    jalapeño, in J-Rob's barbecue sauce, 171
    red, rouille, 148
Peruvian potato, purple, chilled soup with chives, 22

petits fours, 251–56
    cannelés, 256
    cinnamon-cayenne truffles, 253
    Cracker Jack with dried cherries, 251
    hickory and short bread, 252
    honey-and-lemon tea lollipops, 255
pickled:
    rhubarb, 91
    sunchokes, chilled sunchoke velouté, sevruga caviar and,
        118
pig-tail roulade, 167
pineapple:
    peppered, relish, 106
    peppered, relish and fun buns, cured foie gras au torchon
        with, 103–6
    roasted carpaccio with key lime sherbet, 239–42
pink peppercorn-crusted bluefin tuna with tomato marmalade
    and buttermilk crackers, 12–13
pistachio chili tuiles, 237
Pleasant Ridge Reserve with organic honey and panforte, 210
poached, poaching:
    arctic char, in duck fat with spinach-almond puree, 140–42
    liquid, sweetbread, 164
    lobster tails and claws, 81
    and pressed sweetbreads, 75
pomegranate:
    -lacquered Muscovy duck with foie gras ravioli,
        193–95
    molasses, seared foie gras with rhubarb ice cream, pickled
        rhubarb and, 91–93
popcorn, in Cracker Jack with dried cherries, 251
porcini:
    emulsion, 67
    puree, 67
pork:
    belly, cured, 167–69
    smoked, jus, 170
    smoked belly, tenderloin, and pig-tail roulade:
        Tramonto's backyard BBQ, 167–71
portobellos in mushroom stock, 267
port wine reduction, 165
potato(es):
    in braised 31-vegetable ragout with chervil butter, 61–63
    diced purple, 139
    duck fat confit, 70
    olive oil confit, 132
    puree, truffled, 156
    puree, truffled, roasted beef tenderloin and bone marrow
        foam with red wine sauce, 154–56
    puree, Yukon Gold, 80
    purple Peruvian, chilled soup with chives, 22
    truffle mashed "Martini," butter-poached Maine lobster
        and, 80–81
potato(es), sweet:
    boniato mash, 170
    in fried vegetable chips, 41
poultry, sources of, 284
poussin:
    jus, natural, 180

    roasted, and French lentils with bacon lardons and
        truffled green Brussels sprouts, 177–80
produce, sources of, 284–85
prosciutto di Parma with tricolor melon and mascarpone, 32
pudding, truffled bread-and-butter, 174–75
puree:
    asparagus, 154–56
    avocado, 40
    basil, 7
    broccoflower, 175
    cauliflower, 66
    parsnip, 159
    parsnip, braised beef short ribs with, 157–60
    porcini, 67
    scallion, 136
    spiced carrot, 133
    spiced carrot, roasted sturgeon with braised oxtail and,
        131–33
    spinach-almond, 142
    spinach-almond, arctic char poached in duck fat with,
        140–42
    squash, 191
    truffled potato, 156
    truffled potato, roasted beef tenderloin and bone marrow
        foam with red wine sauce, 154–56
    Yukon Gold potato, 80

q
quail egg(s):
    deviled, assortment of, 7
    oozy, ravioli, with porcini mushrooms, 64–67
    ravioli, 66
    in Rick's steak and eggs, 5

r
rabbit:
    jus, 192
    leg confit, 190
    leg confit, in rabbit roulade with salad of frisée, French
        beans, and radish, 19–20
    livers, in roasted rabbit loins, 191
    rabbit, rabbit, 188–92
    roasted loins, 191
    roulade with a salad of frisée, French beans, and radish,
        19–20
radish(es):
    baby, in braised 31-vegetable ragout with chervil butter,
        61–63
    rabbit roulade with a salad of frisée, French beans and,
        19–20
raisins, in banana chutney, 100
ramps, baby, in braised 31-vegetable ragout with chervil
        butter, 61–63
raspberry micro mint salad, clementine granita with, 222
ravioli:
    foie gras, 195
    langoustine, 82–83
    langoustine, with buttered leeks, foie gras sauce, and
        blood orange reduction, 82–83

ravioli (*cont'd*):
   oozy quail egg, with porcini mushrooms, 64–67
   pomegranate-lacquered Muscovy duck with foie gras,
      193–95
reduction:
   blood-orange, 83
   muscat, 96
   muscat, sautéed foie gras with honeydew melon soup and,
      94–96
   organic soy, 47
   port wine, 165
relish, peppered pineapple, 106
   and fun buns, cured foie gras au torchon with, 103–6
rhubarb:
   ice cream, 93
   ice cream, seared foie gras with pickled rhubarb,
      pomegranate molasses and, 91–93
   pickled, 91
rice:
   in black truffle risotto with lobster, French beans, and
      lobster emulsion, 84–85
   in frog leg risotto with parsley and lots and lots of garlic,
      77–79
ricotta gnocchi, Swan Creek ricotta, with Parmigiano-
   Reggiano cream and shaved white truffles, 58–60
risotto:
   black truffle, with lobster, French beans, and lobster
      reduction, 84–85
   frog leg, with parsley and lots and lots of garlic, 77–79
roast(ed):
   beef tenderloin, truffled potato puree, and bone marrow
      foam with red wine sauce, 154–56
   lemonade shooters, 223
   loin, assiette of milk-fed veal: butter-poached breast,
      crispy sweetbreads, 161–66
   oven-, tomatoes, 213
   pineapple carpaccio with key lime sherbet, 239–42
   poussin and French lentils with bacon lardons and truffled
      green Brussels sprouts, 177–80
   rabbit loins, 191
   spaghetti squash, 198
   spiny lobster with vanilla-saffron beurre blanc, 137–39
   squab with sweet corn flan and gingered spaghetti squash,
      196–200
   sturgeon with braised oxtail and spiced carrot puree,
      131–33
   sweetbread salad with walnut vinaigrette and beet paint,
      73–76
   vegetables and fried celery leaves, 163
roasted chicken demi-glace, 269
   in natural poussin jus, 180
Roquefort, with pear chips and hot honey walnuts, 214–16
rosemary:
   and garlic oil, 276
   rose petal ribbons, 227–28
   Wabash Cannonball with cherries and, 217
rouget, 24-karat gold leaf, with shellfish and saffron broth,
   143–45
rouille, red pepper, 148

roulade, rabbit, with a salad of frisée, French beans, and
   radish, 19–20
rutabaga mash, duet of venison with, 185–87

s
saffron:
   broth, 145
   foam, 44
   foam, mosaic of seafood with, 42–44
   and shellfish broth, 24-karat gold leaf rouget with,
      143–45
   -vanilla beurre blanc, roasted spiny lobster with, 137–39
salads:
   Asian pear, 150
   black garbanzo bean and celery, 31
   carrot, Hawaiian ginger and carrot soup with, 122
   cucumber-mango, 40
   curried Peekytoe crab, kumquats stuffed with, 11
   of frisée, French beans, and radish, rabbit roulade with a,
      19–20
   frisée and watercress, 199
   lemon balm, hijiki seaweed, and yuzu soy dressing, Thai
      snapper with, 24
   lentil, 105
   micro green, 45
   Peekytoe crab, with crispy Sawagani crab and micro
      greens, 45
   raspberry micro mint, clementine granita with, 222
   roasted sweetbread, with walnut vinaigrette and beet
      paint, 73–76
   yellow watermelon, red watermelon-lavender juice with,
      17
salmon:
   hamachi and marinated tuna, 40
   -hamachi tartar spoons, 6
salsify, braised, 136
sambal, in Malaysian-crusted rack of lamb with truffled
   bread-and-butter pudding and mint paint, 172–76
sauces:
   chocolate, 100
   chocolate, macadamia nut-crusted foie gras with banana
      French toast and, 100–102
   foie gras, 83
   foie gras, langoustine ravioli with buttered leeks, blood
      orange reduction and, 82–83
   J-Rob's barbecue, 171
   Madeira, 166
   Maine blueberry, 89–90
   red wine, 271
   red wine, lamb, 175–76
   short rib, 159–60
   veal, 71
   venison, 187
sauté(ed):
   baby spinach, 170
   foie gras with honeydew melon soup and muscat
      reduction, 94–96
   shiitake mushrooms, zucchini, and scallion, 149
savory anglaise, 93

Sawagani crabs, crispy, 47
    and micro greens, Peekytoe crab salad with, 45
scallion(s):
    in Asian bouillabaisse with coconut broth and sea beans, 147–48
    in braised 31-vegetable ragout with chervil butter, 61–63
    and fava bean stew, black trumpet mushroom-crusted ahi tuna with, 134–36
    puree, 136
    stew, 136
scallops:
    bay, in 24-karat gold leaf rouget with shellfish and saffron broth, 143–45
    sea, in Asian bouillabaisse with coconut broth and sea beans, 147–48
    sea, in Mosaic of seafood with saffron foam, 42–44
sea beans, Asian bouillabaisse with coconut broth and, 147–48
seafood:
    sources of, 283–84
    see also fish and seafood
seared:
    foie gras with caramelized white peaches and Maine blueberries, 89
    foie gras with rhubarb ice cream, pickled rhubarb, and pomegranate molasses, 91–93
seaweed:
    hijiki, lemon balm salad and yuzu soy dressing, Thai snapper with, 24
    in mosaic of seafood with saffron foam, 42–44
semifreddo chocolate-malted, with chocolate-bergamot paint, 235–38
shallots, in roasted vegetables and fried celery leaves, 163
shellfish:
    and saffron broth, 24-karat gold leaf rouget with, 143–45
    see also fish and seafood
sherbet, sorbet:
    buttermilk-key lime, 241
    coconut, 230
    coconut, Concord cakes with, 229–30
    key lime, roasted pineapple carpaccio with, 239–42
    olive oil, deconstructed insalata caprese with, 28
    toasted almond milk, 233
    toasted almond milk, warm chocolate tart with, 231
sherry vinaigrette, 19–20
shiitake mushrooms:
    in mushroom stock, 267
    zucchini, and scallion sauté, 149
shooters, roasted lemonade, 223
shortbread, hickory nut, 252
short rib(s):
    beef, braised with parsnip puree, 157–60
    sauce, 159–60
shrimp:
    in Asian bouillabaisse with coconut broth and sea beans, 147
    in mosaic of seafood with saffron foam, 42–44
    ravioli with buttered leeks, foie gras sauce, and blood orange reduction, 82–83

simple syrup, 279
smoked:
    pork belly, pork tenderloin, and pig-tail roulade: Tramonto's backyard BBQ, 167–71
    pork jus, 170
snapper:
    red, in 24-karat gold leaf rouget with shellfish and saffron broth, 143–45
    Thai, with hijiki seaweed, lemon balm salad, and yuzu soy dressing, 24
sorbet, see sherbet, sorbet
soubise, onion, 136
soups, 110–26
    carrot and Hawaiian ginger, with carrot salad, 122–24
    chilled purple Peruvian, with chives, 22
    chilled sunchoke velouté, pickled sunchokes, and sevruga caviar, 118
    chilled tomato water with baby heirloom tomatoes and olive oil, 121
    curried cauliflower, with cumin cracker, 116–17
    honeydew melon, 94
    honeydew melon and muscat reduction, sautéed foie gras with, 94–96
    lobster bisque with a spoon of lobster ceviche, 110–12
    Tramonto's totally insane black and white truffle, 125–26
    Walla Walla onion, with orange-kissed beignets, 113–15
sources, see ingredients and equipment, sources of
sour cream ice cream, 247
soy:
    sauce in pomegranate-lacquered Muscovy duck with foie gras ravioli, 193–95
    yuzu, dressing, Thai snapper with hijiki seaweed, lemon balm salad and, 24
spaetzle, squash, 191
specialty products, sources of, 286–87
spiced:
    carrot puree, 133
    carrot puree, roasted sturgeon with braised oxtail and, 131–33
spinach:
    -almond puree, 142
    -almond puree, arctic char poached in duck fat with, 140–42
    in blueberry and Perfection tangerines with basil syrup, 222
    in mint syrup, 102
    in roasted squab with sweet corn flan and gingered spaghetti squash, 196–200
    sautéed, baby, 170
squab:
    jus, 198
    legs, braised, 199
    roasted, with sweet corn flan and gingered spaghetti squash, 196–200
squash:
    gingered spaghetti, roasted squab with sweet corn flan and, 196–200

squash (*cont'd*):
    puree, 191
    roasted spaghetti, 198
    spaetzle, 191
star anise, oranges in, 238
steak and eggs, Rick's, 5
steamed halibut with cucumber broth and Asian pear salad,
    149–50
stew:
    blueberry, 245
    scallion, 136
    scallion and fava bean, black trumpet mushroom-crusted
        ahi tuna with, 134–36
stock:
    beef, 261
    beef, in consommé, 53
    beef and veal, 262
    chicken, 265
    duck, 265
    fish, 266
    game, 264
    lamb, 263
    mushroom, 267
    veal, 261
    veal, in veal tongue, 71
    vegetable, 266
    venison, 264
strawberry(ies):
    balsamic butter, 233
    gelée, 243
    juice, 233
    in warm chocolate tart with toasted almond milk sherbet,
        231–34
stuffed (stuffing):
    kumquats, with curried Peekytoe crab salad, 11
    red and yellow teardrop tomatoes, with goat cheese with
        100-year-old balsamic, 27
sturgeon, roasted, with braised oxtail and spiced carrot puree,
    131–33
sugar in lemon verbena syrup, 200
sunchoke velouté, chilled, pickled sunchokes, and sevruga
    caviar, 118
sweetbreads:
    crispy, assiette of milk-fed veal: roasted loin, butter-
        poached breast, 161–66
    poached and pressed, 75
    poaching liquid, 164
    roasted, salad with walnut vinaigrette and beet paint,
        73–76
    torchons of, 164
Swiss chard, in Malaysian-crusted rack of lamb with truffled
    bread-and-butter pudding and mint paint, 172–76
syrup:
    coconut-cilantro, 239
    corn, in mint syrup, 102
    ginger, 122
    lemon verbena, 200
    mint, 102
    simple, 279

simple, in green apple chips, 99
24-karat gold, 237
Szechuan peppercorn crème brûlée spoonfuls, 221

t
tangerines, Perfection, and blueberry, with basil syrup, 222
taro root, in fried vegetable chips, 41
tart(e):
    apricot, tatin, 246–47
    warm chocolate, with toasted almond milk sherbet, 231
tartar:
    beef, with quail egg and beef gelée, 51–54
    spoons, hamachi-salmon, 6
tenderloin, roasted beef, truffled potato puree, and bone
    marrow foam with red wine sauce, 154–56
tequila granita with yuzu cream and grapefruit, 227–28
terrine, octopus, 49–50
Thai snapper with hijiki seaweed, lemon balm salad, and yuzu
    soy dressing, 24
toasted:
    almond milk sherbet, 233
    almond milk sherbet, warm chocolate tart with, 231–34
tomato(es):
    in Asian bouillabaisse with coconut broth and sea beans,
        147–48
    baby heirloom, chilled tomato water with olive oil and,
        121
    in butter-poached veal breast, 165
    cherry, in braised 31-vegetable ragout with chervil butter,
        61–63
    and green olives, marinated white anchovies with, 29
    marmalade, pink peppercorn-crusted bluefin tuna with
        buttermilk crackers and, 12–13
    in oven-dried tomato rings, 70
    oven-roasted, 213
    oven-roasted, oil-marinated Manchego with, 213
    red and yellow teardrop, stuffed with goat cheese with
        100-year-old balsamic, 27
    red teardrop, in octopus carpaccio with niçoise
        vinaigrette, 49–50
    rings, oven-dried, 70
    in vegetable stock, 266
    water, chilled, with baby heirloom tomatoes and olive oil,
        121
    yellow teardrop, in octopus carpaccio with niçoise
        vinaigrette, 49–50
tomato paste:
    in lobster bisque, 110
    in lobster glace, 268
tongue:
    braised veal, and artichoke napoleon with Asian pear and
        fennel pollen, 68–72
    veal, 71
torchons of sweetbreads, 164
Tramonto's:
    backyard BBQ: smoked pork belly, pork tenderloin, and
        pig-tail roulade, 167–71
    caviar staircase with homemade crème fraîche, 37
    lemon dust, 272

lime dust, 272
orange dust, 272
ruby red grapefruit dust, 272
truffle(s), black:
in oil, 175
risotto with lobster, French beans, and lobster emulsion, 84–85
in veal sauce, 71
truffle(s), truffled:
bread-and-butter pudding, 174–75
bread-and-butter pudding and mint paint, Malaysian-crusted rack of lamb with, 172–76
butter, 106
cinnamon-cayenne, 253
goat cheese gougères, 8–9
green Brussels sprouts, roasted poussin and French lentils with bacon lardons and, 177–80
green Brussels sprouts with purple kale, 179
juice, in Madeira sauce, 166
mashed potato "Martini" and butter-poached Maine lobster, 80–81
potato puree, 156
potato puree, roasted beef tenderloin and bone marrow foam with red wine sauce, 154–56
soup, Tramonto's totally insane black and white, 125–26
vinaigrette, 105
truffle(s), white:
emulsion, 72
oil, in black truffle risotto with lobster, French beans, and lobster emulsion, 84–85
shaved, Swan Creek ricotta gnocchi with Parmigiano Reggiano cream and, 58–60
tuiles:
coconut, 245
Parmesan, 126
pistachio chili, 237
tuna:
ahi, black trumpet mushroom-crusted, with scallion and fava bean stew, 134–36
bluefin, pink peppercorn-crusted, with tomato marmalade and buttermilk crackers, 12–13
marinated, salmon, and hamachi, 40
in mosaic of seafood with saffron foam, 42–44
turnips, baby:
in braised 31-vegetable ragout with chervil butter, 61–63
in venison navarin, 186
24-karat gold syrup, 237

v
vanilla:
brandy, 237
oil, 274
-saffron beurre blanc, roasted spiny lobster with, 137–39
veal:
and beef stock, 262
braised tongue and artichoke napoleon with Asian pear and fennel pollen, 68

milk-fed, assiette of: roasted loin, butter-poached breast, crispy sweetbreads, 161–66
sauce, 71
tenderloin, in veal sauce, 71
tongue, 71
veal demi-glace, 268
in Madeira sauce, 166
in red wine sauce, 271
in smoked pork jus, 170
in veal sauce, 71
in venison navarin, 186
vegetable(s):
braised 31-vegetable ragout with chervil butter, 61–63
fried chips, 41
oil, for fried leeks, 150
roasted, and fried celery leaves, 163
see also specific vegetables
vegetable stock, 266
in black garbanzo beans, 31
in black truffle risotto with lobster, French beans, and lobster emulsion, 84–85
in braised 31-vegetable ragout with chervil butter, 61–63
in carrot and Hawaiian ginger soup with carrot salad, 122–24
in chilled purple Peruvian potato soup with chives, 22
in curried cauliflower soup with cumin crackers, 116
in French green and crimson red lentils, 179
in frog leg risotto with parsley and lots and lots of garlic, 77–79
in Madeira sauce, 166
in poached and pressed sweetbreads, 75
in porcini puree, 67
in sweetbread poaching liquid, 164
in Walla Walla onion soup with orange-kissed beignets, 113–15
in white truffle emulsion, 72
velouté, chilled sunchoke, pickled sunchokes, and sevruga caviar, 118
venison:
demi-glace, 270
navarin, 186
with rutabaga mash, duet of, 185–87
sauce, 187
stock, 264
verjuice, red, in pickled rhubarb, 91
vermouth:
dry, in porcini emulsion, 67
red, in roasted chicken demi-glace, 269
vinaigrette:
citrus, 124
lemon, 71
niçoise, octopus carpaccio with, 49–50
passion fruit, 26
sherry, 19–20
truffle, 105
walnut, 75
vin blanc, 272

vinegar:
    red wine, in pickled rhubarb, 91
    rice wine, in pomegranate-lacquered Muscovy duck with
        foie gras ravioli, 193–95
    white wine, in court bouillon, 267

w
Wabash Cannonball with cherries and rosemary, 217
wakame, marinated, in mosaic of seafood with saffron foam,
    42–44
Walla Walla onion soup with orange-kissed beignets, 113–15
walnut(s):
    hot honey, 214
    hot honey, Roquefort with pear chips and, 214–16
    vinaigrette, 75
warm chocolate tart with toasted almond milk sherbet,
    231–34
watercress and frisée salad, 199
watermelon, red:
    -lavender juice with yellow watermelon salad, 17
    in prosciutto di Parma with tricolor melon and
        mascarpone, 32
watermelon, yellow, salad, red watermelon-lavender juice
    with, 17
wine, port:
    in braised red cabbage, 163–64
    in lamb demi-glace, 270
    reduction, 165
    in red wine essence, 142
    in red wine lamb sauce, 175–76
    in venison stock, 264
wine, red:
    in beef and veal stock, 262
    in beef stock, 261
    in braised beef short ribs, 157–59
    in braised red cabbage, 163
    essence, 142
    lamb sauce, 175–76
    in lamb stock, 263
    sauce, 271
    sauce, roasted beef tenderloin, truffled potato puree, and
        bone marrow foam with, 154–55

    in squab jus, 198
    in veal demi-glace, 268
    in veal sauce, 71
    in veal stock, 261
    in venison navarin, 186
    in venison stock, 264
winc, white:
    in artichoke hearts, 70
    in black truffle risotto with lobster, French beans, and
        lobster emulsion, 84–85
    in fish stock, 266
    in frog leg braise, 79
    in frog leg risotto with parsley and lots and lots of garlic,
        77–79
    in game stock, 264
    in garlic-chive emulsion, 192
    in Madeira aspic, 44
    in mushroom stock, 267
    in natural poussin jus, 180
    in poached and pressed sweetbreads, 75
    in rabbit jus, 192
    in roasted chicken demi-glace, 269
    in saffron broth, 145
    in steamed halibut with cucumber broth and Asian pear
        salad, 149–50
    in sweetbread poaching liquid, 164
    in veal tongue, 71
    in vegetable stock, 266
    in vin blanc, 272
wonton wrappers, in foie gras ravioli, 195

y
Yukon Gold potato puree, 80
yuzu:
    cream, 227
    cream, tequila granita and grapefruit with, 227
    soy dressing, 24
    soy dressing, Thai snapper with hijiki seaweed, lemon
        balm salad and, 24

z
zucchini, shiitake mushrooms, and scallion sauté, 149

ABOUT THE AUTHORS

AND THE PHOTOGRAPHER

RICK TRAMONTO, the executive chef/partner of Tru in Chicago, was named one of *Food & Wine*'s Top Ten Best New Chefs in the country in 1994 and selected as one of America's Rising Star Chefs by Robert Mondavi in 1995. He has also been nominated four times for the James Beard Award for Best Chef in the Midwest, winning the award in 2002. Tru, which opened its doors in May 1999, was nominated for the 2000 James Beard Award for Best New Restaurant and named one of the Top 50 Best Restaurants in the World by *Condé Nast Traveler*. Tramonto is the author of *Amuse-Bouche*, and coauthor, with his partner Gale Gand, of *American Brasserie* and *Butter Sugar Flour Eggs*. Tramonto lives in Chicago with his wife, Eileen, and their three sons.

GALE GAND is widely considered one of the best pastry chefs in the United States. In 2001, she received the James Beard Award for Outstanding Pastry Chef. She was also named top pastry chef of the year in *Bon Appétit*'s annual Best of the Best awards in 2001. In 1994, Gale received the Robert Mondavi Award for Culinary Excellence. That same year, she and partner Rick Tramonto were named among the Top Ten Best New Chefs by *Food & Wine*. Gale and Tramonto were nominated for the 1998 James Beard Award for Best Chefs in the Midwest and also nominated (for Tru) for the 2000 James Beard Award for Best New Restaurant. She also received a James Beard Award nomination for *Butter Sugar Flour Eggs* in the Baking and Desserts category for cookbooks. Gand is also the author of *Just a Bite* and *Gale Gand's Short and Sweet* and the host of the Food Network's *Sweet Dreams*. She lives outside Chicago with her husband, Jimmy, and son, Gio.

MARY GOODBODY is a nationally known food writer and editor who has worked on more than forty-five books. Her most recent credits include *Taste Pure and Simple*, *Williams-Sonoma Kitchen Companion*, *Lobel's Prime Cuts*, and *Back to the Table*. She has contributed significantly to other books, such as *The Naked Chef*, *How to Be a Domestic Goddess*, and *Alfred Portale's Twelve Seasons Cookbook*. She is the editor of the *IACP Food Forum Quarterly* and was the first editor in chief of *Cook's* magazine.

TIM TURNER is a nationally acclaimed food and tabletop photographer. He has been nominated five years in a row for James Beard awards for Best Food Photography, winning in 1999 for *Charlie Trotter's Desserts*. He has also received many IACP, Clio, and ADDY awards and nominations for his work. His previous projects include books in the Charlie Trotter's series; *The Inn at Little Washington Cookbook: A Consuming Passion*; Norman Van Aken's *Norman's New World Cuisine*; *Jacques Pepin's Kitchen*; and *Weber's Art of the Grill*. Turner lives in relative sanity in Chicago with his wife and three exuberant daughters.

This book is set in Fournier, a typeface named for Pierre
Simon Fournier, the youngest son of a French printing family.
He started out engraving woodblocks and large capitals,
then moved on to fonts of type. In 1736 he began his own
foundry and made several important contributions in the field
of type design; he is said to have cut 147 alphabets of his own
creation. Fournier is probably best remembered as the designer
of St. Augustine Ordinaire, a face that served as the model
for Monotype's Fournier, which was released in 1925.